On the Waterfr

Alice Hart-Davis was born in Wales and grew up on a farm in the Chilterns. She studied history at Oxford University, and went on to work at *Vogue*. In 1987, she joined the *Telegraph* Magazine, where she edited the Shop Front section for two years before moving on to more diverse projects. She is married and lives in London.

On the Waterfront
1991

Edited by
Alice Hart-Davis

Researchers: Andrew Baker, Michèle Batcabe,
Sarah Bradnock, Penelope Gibbs,
Guy Hart-Davis, Vanessa Horne, Rachel Perkins,
David Prout, Jane Schofield, Nicci Selby,
Mark Swallow, Kate Valentine, Gareth Williams
and Rupert Winchester

Fontana
An Imprint of HarperCollins*Publishers*

A FONTANA ORIGINAL

First published in Great Britain in 1991 by Fontana,
an imprint of HarperCollins Publishers,
77/85 Fulham Palace Road,
Hammersmith, London W6 8JB.

9 8 7 6 5 4 3 2 1

BRITISH LIBRARY CATALOGUING IN PUBLICATION DATA

On the waterfront
1. Great Britain. Catering establishments
647.954105
ISBN 0 00 637724 6

Printed and bound in Great Britain by
HarperCollins Book Manufacturing, Glasgow

Grateful acknowledgement is made to the following for
permission to reproduce their photographs:
Tom Dobbie: The Waterfront Wine Bar, Portmeirion Hotel,
New Hall Hotel; John Higginson: The River House Restaurant,
The Butt and Oyster Pub, Waterton Park Hotel, Kirkby
Fleetham Hall; Erik Russell: Eddrachilles Hotel, Green Park
Hotel, Altnaharrie Inn; Jeremy Young: Warehouse Oyster Bar,
The Royal Oak, St Michael's Manor House, The Trout Inn,
Black Jack's Mill, The Old Manse Hotel, The Pump House,
Watermill Coffee Shop

Contents

Foreword by Libby Purves

For as long as I can remember, no view has ever seemed complete to me without a fringe of blue or green around its edges. Even grey would do. I would rather be walking on a shingle beach beside a gunmetal sea than landlocked in the prettiest garden or glade. If I climb a mountain, the reward I want is a view of the sea; follow a marshy footpath for miles across flat Suffolk, and the effort becomes worthwhile only when it ends in a rising dune, a few tufts of marram grass and watery infinity. Writing this in the year when the tunnellers under the Channel broke through the rock and exchanged flags, a part of me retains a fierce atavistic satisfaction at the thought that mainland Britain is an island and always will be. As the Irish song has it, 'T'ank God we're surrounded by water!'

It is not a lonely eccentricity. Wherever the sea joins the land in Britain, if you wait long enough somewhere on the horizon will appear a human figure looking outward. Few nations have ever taken their beaches to their heart as we have, building a whole elaborate culture of windbreak and deckchair, winkle and slot-machine and sandcastle flags around nothing more than the naturally eroded fringes of the land. At the other extreme, nobody has produced more poets and authors willing to use the imagery of cliffs, rocks and harbours. We claim the sea as a symbol of eternity lapping dangerously around the edges of time. One of the earliest and most haunting poems in the language is the Anglo-Saxon 'Seafarer', in which the writer alternately dreads a voyage and longs for it:

> And yet my heart is now restless in my breast, my mind
> is with the sea-flood over the whale's domain . . . the lone

gull screams, urges the heart to the whale's path over the stretch of seas.

We are obsessed, in other words, with our edges. And rightly so. As far as I am concerned there is no absurd contrast between the bucket-and-spade approach to the sea and the poet and dreamer on his cliff. It seems to me a lovely continuum: the baby throwing pebbles in a bucket amid the cosy domestic surroundings of a resort looks up and notices the huge sea with its oddly straight horizon and its perpetual, restless movement. He ups and toddles off to find that this vast entity will coolly tease his feet. He falls in love. The taste of the ice cream, the smell of chips, become not a distraction but part of the salty pleasure of it: always he looks wonderingly out at the water beyond his crumbling sandcastle.

The romantic teenagers walk by the sea, delighted at the wind in their hair and the excuse to take off a lot of clothes. Energetic young men and women prefer to get more intimately, damply involved, and skim across it on surf or sailboards. Dreamers launch little dinghies, silently identifying with Cook and Bligh. It gives whatever we ask, tests whatever we claim.

Adults, to be honest, often half forget the sea. They go skiing or to the gritty, tideless Mediterranean; they half believe the old canard that the British coast is 'ruined'. But when they come back the first sight reminds them of old feelings and longings, and they find it oddly comforting.

The sea belittles our troubles. We like to see it calm and remember how threatening it was in the winter storms; equally to have waves curling over the promenade while we remember the glassy calms of summer. We like to see the tide come up and wash away our footprints, and to see it ebb and leave the ribbed sand clean. The sea is a calming, cleansing metaphor, guarantee of life's fluidity. It keeps us in our place. After all, every child's favourite history story is the one about Canute. It was no accident that the Victorians, compulsive tamers of nature, delighted in building piers far out to sea, for trippers to pretend a daring voyage without risk of mal-de-mer; it is no accident, either, that when we are old and frail and need to contemplate the longest voyage of all, so many of us try to arrange to spend our last days looking out to sea from the bath-chairs of the south coast.

One of the peculiar pleasures of the British coast is that all these phases and attitudes are catered for by historical development, by geology and sheer chance. If you want a tang of salt air, a bag of chips and a giggle, there are the fantasy towns of Brighton and Blackpool, built in homage to the pleasure principle. If you want the romance of docks and harbours, your choice ranges from modern container ports to idyllic survivors like Charlestown, Cornwall. If you want to hear nothing but the crash of sea and rock, then Wales or Scotland waits for you. If you want shifting, muddy wastes of wading birds under wide empty skies, Norfolk is there.

And in between are thousands of compromises, oddities, washed-up bits of history; heritage museums and parks for the literal-minded who like to be guided, and weird unlisted, unrepeatable peepholes into the past for those who don't. On the beach at Dunwich in Suffolk, where scores of churches and their cemeteries have been washed into the sea in the last four hundred years, you may take a stroll to work off the excellent fish and chips from the Flora tea rooms and think yourself on an ordinary, bracing, 20th-century day out. Then your foot hits something, and you stoop, and it is a human bone, sea-washed, white and beautiful, and God knows how old. You mutter a prayer for its owner, perhaps, and walk on in another dimension.

Or you might be in a small, respectable Scottish town like Lochinver on a Saturday night, when all seems already closed down for a strict Sabbath and nothing moves except an idly patrolling harbour seal. Then the skirl of pipes comes across the water, and you follow it, and moments later are watching a sword-dance in a fish shed, the air around you crackling with life and colour and music as the band plays a celebratory concert for a fishing boat being sold to the South.

This last incident happened when I and my family made an expedition in 1988, sailing round mainland Britain in our boat *Grace O'Malley* (story told in *One Summer's Grace*). It was a journey intended, in some ways, to exorcise my lifelong fascination with the sea-borders of our big jagged island. Instead it redoubled that fascination. Now I know that if I could circle Britain every year, stopping at different ports and anchorages, so I would. The diversity of it was so breathtaking, the entertainment so rich and the inspiration so concentrated that it is hard to consider going anywhere else.

Each sector of coast has such a different character that you can never become bored. There you are in the shifty, sandy south-east, contemplating the rise and fall of ancient harbours (Hastings was a Cinque Port; now it is a beach). You shift along to the Solent and there begin to be rocks, and dramatic striped cliffs at Alum Bay, and the chalky Needles opening the way to a new stretch of Dorset coast: as Frank Cowper wrote, 'Promontory on promontory, peak upon peak, stretching away to the golden West'. And there is Portland Bill, terrible tidal Cape Horn of the south coast: and beyond it Lyme Bay and its fossils, as poignant in their way as the Dunwich bone. Nobody could confuse any section of coast with the next: even when you come to Devon and Cornwall with their towering cliff scenes, each twenty miles has its own, very different character.

North of Land's End we jumped a hundred miles to Wales: leaving out stretches of the Bristol Channel banks which now we know from landward exploration: the Gower peninsula, glowing in the sunset as if lit from inside, and north Cornwall, the wild and unforgiving coast with what Chaucer called its 'grisly rokkes blake'. We went instead quickly to North Wales, to the extraordinary contrasts of the Lleyn peninsula, where holiday chalet-land lies under the brooding shadow of Iron Age fortifications; then slid into the Menai Strait, with high Wales on one hand and the sandy dunes and donkeys of Anglesey on the other.

The joy of the voyage was that all along the coast new vistas opened and new riches were cast, as it were, at our feet. Geology has been capriciously kind to Britain: estuaries and odd pockets of mud and sand like the River Lune and the Solway Firth present themselves as a change between towering rocky landscapes. Long, quiet sea lochs wind miles inland in Scotland, bringing the coastal walker or sailor from the sight of cold, wild seas to calm landlocked idylls within ten minutes. To see seals and water lilies, breakers and mirror-calm water within such short spaces is a very Scottish miracle: yet over on the straight, apparently featureless east coast we found similar conjuring tricks played by rivers which bent suddenly inland, taking you in half a mile from a grey harbour to a flat green river fringed with willows, with an ancient hermit's cell carved out of the rock wall in the stillness.

We have a fabulous coastline: city and wilderness, rock and sand, estuary and cliff. As yet, we have ruined very little of it with overdevelopment, and a bit more with pollution. The latter, at least, is reversible. I once believed it wrong to encourage tourism on the coast, fearing overcrowding and reckoning that anybody who deserved to see it should find their own way there and make their own arrangements. The threats of pollution and vandal development, however, have changed my mind. The more of us who go to the seaside and love it the better. We shall go home prepared to fight for it, to help the National Trust buy up chunks of it, to assist local efforts to keep small harbours open, and pressure governments to take pollution and overfishing seriously. We are a lobby: we must give the coastline – whether wild or historic – a vote in public life. Going to it, enjoying it, gives us the resolution to do just that.

Not everyone can visit the coast by sea, and not all the coast, indeed, is the kind a boat dare approach. This pilot book for shorebound visitors should ease the landward approach and offer some safe and comfortable havens. Good luck to it.

Notes for Readers

Booking is advisable for all hotels and restaurants. You should specify water-view rooms when booking – some hotels add a small surcharge for these. Many hotels and guest houses offer special rates for weekend breaks. Many places have disabled access, but few have full disabled facilities: details for each establishment are included in the description. Unless stated otherwise, hotels and pubs with accommodation have dining facilities for residents. Non-resident diners are welcome at many hotels. All establishments can cater for vegetarians, though smaller hotels may need advance notice. You are advised to check when booking. Pub hours given are for summer opening; winter opening hours may be shorter. All establishments have been visited to ensure that their situation is memorable. Readers are advised that this is a selective guide. The researchers did not eat or stay at the establishments mentioned, nor did they accept free hospitality. All information and prices correct at time of going to press.

Symbols

🏨 Hotel

🍴 Restaurant

🍺 Public house

inn Inn (that is, a pub with accommodation)

$\frac{5/10}{\approx}$ Five out of 10 bedrooms have a view of the water

🏠 Children welcome

🏠 No children

🏠 5 Only children aged five and over welcome

🐾 Dogs/pets welcome

🚫 No dogs/pets

▬ One or more of the major credit cards are accepted

▬ No credit cards accepted

The South-west

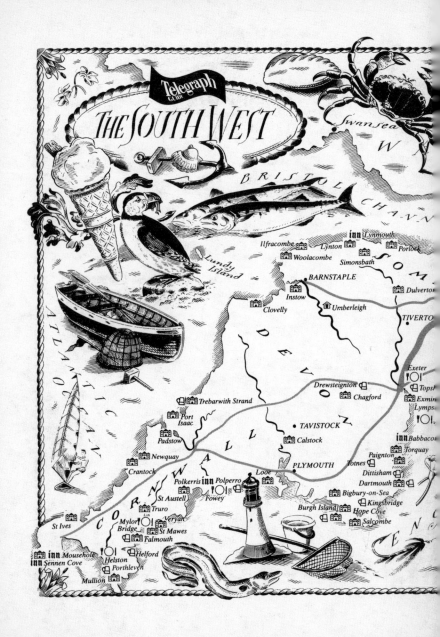

Telegraph GUIDE
THE SOUTH WEST

Swansea

WA

BRISTOL CHANNEL

Lundy Island

ATLANTIC OCEAN

inn Lynmouth
Ilfracombe · Lynton · Porlock
Woolacombe · Simonsbath
BARNSTAPLE · Dulverton
Instow · Umberleigh · TIVERTON
Clovelly

SOM

DEVON

Exeter
Topsh
Drewsteignton · Chagford · Exmin
Lymps

Trebarwith Strand
Port Isaac · **TAVISTOCK**
Padstow · Calstock · **inn** Babbacom
Newquay · Paignton · Torquay
Crantock · **PLYMOUTH** · Totnes · Dittisham
Polkerris · Polperro · Looe · Dartmouth
St Austell · Fowey · Bigbury-on-Sea
Truro · Veryan · Burgh Island · Kingsbridge
St Ives · Mylor Bridge · St Mawes · Hope Cove
inn Mousehole · Helford · Salcombe
inn Sennen Cove · Helston · Porthleven
Mullion

CORNWALL

ENG

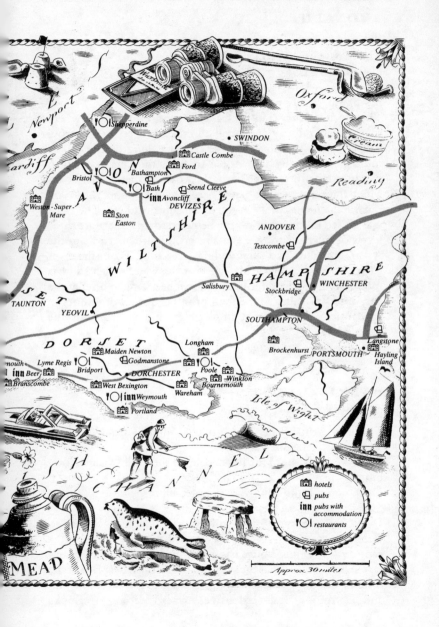

Newport

Shepperdine 🍷

SWINDON

Oxford

Cardiff

Bristol

Castle Combe 🏨
Ford 🏨

Cream

Reading

A V O N

Bathampton 🏨
Bath 🍷
inn Avoncliff

Seend Cleeve 🏨

DEVIZES

Weston-Super-Mare 🏨

Ston 🏨
Easton

W I L T S H I R E

ANDOVER

Testcombe 🍷

HAMPSHIRE

Salisbury

WINCHESTER
Stockbridge 🍷

D O R S E T

TAUNTON

YEOVIL

SOUTHAMPTON

Longham 🏨

Brockenhurst 🏨

Langstone 🏨

Maiden Newton 🏨

Lyme Regis 🍷
inn Beer 🏨
Branscombe 🏨

Bridport 🍷
Godmanstone 🍷

DORCHESTER

West Bexington 🏨

Poole 🏨

Winkton 🏨
Bournemouth

Wareham 🏨

PORTSMOUTH
Hayling Island 🍷

🍷 inn Weymouth

Portland 🏨

Isle of Wight

C H A N N E L

hotels 🏨
pubs 🏠
inn pubs with
accommodation
🍷 restaurants

MEAD

Approx 30 miles

AVONCLIFF

inn $\frac{3/3}$ 🏠 ⊘ 🔲

The Cross Guns, Avoncliff, Bradford-on-Avon, Wilts
(Tel. 02216 2335)
Open 11am–3pm, 6.30pm–11pm all week
£14 pp single, £17 pp double b&b

This 16th-century inn is the only one in England where road, river, railway and canal all cross; it is set in a narrow valley, where the power of the river has long been used for milling. Practically impossible to find, though well worth making the effort, it is approached by a perpendicular road. Much the easiest way to arrive here is by the Kennet and Avon canal, which crosses the Avon on an aqueduct here. The canal was closed in 1956, but is now being restored. There are three levels of riverside terrace and a riverside garden, views of the Avon, aqueduct and surrounding steep hills. From the river banks, there is a spectacular view of the weir, which still has mills at both ends of it. Six traditional beers are on offer at the bar, and the quality of the food prompts queues of visitors to appear from nowhere at meal times. No facilities for the disabled.
Walks; watersports; fishing

BABBACOMBE

🛏 $\frac{4/4}$ 🏠 🐟 🔲

The Cary Arms, Beach Road, Babbacombe, Torquay
TQ1 3LX (Tel. 0803 327110)
From Torquay, head for Babbacombe, then follow signs for beach
Open noon–11pm Mon–Sat; noon–2.30pm, 7pm–10.30pm Sun

Down the fearsomely steep (one in three) single-track road to Babbacombe Beach (car park at the bottom), this eighteenth-century smuggling house has a fine view over the beach and Lyme Bay. The bar has the stone walls and open fireplace of the original building, faces the water and serves Dartmoor Strong and Dartmoor Best. Extensive terraced garden overlooks

beach and bay. Bar meals are available at lunchtime, and can be eaten out at the seaside tables. No facilities for the disabled.
Beach a few yards away; fishing, pedal-boats and motorboats all nearby

BATH
1O1 🏠 ✍ 💳

Bath Puppet Theatre, Riverside Walk, Pulteney Bridge, Bath   (Tel. 0225 312 173)
Open 9.30am–6pm, later in summer
This excellent puppet-theatre-cum-coffee-shop looks directly on to the Avon and the weir beneath Pulteney Bridge, right in the centre of Bath. Puppet shows are held at 3.30pm on Saturdays and daily during school holidays (it is advisable to telephone in advance to check when the shows are on). The coffee shop has room for up to 40 people and serves tea, cakes and wholesome snacks. Most of the inside tables have a view of the water; in summer, go for two tables outside. A delightful and unusual place. No facilities for the disabled.
Small maze nearby (favourite with children); canal; boat trips; car park five minutes away

BATHAMPTON
🍺 🏠 ✍ 💳

The George Inn, Mill Lane, Bathampton, Bath BA2 6TR
(Tel. 0225 425 079)
Off A36 Warminster Road in village of Bathampton; or over tollbridge
Open 11am–2.30pm, 6pm–11pm Mon–Sat; 12pm–3pm, 7pm–10.30pm Sun
An attractive, creeper-clad 15th-century inn by the Kennet & Avon canal. There are two gardens, one enclosed and one looking on to the water and towpath. A charming place, and genuinely 'olde worlde'. Inside is beamed and cosy, with views of water from first floor and family room. The menu of snacks

includes four or five daily specials, but no chips. No bookings taken. No facilities for the disabled.
Walks along towpaths to Bath and Devizes

BEER
inn

The Anchor Inn, Fore Street, Beer, East Devon
(Tel. 0297 20386)
Open 11am–11pm
£21–£27 pp b&b
A traditional small inn, situated at the top of the slipway down to the beach in a quaint seaside village. The accommodation is comfortable and unpretentious, with fitted furniture and floral fabrics. Most of the rooms have good sea views, and you can watch the fishing boats in the harbour from the pub garden. The bar serves a range of traditional ales; bar meals are available, and there is a full menu on offer in the restaurant, with seafood a speciality. No facilities for the disabled.
Beer beach is small and primarily a working beach, but motorboats, deck chairs and beach huts can be hired, and fishing trips can be arranged. Cliff walks recommended for the energetic; golf, riding, squash and scuba diving can all be found nearby

BIGBURY-ON-SEA

Henley Hotel, Folly Hill, Bigbury-on-Sea, Devon TQ7 4AR
(Tel. 0548 810240)
At the coast end of the B3392
£20.50 pp b&b
The hotel looks out from its clifftop across the mouth of the Avon estuary. The view is very spectacular, and Turner is said to have painted it; certainly the Long Stone, a high landmark at the end of the beach, can be found in one of his works. The dining room is open to non-residents and seats up to 20; two window tables look out to sea. A non-smoking establishment. No facilites for the disabled.

Fishing off the steps at high tide; watersports at the beach; diving (mostly professional) nearby; coastal path walks. Private cliff path of 127 steps leads down to the beach (the road offers a gentler descent)

BOURNEMOUTH

🏠 80/131 🏘 🚫 🛏

Royal Bath Hotel, Bath Road, Bournemouth BH1 2EW
(Tel. 0202 555 555)
£85–£210 per room
Situate in the town centre near the pier, this large, five-star Victorian hotel owes some architectural debt to the Brighton Pavilion, especially on the inside. There is a first-rate leisure club, 'The Leisure Pavilion', in the grounds, which is open to residents from 7.30 am–10.30 pm. The hotel's five-star rating is evident in the high-quality decor, and the staff's willingness to arrange activities and excursions for visitors. Separated from the sea by three acres of gardens, the hotel has good, but not spectacular, views over Poole Bay. Oscar's Restaurant (inside the hotel) seats 65–70 people; a set lunch costs £16.10, a three-course dinner £23. Teas are served in the gardens. Full conference and banqueting facilities are available. The hotel has some ground-floor bedrooms but no special facilities for the disabled.
Nearby theatres, sailing, fishing, three golf clubs, cinemas, water-skiing, horse riding, ice skating

BRANSCOMBE

🏠 6/6 🏘6 🖐 🛏

The Look Out, Branscombe (near Lyme Regis), Devon
EX12 3DP   (Tel. 029780 262)
From Branscombe, approach through the shallow ford between two 'Private: Access Only' signs, then follow the cliff-side drive to the hotel.
£45 single, £80 double
The perfect, 'away-from-it-all' location; rugged, beautiful and highly photogenic. Six coastguards' cottages perched on the

side of a cliff have been converted into a small private hotel with superb unspoilt views over Lyme Bay. Branscombe is picturesque and popular, and the beach is packed in summer, though guests, up on their private terrace, are well away from all of this. The conversion has managed to retain much of the cottages' original charm and provides personal and intimate surroundings among good antique and period furniture. The restaurant seats 24 people – with no water views, and open for dinner only – non-residents are welcome. No facilities for the disabled.

Coastal path walks; beach; windsurfing; fishing; boats for hire

BRIDPORT

IOI 🏠 ◇ ▭

Riverside Café and Restaurant, West Bay, Bridport, Dorset DT6 4EZ　(Tel. 0308 22011)
On island across footbridge in centre of village
Open 10.30am–3.30pm; 6.30pm–8.30pm; closed Monday, and generally closed from November to March (Telephone to check first)

Popular eating place specializing in ultra-fresh seafood, located on a small island where the River Brit meets the harbour. West Bay may not appear to embody the best aspects of the Great British seaside, but this restaurant is well worth a detour if you happen to be in the area: the Watsons' cooking and service merits an enthusiastic entry in *The Good Food Guide*. The restaurant seats 80, nearly all tables look out at the water. Tables can be booked (at a small charge) in the restaurant; the café is self-service. Pets are welcome as long as they have not just been for a swim in the sea or the river. There are ramps to all areas for disabled visitors.

Beach nearby; walks; watersports; fishing

BRISTOL
IOI 🏠 🚫 ▱

Arnolfini Café Restaurant, 16 Narrow Quay, Bristol
BS1 4QA   (Tel. 0272 279330)
Next door to the Bristol Tourist Information Centre
Open 10am–11pm Mon–Sat; 12pm–10.30pm Sun
This sleek and popular café, with its etched glass and steel
interior, has established itself in an arts complex converted
from dockside warehouse. The late-eighties designer atmosphere is enhanced by the 180 different spirits on offer at the bar.
There is seating for up to 60 people, and tables provide good
views of Narrow Quay. There are also four picnic tables
outside by the quay. Creative light meals include soups, salads
and cakes. Beside the spot where the Kennet & Avon canal
joins the sea, there are moorings for those arriving by canal
boat or yacht. A new section of the canal was opened earlier
this year, joining Bristol to Bath and London. The bar and a
small dining area are on the ground floor, but there are no
special facilities for the disabled.
Walks; 15-minute walk to watersports

BRISTOL
IOI 🏠 🚫 ▭

The Glass Boat Restaurant, Welsh Back, Bristol BS1 4SS
(Tel. 0272 290 704)
At the Bristol Bridge end of Welsh Back and Baldwin Street
Open 7.30am–10am, 12pm–2.30pm, 7pm–11pm Mon–Fri;
7pm–11pm Sat; 12pm–3pm, 7pm–10pm Sun
A converted boat resting at the dockside in the heart of Bristol.
Most of the 70 seats in upper-deck restaurant command fine
water views. (There is a wine bar on the lower deck, though
this is now only used for functions.) The cuisine is French/
Continental. High chairs can be provided for children. No
facilities for the disabled.
Walks; watersports; fishing; boat trips 100 yards along quay

BROCKENHURST

Master Builder's House Hotel, Buckler's Hard, Beaulieu,
Brockenhurst, Hants   (Tel. 0590 616253)
From Beaulieu, follow signs to Brockenhurst Maritime
Museum
£45 single, £75 double, £95 four poster
Attractive hotel gardens slope down to the wide curve of the
River Beaulieu and an exclusive marina where many yachts are
moored. The hotel was once a master ship-builder's home –
hence the name. There are tasteful rooms in the Old Wing,
with views of the river and film-set-pretty village: some have
four-poster beds. Avoid rooms in the new wing which mostly
have views of the car park. Almost all of the tables in the smart
restaurant have a view of the river, and there is also a restaurant
terrace which overlooks the water (the table d'hôte dinner
costs £12). Watch out, when approaching, for the New Forest
ponies that wander freely across the roads. There are some
ground-floor rooms, and ramps, though no specific facilities
for the disabled.

BURGH ISLAND

Burgh Island Hotel, Burgh Island, Bigbury-on-Sea,
South Devon TQ7 4AU   (Tel. 0548 810 514)
Open all year
Suites £64–£88 pp for dinner and b&b
This unique Art Deco hotel was famous in the twenties and
thirties, and has recently been restored to its former, full-
blown glory by Tony and Beatrice Porter. Telephone from the
mainland, and you can be fetched across to the island by Land
Rover at low tide, or by the giant sea-tractor at high tide. All of
the accommodation is in suites of rooms (the finest are two
double suites) and has sea views, and there is a helipad for high-
flying arrivals. The chef and pastry chef are Roux brothers
trained; their classic French cuisine features fresh local
produce, and in summer island-caught shellfish. Jackets and

ties are required at dinner. Some suites are served by a lift, but there are no special facilities for the disabled.

Watersports; windsurfers and diving boats for hire nearby; indoor exercise machines; bird sanctuary; tennis on the island; golf on the mainland

BURGH ISLAND

Pilchard Inn, Burgh Island, Bigbury-on-Sea, South Devon TQ7 4AU   (Tel. 0548 810 344)

Open in spring and summer 11am–11pm Mon–Sat; noon–3pm, 7pm–10pm Sun. In autumn and winter 11am–3pm, 6.30pm–11pm Mon–Sat; noon–3pm, 7pm–10pm Sun

If you want to make a day trip to Burgh Island, you can visit the Pilchard Inn. This pub dates from 1336, and is run by the hotel above: it is the only other building on the island. The pub has two bars overlooking the water, and a waterside garden; Ruddles, Ushers Best, and draught cider are on offer. Bar snacks are available at lunch and in the evenings. No facilities for the disabled.

Walks on the island or around the coast; watersports; fishing; beaches on mainland

CALSTOCK

Danescombe Valley Hotel, Lower Kelly, Calstock, Cornwall PL18 9RY   (Tel. 0822 832414)

Half mile west of Calstock Village, along River Road

Open Easter to end October

£77 pp per night (inc. four-course dinner and breakfast)

Set on a sweeping bend of the River Tamar, this beautiful, Grade II listed house was built for Lord Ashburton in 1850. An extremely tranquil place to stay, thanks to the absence of televisions and small children. A slate-floored bar leads out to a terrace with panoramic river views. Even more impressive than the setting and the rooms is the food, cooked by Anna

Smith and widely praised. Guests present themselves for dinner each evening at 7.30 for 8pm, and are served four-course 'West Country' dinners. Four of the tables in the dining room look on to the river. (Only two non-residents can be accommodated for dinner each evening.) No facilities for the disabled.

Canoeing nearby; riverboat rides from Calstock village; National Maritime Museum nearby; Cotehele House (National Trust property) is a 15-minute walk away

CASTLE COMBE

25/34

The Manor House, Castle Combe, Chippenham, Wilts
(Tel. 0249 782206)
Off B3049
£95–£250 per room b&b
Situated in the beautiful village of Castle Combe, this hotel is a splendid 17th-century manor house, festooned with creepers. The public rooms are large, light, tastefully decorated, and most have lovely views of the lawns, the valley and the river Bybrook – the bedrooms are even better. There is also a cottage in the grounds for guests. Though the river is not the focal point of the place, it is always there in the background. The dining room seats 110. Non-residents can savour the atmosphere and the surroundings by dropping in for tea in the panelled lounge or, in fine weather, out on the lawn. There are some ground-floor rooms, though no specific facilities for the disabled.

Fly fishing (hotel provides rods); riverside walks; riding

CHAGFORD

9/14

Gidleigh Park, Chagford, Devon TQ13 8HH
(Tel. 0647 432367)
Two miles from village of Chagford; telephone for directions
£200–£350 double occupancy, dinner and b&b; cottage, £425 for two guests; £510 for four

An extremely luxurious and relaxing country-house hotel (Relais et Chateaux member), set in 40 acres of secluded grounds inside the Dartmoor National Park. The River Teign has been landscaped and re-routed directly in front of the house: a pleasant but not dramatic water view. Great attention is paid to all those small details that makes the visitor feel at home, but not overwhelmed. Gidleigh Park was decreed Egon Ronay Hotel of the Year 1990, and in 1989 received the César award for the most sumptuous traditional country-house hotel. The highly praised restaurant seats 40 (three tables have a water view). Pets are allowed, though only in owners' bedrooms. Children are welcome, but only if they behave themselves. No facilities for the disabled.

Four croquet lawns, all-weather tennis court. Plenty of scope for walking; fishing and riding can be arranged

CHAGFORD

Mill End Hotel, Sandy Park, Chagford, Devon TQ13 8JN
(Tel. 0647 432282)
Exeter–Okehampton Road (A30) to Whiddon Down, then A382 to hotel
£40–£70 per room

Log fires, comfortable public rooms, and lots of nooks and crannies make the Mill End a peaceful spot with an old world feel. A former flour mill, the hotel rests on the bank of the River Teign at the head of Fingle Gorge. All bedrooms have fine views of the river valley, though only two look directly over the water. The courtyard and working water-wheel form a pleasant scene for diners in the 40-seat restaurant; three tables have a river view. The hotel runs special wine and food weekends (gourmet menus and accommodation for two people for two nights costs £275), and is also very strong on fishing: rods can be hired, and a ghillie is on call for guidance on the river. The bar, dining room and some bedrooms are on the ground floor, but there are no special facilities for the disabled.

Six miles of salmon and seatrout fishing on River Teign; trout fishing on reservoir and golf nearby; swimming; tennis; shooting; riding; Castle Drogo and other National Trust properties nearby

CLOVELLY

11/11

Red Lion Hotel, Clovelly, Devon EX39 5TS
(Tel. 02373 237)
Off the A39 between Bude and Bideford
£25 b&b
The hotel sits on the very steep hill that descends through the picturesque village to the pebble beach and quay. Small, old, traditional, unassuming, and a good place to eat if visiting Clovelly: the dining room seats 60, and four tables overlook the water. A pleasant place to stay, and soon to be more comfortable: the hotel is moving upmarket and being totally refurbished. All bedrooms will have bathrooms *en suite*. No facilities for the disabled.
Good walks; sea fishing; riding, surfing, golf and safe beach nearby

CRANTOCK

27/36

Crantock Bay Hotel, Crantock, Newquay, Cornwall
TR8 5SE   (Tel. 0637 830229)
From A3075, head for Crantock, then West Pentire
Open March–November
£31–£41 pp dinner and b&b
Traditional seaside hotel, with gardens that run down to the western end of the beautiful, sandy Crantock Beach. The setting is tranquil, and the views across the bay are fabulous. Most tables in the dining room look out to sea, and so does the bar. Visible in the bay is the Goose (a rocky island, and a target for intrepid swimmers). The hotel boasts a new extension complete with a games room, indoor pool (free to non-residents if they have a meal), sauna, and sun terrace. The croquet lawn should be ready by the summer. No facilities for the disabled.
Outdoor tennis court; hotel boat available for water skiing; windsurfing at Newquay (3 miles); rock fishing, freshwater fishing on inland waterways and reservoir; walks on (ubiquitous) coastal path; exercise room and putting green at hotel

DARTMOUTH

🍴 🏠 ⊗ 💳

Carved Angel, 2 South Embankment, Dartmouth, Devon
TQ6 9BH   (Tel. 0803 83 2465)
In the middle of town, opposite the passenger ferry
Open for lunch 12.30pm–1.45pm Tues–Sun, and for dinner
7.30pm–9.30pm Tues–Sat
This highly rated restaurant looks across the road and a broad
promenade to the River Dart. There is seating for 55 people;
five of the tables have a direct view of the river; six more look
on to the quayside scene of boats, ferry and promenade. There
are wide picture windows on the ground floor; the outlook is
better from upstairs, from where there are splendid views
down to the mouth of the river. One room upstairs can be
booked for private parties. The cooking is described as
'Modern English' – fish, shellfish, poultry, meat and game all
find their way on to the menu, and the emphasis is on using
local produce, depending on the season. The set menu at lunch
costs £22–£24; set dinner is £30–£35 for three courses, plus
sorbet, cheese, petits fours, and coffee. Sunday lunch £27.50.
The ground-floor dining room is up two steps, and the
lavatories are on the first floor. No special facilities for the
disabled.
Fishing, rowing and sailing can be found in the vicinity; there is a
yacht club nearby, a marina ten minutes' walk up the road, and boat
trips leave from the promenade

DARTMOUTH

🏨 10/24 🏠 🔔 💳

Royal Castle Hotel, The Quay, Dartmouth, Devon TQ6 9PS
(Tel. 0803 83 3033)
£30–£45 pp b&b
Dating from the 16th century, this listed building on the quay
is bursting with character. The façade is Regency and
crenellated but the core of the hotel is an old coaching inn,
popular as a location for films and television drama. There are
open log fires, antique furnishings and several four-poster beds

(three with a water view). The two bars just overlook the water and have a good atmosphere (locals, lots of dogs) and serve local beers. The Galleon lounge takes children at one end, and serves lunch, cream teas, and bar snacks. The first-floor restaurant specializes in seafood, and has the same view (slightly better because of the elevation); it seats 60, and five tables look on to the river. No facilities for the disabled.

Sailing; fishing; hotel can arrange watersports; walks to Castle and on coastal path; riding and golf nearby

DARTMOUTH

Wavenden House, Compass Cove, Dartmouth, Devon
TQ6 0JN   (Tel. 0803 83 3979)
Off the A379, Dartmouth–Kingsbridge
£15 pp b&b (four-course dinner £10)

A gem of a hideaway, set in an isolated position on the clifftop, on the site of a gun emplacement (to ward off the Spaniards, French, Germans, etc.) and so with a marvellous view of the Dart Estuary and the bay. Wavenden House does not pretend to be a hotel or guest house; the owners simply take in paying guests (there are only three rooms, all of which have a sea view) and cook them delicious dinners on request. The large dining table seats 10 (residents only) and looks out across the estuary to Kingswear Castle. The surrounding countryside is National Trust owned, and Wavenden House is the only building in the vicinity. The house is on a precipitous hill, so it is unsuitable for young children and the disabled.

Lots of walks (the coastal path runs right by the gate); sailing can be arranged; sailing courses in Dartmouth; fishing off rocks below; Sugary Cove beach (five-minute walk)

DITTISHAM

The Ferry Boat Inn, Dittisham, Dartmouth, South Devon
(Tel. 080422 368)
Follow Ferry sign from Dartmouth; access also by boat
(and ferry)

Open 11am–3pm, 6pm–11pm Mon–Sat; noon–2.30pm, 7pm–10.30pm Sun
White-painted inn at bottom of steep hill, right by water's edge at high tide and popular with yachtsmen. At low tide, the riverbank finds itself providing additional parking spaces. The one bar overlooks the water, and serves real ales and snacks. No facilities for the disabled.
Windsurfing at the Ham; boating; walks

DREWSTEIGNTON

The Anglers Rest, Fingle Bridge, Drewsteignton, Exeter EX6 6PW (Tel. 0647 21287)
Signposted from Drewsteignton
Open in summer 11am–3pm, 6pm–11pm Mon Sat; noon–3pm, 7pm–10.30pm Sun. In winter 11 am–2.30pm Mon–Fri
This 93-year-old pub is set beside an Elizabethan bridge in a quiet wooded valley. It has always been run by the same family, and boasts a fine collection of antique fishing tackle. The one bar overlooks the river; outside, the terraced garden, with seating for 60 people, reaches down to the water. Beers on offer include Wadworth 6X; Cotleigh Tawny, and Dorset IPA. In the summer, the restaurant is open from 10.30am, for morning coffee, to 5.30pm for cream teas, and serves roast lunches on Sundays. Children are welcome in the restaurant or the garden, but not in the pub. No facilities for the disabled.
Trout, salmon, and sea trout fishing (pub hires out rods and sells flies); miles of woodland walks, including one to Castle Drogo (about 45 minutes on foot for the average walker), Hunters' Path and Fishermen's Path

DULVERTON

Tarr Steps Hotel, Hawkridge, Dulverton, Somerset TA22 9PY (Tel. 064 385293)
West of Dulverton–Exford road
£34 pp b&b
A remote sporting hotel, once a Georgian rectory, set in eight

acres of grounds on Exmoor, with lovely views of the River Barle and its valley. Two hundred yards from the house, there is a hewn-stone bridge, Tarr Steps, which is believed to date from the Bronze Age. Inside, the hotel is welcoming, comfortable and homely, with open fires, sporting pictures and the blissful tranquillity engendered by the absence of televisions and telephones. Some of the rooms have splendid river views. Traditional English cooking served in Georgian dining room. Set lunch £15, set dinner £16. There is a ground-floor bedroom available for disabled guests.

Three miles of trout and salmon fishing; rough shooting; clay pigeon shooting; driven pheasant shooting can be arranged, as can riding and hunting

EXETER

🍽 ⚶ ⌀ ▭

The Captain's Table, The Basin, Haven Road, Exeter (Tel. 0392 413678)
Open 11am–2pm, 6pm–10pm Mon–Sat
Strategically positioned in the heart of Exeter's old docks at the entrance to the Maritime Museum, this is Exeter's only floating restaurant. It seats 20 (the seven tables by the portholes have the best views of the quay) and is housed in an unusual and attractively converted tug that worked on the Thames during the Second World War, and made no less than three trips across to Dunkirk. Tony Gulliver aims to keep the cooking crustacean oriented; at lunchtime, the menu is based on galettes, and in the evenings, prawns, crayfish, lobster and steaks are likely to be on the menu.

Haven Banks canoe club has its HQ a few yards away; fishing up and down the canal; windsurfing

EXMINSTER

🏨 ³/³ ⚶ ⌀ ▭

Turf Hotel, Exminster, Exeter EX6 8EE   (Tel. 0392 833128)
Call for directions
£17.50 b&b

This small hotel enjoys a unique position at the point where the Exeter canal emerges into the Exe estuary. There is no road access, so it is a silent haven and a walker's paradise; once there, you are well away from the distractions of the modern world. Wading birds and avocets also find the area attractive, and are evident in numbers: the spot is well known to, and popular with, bird watchers. The dining room seats 30 people; food is home cooked, and all tables have a view of the water. Bar meals are available, and there are 'cook-your-own-barbecue' evenings in the summer. Because of its solitary, watery situation, the area can look a little bleak in winter, though the landlords deny this strenuously. It is certainly an unusual location, and very different to everywhere else on the visiting list. No facilities for the disabled.

Hotel served by its own canal boat, The Water Mongoose, *for trips up the river; sailing, waterskiing, fishing*

FALMOUTH

The Chainlocker, Customs House Quay, Quay Hill, Falmouth, Cornwall TR11 3HG   (Tel. 0326 311085)
Turn left 200 yards past the church in the town centre
Open 11am–11pm Mon–Sat; noon–2.30pm, 7pm–10.30pm Sun

This 250-year-old pub has a great deal of atmosphere and much in the way of ships' paraphernalia (wheels, barometers and such). It is situated next to the lifeboat station and the customs house on a busy working harbour; take your drinks to the tables outside the pub, and watch the comings and goings on the quay. There is a good variety of Steam beers and lagers on offer at the bar, and bar meals are now available at lunchtimes and in the evenings all year round. The Marine Restaurant has recently been converted into two new bars, both of which overlook the harbour. No disabled facilities, though access is not difficult for anyone in a wheelchair.

Sailing and shark-fishing trips from harbour; river trips; beach and windsurfing from Gyllyngvase beach (other side of Falmouth); coastal walks, also walks at Flushing, reached by ferry

FALMOUTH

 23/43

The Greenbank Hotel, Harbourside, Falmouth, Cornwall
TR11 2SR   (Tel. 0326 312440)
Signposted from main roundabout outside town
£42.90–£57.75 pp b&b, set dinner £14.40
A 17th-century building with a comfortable atmosphere, airy
public rooms, and bedrooms named after ships: lots of
maritime bits and pieces (old etchings, brass fittings). In 1640,
the building was a ferryman's house – the ferry to Flushing
leaves from opposite the hotel. The hotel has its own private
quay and fine views of the Penryn river and harbour. The
downstairs bar has tables on the quay in summer. There is
seating for 70 people in the dining room, and both lunch and
dinner are served. Nearly all tables have a water view.
Additional facilities include a beauty salon and solarium. The
hotel has recently undergone a £1 million refit; there are 20 new
bedrooms, an underground car park, a gymnasium, and
conference facilities, but, sadly, no facilities for the disabled
have been considered.
*Watersports at Marina, 10 minutes' walk away; motorboats, yachts;
windsurfing at Custom House Quay; waterskiing at Swanpool
Beach, and on Helford River (five miles away); diving from
dockyard; rock fishing nearby; hotel can arrange sea fishing; beach
(five minutes' drive); five-minute walk to ferry to Flushing, where
there are walks round headland*

FORD

5/11

White Hart at Ford, nr Chippenham, Wilts SN14 8RP
(Tel. 0249 782213)
Off main A420 towards Bristol from Chippenham. Take first
left in the village of Ford
£59 double b&b
This 16th-century inn is a good combination of country pub
and small hotel, with timbered bar and log fire, and honest
portions of pub grub on offer. The bedrooms are civilized and

characterful, if not enormous, and the restaurant is pleasant, though it does not have a view of the river. Outside, there is a river terrace, with tables, beside a bona fide babbling trout stream, all set in beautiful grounds. Don't expect to go fishing, however: the trout are to be fed, not caught. The à la carte restaurant over the river seats 70, all tables with water view. There are no specific facilities for the disabled, though access is 'no problem', and four of the bedrooms are only up one step.
Swimming pool; walks along footpaths through grounds; fishing nearby

FOWEY

Food for Thought, The Quay, Fowey, Cornwall PL23 1AT
(Tel. 0726 83 2221)
Closed Sunday (open bank holidays)
Dinner only, set menu £16
This renowned restaurant is set in a 500-year-old, Grade II listed building almost on the water's edge on the quay in Fowey. The town is delightful, and not congested with traffic thanks to the draconian restrictions on vehicles, banishing them to the car parks on the edge of the town. Food for Thought boasts the distinction of having held a Michelin 'red M' for the last five years. Cooking is classic and French, with much use of fish and shellfish. There is seating for 38 people, and six tables have a good view of the quay. Advance booking is essential. No facilities for the disabled.
Nearby walks on National Trust land; windsurfing and sailing at harbour; beach at harbour mouth

FOWEY

Marina Hotel, Esplanade, Fowey, Cornwall PL23 1HY
(Tel. 0726 833315)
Open March to October
£24–£31 pp b&b
Perched on the harbour with fine views over the river and sea,

this charming hotel has three private moorings, and a small quayside garden with steps down to the beach. If you are planning on driving down the steep hill to the hotel to deliver your luggage (you have to leave your car outside the town, see above), warn the proprietor: when you stop in front of the hotel you will be blocking the whole street. Seven of the 11 rooms have a splendid view of the water, and big windows. Four rooms have balconies which give access to the garden. All 12 tables in the dining room share the panoramic view. The set menu at dinner costs £13; bar meals are available at lunchtime. *Beach at end of hotel garden; sailing, windsurfing, fishing and riding nearby; walks*

GODMANSTONE

Smiths Arms, Godmanstone, nr Dorchester, Dorset
(Tel. 0300 341 236)
Open 11am–3pm, 6pm–11pm
The Smiths Arms is the smallest pub in England, and that's official: it features in the *Guinness Book of Records*, with its external dimensions checking in at 39ft 6in by 11ft by 12ft. The pub can seat 28 customers on old church pews, and there is a stretch of a suitably diminutive River Frome running past, to provide a waterside garden. The building dates from the 15th century. Originally it was a blacksmith's shop, and the story goes that King Charles II once stopped here to have his horse shod, wanted a drink and granted the place a licence. The horse-racing memorabilia in the bar was collected by one landlord, who was an ex-jockey. Good home cooking, especially ham and bread pudding. No children under 14 in bar. No facilities for the disabled.
Interesting walks (for example to Cerne Abbas Giant; ask staff for details)

HAYLING ISLAND

Cockle Warren Cottage Hotel, 36 Seafront, Hayling Island,
Hants PO11 9HL   (Tel. 0705 464961)
£35–£40 single, £56–£64 double room
An oddball of a tiny hotel, which won the AA Best Newcomer of
the Year Award for 1990, with a small dining room set in a conservatory overlooking the outdoor swimming pool. Two of the
bedrooms both with four-posters overlook the Solent, with
lovely views across to the Isle of Wight. A good-looking, home-
cooked menu includes regional French country dishes (residents'
friends are welcome at dinner; non-residents can find coffee and
snacks in the patio café). With no disrespect to the owners, our
researcher, though he was greatly taken with it, thought it a
funny little place and the surroundings, although seaside, are
not particularly picturesque. No facilities for the disabled.
*Six-and-a-half-mile sandy beach; sailing; windsurfing; deep sea
fishing; golf; tennis; squash; badminton; riding*

HELFORD

Shipwright's Arms, Helford Village, nr Helston, Cornwall
(Tel. 0326 23235)
On the road through Helford
Open 11am–11pm Mon–Sat; noon–2.30pm, 7pm–10.30pm
Sun An ancient and highly picturesque thatched pub on
Helford
Passage Creek, with about 15 tables on a terraced patio going
right down to sea wall. Bar food available from noon to 2pm
and 7pm to 9pm (on Sundays in winter, only from noon to
1.30pm). Barbecue dinners are served out on the patio in
summer. Very attractive when the tide is in. Beers include
Cornish Original, Newquay Steam beers, and draught
Guinness. No facilities for the disabled.
*Boats for hire in Helford (and St Anthony, two miles away); walks
on costal path; fishing from rocks, or fishing trips from Manaccan (one
mile away); beach (10 minutes' walk)*

HELSTON
IOI ⚓ 🏠 🚫 🛏

Riverside Restaurant with Rooms, Helford Village, nr
Helston, Cornwall TR12 6JU   (Tel. 0326 23 443)
Open 7.30pm–9.30pm daily, mid-February to
mid-November; also open for lunch on Fri–Sun, May to
September
£70–£87 per double, including a substantial continental
breakfast. Full English breakfast available, £3–£4
Situated 10 yards from the water on a tidal creek in the quiet
Cornish village of Helford, the Riverside Restaurant is housed
in a Grade II listed building, and describes its cuisine as 'French
provincial'. The emphasis on the menu is on fresh produce;
herbs and vegetables come from the garden, the fish is local,
and the croissants and marmalade served at breakfast are home
made. Gourmet oils and vinegars are also made on the
premises; these are for sale by the bottle so guests can
experiment with them at home. There is seating for 40 in the
dining room, and five of the tables have a view out over the
creek. The set menu for dinner – four or five courses – costs
£27.50. No special disabled facilities, but the dining room is on
the ground floor.
*Sailing and windsurfing at St Anthony; golf near Mullion (six miles
away); deep sea fishing can be arranged; National Trust gardens;
walks along the coast; bird watching*

HOPE COVE
🏘 26/35 🏠 ⚐ 🛏

The Cottage Hotel, Hope Cove, nr Kingsbridge, South
Devon TQ7 3HJ   (Tel. 0548 561 555)
From A381 (Kingsbridge to Salcombe), head for Hope Cove,
then Inner Hope
£27.50–£57 dinner and b&b
Originally a small cottage built in 1880, the hotel has been
developed in stages since 1927, and stands in two acres of
grounds. The beautiful gardens lead down to the beach. The
hotel is surrounded by National Trust land, so there is plenty

of scope for walks in glorious surroundings. The restaurant seats 80 (the 14 window tables have the best sea view), and serves bar/snack lunches, and dinner; non-residents are welcome. Devonshire cream teas and after-dinner coffee are served on the sun terrace, which has superb views overlooking Bolt Tail and Bigbury Bay. Two ground-floor rooms suitable for the disabled.

Coastal walks; watersports nearby (bring equipment) or at Thurlestone Sands; fishing (trips in season, or off breakwater), or at Bolt Head; two beaches; favourable rates with nearby golf course; Bigbury golf course 20 minutes by car

ILFRACOMBE

Cliffe Hydro Hotel, Hillsborough Road, Ilfracombe, North Devon EX34 9NP   (Tel. 0271 863606)
From town centre, follow Hillsborough Road
£30–£70 per room b&b
The location is fabulous; views sweep across the harbour and coastline to Wales. The hotel itself is not so impressive: its saving grace is a very smart health complex, equipped with a swimming pool, sauna, steam room, whirlpool spa and weight training machines. The restaurant seats 75; half the room overlooks the sea (seven tables have a direct water view). Non-residents are welcome for meals. There is an à la carte dinner menu; a four-course dinner costs £9.95. Main courses at lunch are about £5. The hotel gardens reach down to the quay. There are no facilities for the disabled.

Raparee beach (five minutes' walk); fishing nearby; coastal path walks

INSTOW

The Commodore Hotel, Marine Parade, Instow, North Devon EX39 4JN   (Tel. 0271 860347)
Off the A39 Barnstaple–Bideford road
£85 double b&b

A long, low, white, villa-style building in an excellent position right on the sea front, with spectacular views of the Taw/Torridge estuary. The gardens are highly manicured, and the bar opens straight on to the patio terrace, which overlooks the estuary. The glass-fronted restaurant seats 80; everyone has a water view, though few tables are actually in the window. The table d'hôte menu is £17.50; the à la carte menu features seafood and game. Children are allowed into the restaurant, as long as they can sit on their own chairs. Saturday night dinner dances are held during the winter. There are no specific facilities for the disabled, though non-resident visitors in wheelchairs will be able to find their way into the restaurant without trouble, as it is all on one level.

Wonderful long sandy beach; coastal path walks; sailing, waterskiing, windsurfing, paragliding; fishing

KINGSBRIDGE

Start Bay Inn, Torcross, Kingsbridge, South Devon TQ7 2TQ (Tel. 0548 580553)
On the A379 between Dartmouth and Kingsbridge
Open 11am–3pm, 6pm–11pm Mon–Sat; noon–2pm, 7pm–10.30pm Sun
The pub is a 14th-century thatched cottage right on the beach, opposite a freshwater ley (an inland lake, about a mile long). The bar and patio look directly out to sea. The bar menu, served at lunch and dinner, is strong on seafood; the landlord dives for as much fish as possible (such as lobster, crabs, scallops) and has won an award for serving the freshest fish in Britain. Beers include Marston's and Flowers IPA. Pets should be kept on leads. There is a ramp to facilitate wheelchair access to the pub, but no specific disabled facilities.

Watersports at Blackpool Sands (two or three miles away); fishing on beach and on ley; coastal path walks; Slapton Sands beach, long, sandy and straight, where many American soldiers died in the war practising for D-Day (a recovered Sherman tank stands in the beach car park near the inn)

LANGSTONE

The Royal Oak, High Street, Langstone, Hants
(Tel. 0705 483125)
From A3M–A27 Chichester Road, follow signs to Hayling
Island
Open 11am–11pm Mon–Sat; noon–3pm, 7pm–10.30pm Sun
A pretty, bona fide old inn situated right on the harbour (on an inlet, rather than sea), with flag floors, heavy beams, real ales and (alas) Muzak. The bar overlooks the water, and there are waterside seats outside, though the view can be uninspiring at low tide. There is a strong 'local' feeling to the pub, plenty of seagulls, and always two great ales and bar food available. Though busy in summer, it is rarely congested. At the back of the pub there is a pet corner (featuring rabbits and ducks), which is popular with children. A free nappy-changing facility has just been introduced. No facilities for the disabled.

LONGHAM

The Bridge House Hotel, Longham, Dorset BH22 9AN
(Tel. 0202 578828)
Off A348 between Poole and Fransham
£53 pp single, £82.50 double b&b
A Mediterranean-style hotel sitting, rather incongruously, right on the river bank in the Stour Valley. Verandas, terraces and balconies add considerably to the atmosphere. The grounds enclose an island, which is linked to the hotel by a bridge. There is a large bar, and the carvery restaurant, which overlooks the river, seats 45–50 people. The rooms which have a view of the river are very comfortable, but ground-floor rooms look on to car park and road (some of the rooms are for non-smokers only). Greek food and music evenings are held on the last Sunday of the month, if the Greek owners are not hosting a wedding. Macrobiotic weekends, with 'special gourmet meals for a balanced life' are held occasionally. There

are conference facilities, and some ground-floor rooms which are suitable for disabled visitors.

Fishing (the hotel has rights on the Stour river; bring equipment); golf at local courses (golf weekends can be organized); walks; beach (six miles away); watersports

LOOE

Talland Bay Hotel, nr Looe, Cornwall PL13 2JB
(Tel. 0503 72667)
Take the Polperro road from Looe. After one mile ignore a signpost pointing left to Talland. Continue on the Polperro road for another mile, then follow the 'Talland Bay Hotel' sign at the crossroads
Closed in January
£46–£80 pp dinner and b&b

Parts of this fine Cornish house date back to the 16th century. It is set in beautiful gardens 150 feet above sea level, with magnificent views over the bay, so it is a five-minute walk to descend to the beach, which is sandy at low tide. Bedrooms are spacious (there is one four-poster), individually furnished and fully equipped. The dining room seats 60, with five tables overlooking the bay. Lunch is served between 12.30pm and 2pm; dinner between 7.30pm and 9pm (set dinner, £15). In the summer there are occasional evening barbecues under the pine trees in the garden. Dogs can be accommodated by arrangement (£3 per night). Children are welcome, though no under-fives are allowed in the dining room – they are provided with high tea, and packed off to bed at a sensible hour. The hotel is strong on special interest holidays, including landscape painting, geology, archaeology, and bridge. The dining room and one bedroom are on the ground floor, and a ramp is available for wheelchair access to the garden; otherwise there are no special facilities for the disabled.

Swimming pool (heated May to November); sauna; solarium; the hotel has its own boat for waterskiing, and a yacht; beach; golf, tennis, riding, watersports and fishing nearby; walks along cliff path (the hotel can provide a booklet of local walks)

LYME REGIS

Alexandra Hotel, Pound Street, Lyme Regis, Dorset
(Tel. 02794 2010)
£40–£55 pp dinner and b&b
Built in 1735, this house has been a hotel since the beginning of
the century. It is very pleasant, and medium sized, with fine
gardens and excellent views of the Cobb and Lyme Bay. The
bedrooms and public rooms are comfortable and tastefully
furnished. Altogether, a very civilized place, though not a
family hotel. The restaurant seats 65 people, and most tables
have a view out to sea. Dorset cream teas served. They have no
disabled facilities, and there are a lot of steps, which makes
wheelchair access difficult.
*Inland and coastal walks; boat hire; sea angling; charter boats; sandy
beach*

LYME REGIS

The Red House, Sidmouth Road, Lyme Regis, Dorset
DT7 3ES   (Tel. 02974 2055)
£34–£42 per room b&b
Another very friendly guest house with prime southerly views
of Lyme Bay, though not right beside the sea. It is situated at
the top of the hill out of town, and thus a good 15-minute walk
uphill from the town and the beach. An excellent spot for
walkers – the house is close to the path that leads through the
Undercliff (which should strike a chord with readers of John
Fowles's *The French Lieutenant's Woman*). Large, comfortable
rooms. Weather permitting, breakfast is served on the balcony
overlooking the bay. There are no facilities for the disabled.
Pets are accepted by prior arrangement only.
*Trout fishing can be arranged; walks; beach; watersports; visits to
National Trust properties and famous gardens*

LYMPSTONE

🍽 ♨6 ✗ ▭

The River House, The Strand, Lympstone, Exmouth, Devon
EX8 5EY   (Tel. 0395 265 147)
Six miles from Exeter on A376 Exmouth road
Closed Sunday dinner, all Monday
All tables water-view, 34 covers
In the heart of the picturesque village of Lympstone on Exe,
the River House provides a friendly welcome for serious diners
in congenial surroundings. The first-floor restaurant has a glass
wall, which gives a magnificent view of Powderham Castle
and the Exe estuary. The cooking is European: a three-course
meal costs about £28.50, and the restaurant is famous for its
vegetable (as opposed to vegetarian) cookery. Cookery
demonstrations and full tasting lunches are held at least four
times a year. There are two rooms available for diners who
wish to go no further: £50 single, £66 double, with a light
breakfast included. No facilities for the disabled.
Walks, sailing, windsurfing; watersports, fishing and beach two miles
away, at Exmouth

LYNMOUTH

🏛 12/16 ♨5 ◁ ▭

The Rising Sun Hotel, Harbourside, Lynmouth, North
Devon EX35 6EQ   (Tel. 0598 53223)
£35–£45 pp b&b
An immaculate 14th-century smugglers' inn right on the
quayside in Lynmouth, with a terraced garden and very
comfortable cottage-style rooms. R. D. Blackmore wrote
Lorna Doone here, and there is the added bonus of the garden
cottage, where Shelley spent his honeymoon (the cottage has a
four-poster, sitting room, and private garden with spectacular
views). The inn overlooks the small picturesque harbour and
the East Lyn salmon river. The oak-panelled dining room and
bar have crooked ceilings, thick walls and uneven oak floors.
Thirty-two people can be seated for lunch and dinner (six
tables have a water view); the chef specializes in local Exmoor

game and seafood. The set dinner costs £17.50. No facilities for the disabled.

The hotel has private fishing; superb walks; hunting nearby; swimming; 10 minutes' walk to beach

LYNTON

Hewitts Hotel and Restaurant, North Walk, Lynton, Devon EX35 6HJ   (Tel. 0598 52293)
£35–£45 pp b&b, lunch £13.50, dinner £19.50
A rambling, late-19th-century house in a wonderfully dramatic location, with tremendous views from the 150-foot terrace overlooking Lynmouth Bay and the Bristol Channel. The panelled two-storey hall with gallery would make a perfect Agatha Christie set: the whole place has a strong country-house feel. Great character throughout, and very secluded, with 27 acres of wooded grounds stretching down to Lynmouth. The restaurant seats 26, all tables have a water view (set lunch £12.50, set dinner £16.50). Children under 12 are only allowed in the dining room between 7pm and 8pm. No facilities for the disabled.

Walks (the coastal path leads into the Exmoor National Park); watersports, fishing, beach; riding; clay pigeon shooting in grounds

LYNTON

The Lynton Cottage Hotel, North Walk Hill, Lynton, Devon EX35 6ED   (Tel. 0598 52 342)
£98–£115 dinner and b&b
Once the residence of a Knight of the Realm, the hotel is set on the cliffs 500 feet above the bay. The views have the extra dimension of the inland aspect up the Lyn valley, so there is a breathtaking panorama of the coastal boundaries of Exmoor, the East Lyn valley, and Lynmouth Bay. The restaurant seats 65, and 10 of the tables have a water view. Cuisine features

modern French dishes. The restaurant is open to non-residents in the evening, serving four-course dinners for £17–£25. Murder and mystery weekends are occasionally arranged, as well as gastronomic house parties. No facilities for the disabled.

Walks on coastal path and to Exmoor; coarse and sea fishing; rocky beach; riding, clay pigeon shooting and tennis can be arranged by the staff at the hotel

MAIDEN NEWTON

Maiden Newton House, Maiden Newton, nr Dorchester
DT2 0AA   (Tel. 0300 20336)
Off the A356 Dorchester–Crewkerne road
Open February to December
£80–£120 double room b&b

This large house, made of local stone, has 21 acres of grounds, a stretch of the River Frome, and enough Hardy connections to satisfy the most ardent aficionado. The village is mentioned in *Tess of the D'Urbervilles*, Hardy's mother worked in the original house on this site, and the house itself is believed to have featured in a Hardy short story, though no one is quite sure which one. If you would prefer an alternative historical reference, Charles I is believed to have stayed here in 1642. There is a strong country-house atmosphere, fostered by immaculate, luxurious rooms, and the small number of guests (there are only six rooms), who all dine together in a fine dining room overlooking the river. In the Edwardian tradition, guests' names, rather than room numbers, are displayed on the doors of the rooms. The evening's gourmet menu is displayed all day so guests have plenty of time to choose their courses or request alternatives. Supper available for children under 12. Highly recommended. No non-residents for dinner. No facilities for the disabled.

One mile of private fishing; rough shooting in grounds; sailing; clay pigeon shooting; riding; golf

MOUSEHOLE

2/3

The Ship Inn, Mousehole, Cornwall TR19 6QX
(Tel. 0736 731234)
Open 10.30am–11pm Mon–Sat; noon–2.30pm,
7pm–10.30pm Sun
£40 double b&b
Parts of this charming pub are 300 years old. There is nowhere
to sit outside, as the road runs right past, but you can stand on
road with your drinks and admire the harbour. Both bars look
out on to the water, and serve St Austell beers (including HSD,
Bosuns, and Mild). Bar snacks are available, but not on
Sunday. The bedrooms (summer only) are basic and cheerful.
The hotel has recently been undergoing a major refit: new
kitchens, cellars and bedrooms with en suite bathrooms are
being added, though there will still not be any facilities for the
disabled.
*Harbour beach right in front of pub; sea fishing trips from harbour, or
fishing from quay; yacht club at Penzance; coastal path walks*

MOUSEHOLE

7/25

The Lobster Pot Hotel, South Cliff, Mousehole, Penzance,
Cornwall TR19 6QX   (Tel. 0736 731528)
Closed in January
£23–£44 pp b&b
You would find it hard to get closer to the water: the hotel
restaurant overhangs the harbour. The hotel itself is made up
of fisherman's cottages – Grade II listed, with some sections
over 200 years old. Though refurbished this winter, the cosy
cramped rooms, low ceilings and rickety floors retain much
'olde worlde' charm: to reach one of the rooms – the Crow's
Nest – you must scale a steep ladder of a staircase. The
restaurant seats 65 people, and six tables have a view of the
harbour. Bar snacks are available at lunchtime; table d'hôte
dinner costs £12.95. Pets accepted by arrangement. No

facilities for the disabled. No hotel car park, though the harbour car park is within view.

Safe harbour beach below hotel; fishing in village; six miles to watersports at Mounts Bay

MULLION

Polurrian Hotel, Mullion, Helston, Cornwall TR12 7EN
(Tel. 0326 240421)
From Mullion, follow signs to Mullion Cove then Polurrian Cove.
Closed December to March
£50–£86 pp b&b

This imposing Edwardian building occupies a wonderful location overlooking Polurrian Cove, on the Lizard Peninsula. There are 12 acres of terraced lawns descending to the sea and a sandy beach. The spring storms in 1989 took a vast bite out of the roof, so there has recently been extensive rebuilding and redecorating to restore the hotel to its former glory. Restaurant seats 100 and has 15 sea-view tables. Five-course dinner costs £15; bar snacks are served at lunchtime. Indoor pool, spa bath, sauna, solarium, squash. Positively welcoming to, and geared up for, children, with play areas inside and out. All public rooms and some bedrooms are on the ground floor, but there are no special facilities for the disabled.

Outdoor pool, tennis, croquet, putting; coastal path walks (walk to The Lizard and the hotel will collect you); watersports (on reservoir, 20 miles away); fishing from cove, or on bigger boats (also from Helford); sandy beach below hotel garden; orienteering from Truro; riding and golf can be arranged (both 3 miles away)

MYLOR BRIDGE

The Pandora Inn, Restronguet Creek, Mylor Bridge, Falmouth, Cornwall TR11 5ST   (Tel. 0326 72678)
For Mylor Bridge, turn off the A39 at Penryn
Restaurant open 7pm–12am. Bars open in the summer 11am–

11pm Mon–Sat (for food, noon–10pm); noon–3pm, 7pm–
10.30pm Sun

An immensely charming building, with thatched roof and
whitewashed walls, low ceilings, heavy beams and many
nautical souvenirs, by Restronguet Creek. One of the lower
rooms floods at (very) high tide, frustrating all attempts to stop
it. The restaurant seats 50 (including the semi-private Captain
Edwardes Room, suitably furnished with portholes). The
menu is strong on seafood, the dish of the day depending on
the local catch (main courses £10–£15). There is space for 60 in
the bars, outside seating for 80 on the floating pontoon patio
and an extensive bar menu. Most tables have views of the
water. Children are allowed in limited areas. Dogs must be on
leads. Local beers include Bowsons, Tinner, Bass, and HSD
(Hicks Special Draught, known to locals as High Speed
Death). No disabled access or facilities.

Sailing tuition nearby at Mylor Yacht Harbour; coastal path walks;
beach at Falmouth (four miles away); pontoon only accessible to
yachts for three hours either side of high water; shower for yachtsmen

NEWQUAY

🏨 ²⁵/₅₀ 🛏 🕊 ▭

Hotel Riviera, Lusty Glaze Road, Newquay, Cornwall
TR7 3AA   (Tel. 0637 874251)
£32–£39.50 pp b&b

Large hotel with friendly staff situated next to Newquay's
Barrow Field. Bedrooms are slightly dated, but some have
excellent views over Barrow Field and the sea; others have
poor views, so specify when booking (there is a supplement of
£2.80 for sea-view rooms). The hotel is very popular for food
(set lunch, £8; set dinner, £11.50; bar snacks can be taken
outside), and with an older clientele. Babysitting can be
arranged (with notice). Pets can be accommodated for a charge
of £4.50 per day. No disabled facilities, and a considerable
number of stairs.

Outdoor swimming pool; squash and racquetball courts; sauna; games
room with full-sized snooker table; children's play area; Lusty Glaze
beach two minutes' walk away; Newquay's speciality is surfing; there

is some windsurfing and waterskiing; hotel can advise on sea and rock fishing; walks on coastal path

PADSTOW

The Old Mill Country House, Little Petherick (nr Padstow), Cornwall PL27 7QT (Tel. 0841 540388)
On A389 by bridge in Little Petherick
Open March to November
£18.50–£23 pp b&b
This converted 16th-century grist mill is now a Grade II listed building, set in its own gardens, next to a stream that dawdles into the Camel Estuary. A new water-wheel has just been installed outside the dining room window; one of the bedrooms looks down on to it (it is turned off at night, for the sake of tranquillity). The dining room seats 16 and serves lunch by arrangement, and dinner at 7pm. No facilities for the disabled.
Sandy beaches on Camel Estuary; sailing, windsurfing and waterskiing nearby; walks around estuary and along National Trust coastline; freshwater (on lakes, six miles away) and sea fishing; pony trekking; golf

PAIGNTON

Redcliffe Hotel, Marine Drive, Paignton, Devon TQ3 2NL (Tel. 0803 526397)
£34–£46 b&b
Built to the design of Colonel Robert Smith (he bought the tower in 1853 and added to it), the hotel is an unusual example of Indo-European architecture, hyped as the jewel in Torbay's crown. The hotel meets the beach at the sea wall: the Colonel built the subterranean passage to the beach as a walkway to his plunge bath. Eight of the rooms have balconies overlooking the sea. The dining room seats 180; 20 tables overlook the water. As well as dinner (table d'hôte £12.50), there are bar meals available, and the restaurant serves Sunday lunch, from

£6.95. The restaurant has recently been mirrored, to make it easier for diners to admire the sea. Ballroom and residents' lounge have sea views. Additional attractions are a putting green and an outdoor swimming pool. NB: All rooms are the same price, though widely varying in size and view, so ask for the best. No facilities for the disabled.

Beach; watersports; fishing (through contacts, in Paignton harbour); walks to Brixham, Paignton, Torquay, and Dartmoor (not too far by car)

POLKERRIS

inn ⌂ ⊗ ▭

The Rashleigh Inn, Polkerris, Par, nr Fowey, Cornwall
PL24 2TL   (Tel. 0726 81 3991)
Signposted from A3082 (road from St Austell to Fowey)
Open 11am–2.30pm, 6pm–11pm Mon–Sat; noon–3pm, 7pm–10.30pm Sun. Summer Saturdays, 11am–11pm; August, 11am–11pm Mon–Sat

You couldn't get much closer to the beach if you tried. The pub has seating for 100 on the sea-wall terrace which looks directly on to the beach, and is attractive inside. The restaurant, which seats 24, serves an extensive buffet lunch, and à la carte dinners Wednesday to Saturday. Prices range from £4 for bar snacks, through about £6 for lunch buffet, to £12 for dinner main courses. Local beers include St Austell HSD, Burtons, and Bolsters Bitter. Live jazz piano entertainment on Friday and Saturday evenings, all year round. Children are allowed in for meals only, by prior arrangement. The bar and restaurant are on the ground floor, but there are no special facilities for the disabled.

Right on the beach; fishing off sea wall; windsurfing equipment and boats for hire on beach in summer; coastal path walks

POLPERRO

The Blue Peter Inn, The Quay, Polperro, Cornwall
(Tel. 0503 72743/72467)
Past Looe, at the end of the A387
Open 11am–11pm Mon–Sat; noon–3pm, 7pm–10.30pm Sun
The 'smallest pub in Polperro' is an attractive whitewashed
building by the harbour, with views of the cliffs and open sea
from upstairs. There is water on two sides; the interior is cosy.
Approach on foot through Polperro's tiny streets (leave your
car in the main car park outside the exclusion zone and believe
the signs that say there are no parking spaces in the town!).
There are just four chairs outside the pub, and seating for 32
inside. There is a variety of home-cooked food at lunch and
dinner; the blackboard menu changes daily: Jennie Craig-
Hallam is Burmese, and prepares authentic curries and lots of
seafood. Live jazz on Sunday lunchtimes. Local scrumpy;
beers include St Austell HSD, Tinners, Wreckers (strong keg
bitter) and a guest beer every week. No facilities for the
disabled.
Safe beach nearby, with caves; boat cruises from Polperro; fishing
from beach and harbour (bring own equipment); fishing trips from
nearby towns; coastal path walks

POOLE

The Salterns Hotel, 38 Salterns Way, Lilliput, Poole, Dorset
BH14 8JR   (Tel. 0202 707 321)
From Poole, take B3369 to Sandbanks/Lilliput
£80–£92 single, £110–£126.50 double
The approach to this hotel does not reveal its best side: it is a
marvellous quasi-Tudor pile, which used to house the Poole
Harbour Yacht Club (the bar is still the PHYC Clubroom). A
family-run hotel, it is situated in the middle of its own marina.
Nearly all the rooms have excellent views of the boats in the
marina, the sandbanks and Brownsea Island beyond. Decor is
standardized, but of a high quality. The restaurant has been

expanded, so that there are now 50 tables, all with a view of the water. The marina can take boats up to 59-foot, and has full back-up facilities. Visitors to the hotel pay the usual mooring fee, and moorings are subject to availability. Meeting room facilities; secretarial services can be arranged. No facilities for the disabled.

Games room; charter motorboats available; sea fishing trips (from Poole); sailing; golf and riding can be arranged; tennis; good walks; small private beach; Sandbanks beach (two miles away)

POOLE

IOI 🏠 🚫 ▭

The Warehouse Oyster Bar, Poole Quay, Poole, Dorset
BH15 1HJ   (Tel. 0202 677238)
Oyster bar open 11am–11pm; restaurant open
noon–2pm, 7pm–10pm (11pm Fri and Sat)
An old warehouse right on the quay has been converted to form this restaurant and oyster bar. It is very comfortably appointed and well-restored, and energetically run. The well-stocked wine cellar, behind wrought-iron gates, is a feature in the bar. The Oyster Bar serves light lunches and snacks (choose your own crustaceans from the live menagerie); the first-floor restaurant has a wider menu (lots of local fish), and even better views of the quay from its 24 tables. No facilities for the disabled.

Walks; watersports; fishing; beach nearby

PORLOCK

🏠 12/24 🏠 ◁ᴅ ▭

Anchor Hotel & Ship Inn, Porlock Weir, nr Minehead, Somerset   (Tel. 0643 862636)
A39 to Porlock
£30–£53 pp b&b
The Ship Inn, a thatched 16th-century converted cider barn, combines with the 19th-century Anchor Hotel to offer both modern comforts and old world charm. Half of the rooms overlook picturesque Porlock Weir harbour and the Severn

Estuary. The Ship opens out to a garden and terrace. Home-made food is available from the bars, which also look out on to the harbour. No facilities for the disabled.

PORTLAND

Pennsylvania Castle Hotel, Pennsylvania Road, Portland, Dorset DT5 1HZ   (Tel. 0305 820 561)
From Weymouth, take the A354, then the B3154 to end of the Portland promontory
£27 pp b&b
An unusual place: a castle with strongly built towers and battlements designed by James Wyatt and completed by 1800, and thought to be Sylvania Castle in Hardy's *The Well Beloved*. George III suggested the building of the Castle, which was later occupied by his daughter, Princess Elizabeth. The new owner has big plans, and though now the place is good in parts, it should soon be very special. One recent addition is a new chef, whose menu is strong on fresh seafood. The main restaurant has 12 tables, half with water views. The garden room restaurant has passion flower creepers and 30 seats, all with a view. Bar meals also available. The sub-tropical garden leads steeply down to a cove. A new swimming pool is under construction, though this may not be finished until the end of 1991. No facilities for the disabled.
Walks; bird-watching; watersports; fishing; beach

PORTHLEVEN

The Ship Inn, Porthleven, Cornwall TR13 9JS
(Tel. 0326 572841)
West side of Porthleven harbour
Open 11.30am–11pm Mon–Sat; noon–3pm, 7pm–10.30pm Sun
A fine, 17th-century smugglers' pub, complete with original stone walls. Both bars overlook the water, as does the garden, which has tables that can seat 60–70 people. Curiosities include

the statutory collection of portholes and sea-faring bric-a-brac, and old (from 1860s) British coins and foreign currency stuck to bar pillars (more coins always welcome). Children are only allowed into family room. The inn is known for its good seafood (served both at lunchtime and in the evening), and the considerable efforts made by the landlord are reflected in the congeniality of the surroundings. No facilities for the disabled.
Coastal path goes right past the door; short surfing break off Porthleven, considered good; windsurfing (eight miles away); boat hire and beach nearby; rock and sea fishing

PORT ISAAC

5/10

Slipway Hotel, The Harbour Front, Port Isaac, Cornwall
PL29 3RH   (Tel. 0208 880264)
By the harbour in Port Isaac
Closed in February
£22–£28 pp b&b
A 16th-century, Grade II listed building, all funny little staircases, oddly shaped rooms, slanting ceilings that bang-your-head level and other manifestations of age, at the bottom of the narrow streets that wind down to the harbour. Since the hotel is small and overlooks the fishing port, the higher floors have the best views. Cosy bar, apparently the scene of many a sing-song. A small stream runs past the side of hotel. The restaurant (no water view) seats 32, and is proud of its reputation for good, fresh food; fish, crabs and lobsters are landed daily. No children under nine years (because of the very steep stairs). No facilities for the disabled.
Coastal path walks; fishing trips; harbour beach right in front of hotel, though Gaverne beach (10 minutes' walk) is better; surfing at Polzeath (three miles away); other watersports on Camel Estuary; two championship golf courses within 10 miles

ST AUSTELL

Carlyon Bay Hotel, Carlyon Bay, St Austell, Cornwall
PL25 3RD   (Tel. 0726 81 2304)
£63–£81 pp b&b

This luxurious and peaceful 1920s hotel occupies 250 acres of gardens overlooking the three-quarter-mile-long Crinnis beach. The bedrooms are comfortable and airy, and many have sea views. The dining room seats 150 people, and 20 tables have a view out to sea. Non-residents are welcome for lunch and dinner (set lunch £9.95; five-course dinner £16.50). Guests should dress smartly in the evenings: jacket and tie required in public rooms after 7pm. There is a playroom and 'play paddock' for children; in summer the hotel organizes games and entertainment. Some rooms are served by a lift, but there are no special facilities for the disabled.

Hotel has its own 18-hole golf course, nine-hole approach and putting lawn, indoor and outdoor pools, spa/solarium and sauna room, two tennis courts; nearby walks along coastal path or beach and golf course; watersports; fishing in Fowey; beaches (five minutes' walk); helipad

ST AUSTELL

Porth Avallen Hotel, Sea Road, Carlyon Bay, St Austell,
Cornwall PL25 3SG   (Tel. 0726 81 2802)
On sea road, call for directions
Closed for 10 days at Christmas
£41.50 single, £66 double

A private house built in 1930, the hotel enjoys excellent unimpeded views of the sea. As the crow flies, the water is only 100 yards away, but for pedestrians, it is a ten-minute walk. Friendly staff and comfortable decor add to the relaxed country-house atmosphere. Bedrooms are comfortable and well furnished; two have four-poster beds. The dining room seats 45, with the best views from four window tables. A set lunch costs £7.50; a five-course dinner, £12.50. The bar and sunny conservatory also have excellent sea views. There are no special facilities for the disabled.

Coastal path walks (the hotel can provide a ramblers' booklet); riding; windsurfing at Newquay, canoeing and jetskis at Pentewan (five miles away)

ST IVES

🏨 10/33 ⌂ ✍ ▭

Carbis Bay Hotel, Carbis Bay, St Ives, Cornwall TR26 2NP (Tel. 0736 795311)
Open 30 March to November
£30–£50 pp dinner and b&b
A large hotel set in grounds just above the sweeping curve of Carbis Bay. The hotel owns and manages the beach, and rents out deck chairs, windbreaks and so on. As well as the rooms in the hotel (one of which has a four-poster bed as well as a sea view), the hotel has some self-catering flats for rent. These tend to be booked up early, so move fast if you want one for next year. A kidney-shaped heated outdoor pool on a sun-trap terrace also looks out over the beach. The restaurant seats 100; 10 tables overlook the sea. Special diets catered for. High season entertainments here include Punch and Judy shows, live Country and Western music evenings, and barbecues. No facilities for the disabled.

Outdoor pool; coastal path walks; waterskiing and surfing (bring own equipment); sea fishing off beach, or hotel can organize fishing trips from Penzance; golf nearby; trips to the Scilly Isles

ST MAWES

🏨 12/23 ⌂ ✍ ▭

Idle Rocks Hotel, Tredenham Road, St Mawes, Cornwall TR2 5RD   (Tel. 0326 270771)
On A3078
£38.50–£59.50 pp dinner and b&b (b&b without dinner £7 less)
This bright and cheerful hotel enjoys a fine situation, right on the sea wall. The rooms are full of character, and there is a cocktail bar and terrace that look out to the harbour and the sea,

and makes the perfect spot for a pre-dinner drink. There is seating for 80 people in the restaurant, and all of the tables have a sea view. The castle opposite the hotel was built for Henry VIII, and makes up a matching pair with Falmouth Castle. Pets can be accommodated by arrangement. No facilities for the disabled.

Beach (three minutes' walk); coastal path walks and marked trails along Percuil river (National Trust); sailing classes, fishing from quay and shark fishing nearby

SALCOMBE

🏨 18/18 ⛲ ⬦ 🎴

Sunny Cliff Hotel, Cliff Road, Salcombe, Devon TQ8 8JX (Tel. 054 884 2207)
£23.50–£31.50 pp b&b
Open all year: November to April b&b; April to November half-board

Set on the side of the estuary, this friendly hotel, five minutes' walk from the town centre, has large, bright family rooms. From its vantage point 100 feet above the water, there are superb views straight across estuary and out to the sea; the gardens slope down to the water, where there are six moorings and a landing stage. There is a heated salt-water swimming pool by the sea wall. The dining room seats a maximum of 44 people (the five window tables have the best view of the water). No facilities for the disabled.

Beaches at North Sands (10 minutes' walk), South Sands (further), and across estuary by ferry; windsurfing and sailing nearby, but no waterskiing in the bay (8 mph speed limit); and, of course, plenty of coastal walks along the spectacular coastline

SALCOMBE

🏨 20/40 ⛲ ⬦ 🎴

South Sands Hotel, South Sands, Salcombe, Devon TQ8 8LL (Tel. 054884 3741)
From Salcombe, follow signs to South Sands
Sea-view rooms £55–£65 pp dinner and b&b

Comfortable and friendly hotel in a small sandy cove: the water actually comes up to the hotel at high tide. There is an excellent view from sea-facing rooms and the dining room, where there is seating for 100 people, and all tables have a sea view. All bedrooms are well-equipped; half of them look out to sea, and cost a little more than the others. If you feel like a change from the dining room, you can choose to eat in the new bistro. There is a charge for dogs: £3 a day, food extra. One hundred yards from Tides Reach Hotel, and not much to choose between the two. No facilities for the disabled.

Pool; sauna and solarium; beach starts where hotel stops; ferry from beach to Salcombe (10 minutes away); watersports from boat house next door; coastal path walks; sea fishing nearby

SALCOMBE

34/41

Tides Reach Hotel, South Sands, Salcombe, Devon TQ8 9LJ (Tel. 054884 3466)
From Salcombe, follow signs to South Sands
Closed November to February
£55–£90 pp dinner and b&b
An elegant, family-run hotel on a sandy cove and just across the road from the beach. Some of the attractive bedrooms have sea-view balconies, the staff are attentive, and there is a sheltered water garden by the hotel. The sea aquarium in the cocktail bar displays a number of locally caught fish. The dining room seats 94 people, and the 15 window tables have the best view of the sea. Non-residents are welcome for meals; a four-course dinner costs £20. Snacks are available in the bar at lunchtime. Within the hotel, there is an impressive indoor leisure complex complete with heated pool, sauna, squash court, multi-gym and hair salon. All floors are served by a lift, and doorways are wide enough to accommodate wheelchairs, but there are no special facilities for the disabled.

Coastal and country walks (the hotel can supply a booklet that gives details of 15 walks); ferry from beach to Salcombe (10 minutes); sailing; windsurfing; waterskiing; scuba diving, and sea or freshwater fishing can be arranged; beach immediately across the road

SALCOMBE

🏘️ 19/28 🏠 ✍️ 💳

Bolt Head Hotel, South Sands, Salcombe, Devon TQ8 8LL
(Tel. 054884 3751)
Call for directions
Closed November to end of March
£48–£69 pp per night dinner and b&b
Perched on a headland 140 feet above sea level, the hotel
overlooks the sea and the Salcombe Estuary. The hotel
grounds slope down a steep hill, and the beach is 50 yards
beyond. Bedrooms are modern and furnished with a good deal
of pine. The terrace, lounge and bar all have magnificent views
over Salcombe Estuary. Fifteen tables in the 60-cover dining
room overlook the water. Non-residents are welcome for
dinner; four courses cost £18.50. There are some ground-floor
rooms but no special facilities for the disabled.
Cliff walks on National Trust property next to the hotel grounds;
windsurfing from the beach (equipment for hire); fishing; heated
swimming pool

SALCOMBE

🏘️ 9/14 🏠 ✍️ 💳

Soar Mill Cove Hotel, Salcombe, Devon TQ7 3DS
(Tel. 0548 561566)
Off the A381; call for directions
Closed for five weeks in January and early February
£50–£82 pp dinner and b&b
A long, low one-storey building in an idyllic remote setting
high above the sea. Extensive grounds lead down to the sandy
sun-trap beach. The bar is cosy, and the lounge has wonderful
views: sliding glass doors can be opened up for an even better
impression of the bay on warm summer evenings. Bedrooms
are soothing and airy, and all open on to private terraces and
the garden. Most tables in the 50-cover dining room have sea
views. Cuisine is 'modern English' and focuses on the fresh
shellfish caught by the hotel's own lobster boat, though the
owner warns that the crabs 'get a bit thin in mid-winter'. Local

lamb is also a speciality. Light seafood meals are available at lunchtime. Set dinners cost £26, and lunches about £15. Rooms are on the ground floor, but there are no special facilities for the disabled.
Outdoor and indoor swimming pools (the indoor one is kept at 88°F all year); walking; sailing; windsurfing; waterskiing; fishing; putting; tennis

SALISBURY

The Mill House, Berwick St James, Salisbury, Wilts SP3 4TS (Tel. 0722 790 331)
One mile from A36 at Stapleford; one mile from A303 at Winterbourne Stoke
£18–£27 pp b&b (less for students)
In a word: priceless. Charming, traditional bed and breakfast accommodation, in a small and picturesque village. The Mill House was built in 1785, adjacent to the Old Mill; enlargements and modernizations 30 years ago have not detracted from its character. The Mill still works, pumping water for the farm. Surrounded by lovely gardens and the babbling river Till, the house is virtually on an island, and is approached by bridges from all sides. Inside, hunting pictures and family portraits abound. The views are super; guests can admire the river from the waterside terrace outside. Admittedly, the river dried up last summer, but that was due to the drought. The dining room (for breakfast only) seats eight people, with one table that looks out on to the river (there are several good pubs nearby where guests can find an evening meal). No facilities for the disabled.
Three golf courses within 10 miles; brown trout fishing; walks in the 12-acre nature reserve nearby; swimming in mill pool; riding

SALISBURY

🏠 ~23/28~ 🛏 🍴 💳

The Rose and Crown Hotel, Harnham Road, Harnham, Wilts
SP2 8JQ   (Tel. 0722 27908)
Approach on A354 Coombe Road, turn left on the A3094 New
Harnham Road, right on Harnham Road; Rose and Crown is
just before bridge, on the left
£85.50–£95.50 double
A fine 13th-century inn, with original half-timbering, set in a
rose garden on the banks of the river Avon, with a modern
restaurant and a new accommodation wing attached. Pleasant
gardens, with geese and ducks. All the rooms – in the old wing
as well as the new wing – have recently been refurbished, and
all are individually decorated; some have four-poster beds, and
most have views of the river and of Salisbury Cathedral. The
hotel is a trifle bland, but the views are lovely, and the outlook
from the restaurant, across the river Avon to Salisbury
Cathedral, is spectacular. In the 18th century a drinker tried to
cut off a piece of ham while the landlady was out of room, but
his hand slipped: he cut off his finger by mistake and fled. The
landlord still has the knife and finger as souvenirs. Beers on
offer in the bars include Ushers and Bass IPA; one of three bars
overlooks the water. There are two bedrooms with facilities
for the disabled, and a lavatory for the disabled in the foyer.
Walks, fishing

SALISBURY

🏠 ~4/7~ 🛏 🚫 💳

Old Mill Hotel, Town Path, West Harnham, Salisbury, Wilts
SP2 8EU   (Tel. (0722 27517)
Just off the A3094, from Salisbury to Wilton
Open April to late November
£16.50–£17.50 pp b&b
This hotel was originally a warehouse; the cosy restaurant is
housed in a 12th-century water mill, with plenty of rushing
water and loads of ducks outside. As the restaurant has few
windows, the views are not outstanding, but there are lovely

views of the river from some of the rooms, which are of simple bed and breakfast standard. The restaurant seats up to 55 people, and is open all year. No facilities for the disabled. New owners took over in December 1990, so some details may change; there are tentative plans to add four more bedrooms.
Good trout fishing; interesting walks; riding nearby; squash; nice walks and views of the Cathedral

SEEND CLEEVE

The Barge, Seend Cleeve, Wiltshire   (Tel. 0380 828230)
Open 11am–2.30pm, 6pm–11pm Mon–Sat; noon–2.30pm, 7pm–10.30pm Sun
Off the A361, between Seend Village and signpost to Seend Head
A nice, simple pub with pleasant canalside views. There are waterside tables in eating area; amazing floral decoration and barge-painting lends a gypsyish air to the bar, where painted milk churns serve as bar stools. There are Wadworth beers on offer, and good cheap bar food (fresh fish on Fridays, and there are always two vegetarian items on the menu). Outside, there is a terrace and a sizeable lawn, with 22 tables by the canal, which is just as well, as the pub is popular and the bar can become very crowded in summer. Moorings are available on the canal. The pub has wheelchair access and a lavatory for the disabled.
Walks along towpath; fishing (licence needed)

SENNEN COVE

inn 9/11

Old Success Inn, Sennen Cove, Cornwall TR19 7DG
(Tel. 0736 871232)
Open 11am–2.30pm, 6.30pm–11pm Mon–Sat; noon–3pm, 7pm–10.30pm Sun; summer holidays, 11am–11pm Mon–Sat
£27.50 pp dinner and b&b
A 17th-century fishermen's inn, in a fantastic location just north

of Land's End, overlooking Whitesand Bay. The bedrooms include two honeymoon four-poster suites; some views are much better than others, so be sure to ask exactly what you're getting when you book. There is an extensive menu available from the bar; dinner is for residents only, and there is a set menu. Some tables in the restaurant have a view of the sea. The bay is a blue flag beach (which means that there is lots of sand and no dogs are allowed on it). There are two family cottages available for rent (£330 a week in high season), and two flats (£330 a week high season, both sleep four or five). No facilities for the disabled.

Coastal path walks; fishing off pier, or trips from Penzance; surfing, windsurfing and canoeing on beach (equipment for hire); two surfing schools nearby

SHEPPERDINE

IOI 🏠 🚫 ▭

The Windbound Inn, Shepperdine, nr Oldbury-on-Severn, Avon BS12 1RW   (Tel. 0454 414 343)
From Thornbury town centre, follow signs towards Oldbury-on-Severn, Shepperdine and finally the river
Large and popular eating-house pub in an attractive spot on the Severn. Friendly and unpretentious, the Windbound Inn specializes in good home cooking, and there are daily specials for vegetarians. The spacious first-floor dining lounge has panoramic views over the estuary. Downstairs, there is another restaurant, and a bar which also serves food. There is seating outside in the large garden and by the estuary. Children are welcome in both restaurants (high chairs are available). One dining room and lavatory are on the ground floor, but there are no special facilities for the disabled.

Walks (start of 50-mile Severn Way Walk); salmon fishing on the Severn; skittle alley; children's play area in the garden

SIDMOUTH

 22/34

Hotel Riviera, The Esplanade, Sidmouth, Devon EX10 8AY
(Tel. 0395 515201)
£41–£57 pp b&b; with seven-course dinner from £47–£63
The most attractive of Sidmouth's seafront hotels, the Riviera
retains much Georgian character and elegance without
seeming pompous or pretentious. Set right on the esplanade,
with views across Lyme Bay, it is a stone's throw from the
beach, and the recently refurbished rooms are tasteful and well
appointed. The restaurant seats 85, and has an impressive
menu; most tables have a water view. The hotel has recently
been placed, by the AA, in the top five per cent of hotels in the
British Isles. There are some rooms for disabled visitors, and
special bathrooms, that have been designed in conjunction
with disabled organizations.
*Walks; watersports can be arranged at nearby beaches; golf at
Sidmouth Golf Club*

SIDMOUTH

 35/68

Royal York and Faulkner Hotel, The Esplanade, Sidmouth,
Devon EX10 8AZ   (Tel. 0395 513043)
£25–£44 dinner and b&b
A fine Regency building at the centre of the Esplanade, dating
from 1809, the Royal York and Faulkner was Sidmouth's first
purpose-built hotel. King Edward VII stayed here in 1856
(when he was still the young Prince of Wales). The hotel is a
rabbit warren of rooms, and seems to be much larger than it
appears from the outside. In a fine position, right opposite
Sidmouth's main beach, some of the sea-view rooms have
balconies. The restaurant seats 120; about 25 tables have a
water view. Non-residents are welcome in the evening. An
impressive 'health complex' within the hotel comprises a
sauna, spa bath, solarium, and exercise equipment. Dogs can
be accommodated, for a charge of £3 per day, which includes
their dinner. No facilities for the disabled.

Nearby sailing, tennis, cricket, golf, riding, bowls, squash, coastal walks, surfing, windsurfing, sea and some river fishing; beach opposite hotel

SIDMOUTH

The Victoria Hotel, The Esplanade, Sidmouth, Devon
EX10 8RY   (Tel. 0395 512 651)
£98–£183 per room b&b

One of Sidmouth's finest hotels, the Victoria has occupied a commanding position at the end of the Esplanade since shortly after the death of its namesake monarch. A Brend hotel, so decor and service are to the standards one would expect, with friendly staff and rooms that are comfortable, if a touch more utilitarian than tasteful. The restaurant seats 120 people, and most of the tables have a view of the sea. A six-course lunch costs £10; bar snacks are available for those with less robust appetites. The set dinner is also six courses and costs £16. Added attractions inside the hotel include a swimming pool, sauna, solarium, spa bath and snooker room. There are no special facilities for the disabled, but a lift serves all rooms and doorways are wide enough to accommodate wheelchairs.

Indoor and outdoor swimming pools; tennis courts; plenty of walks; watersports (equipment for hire nearby); fishing; beach

SIMONSBATH

Simonsbath House Hotel, Simonsbath, Exmoor, Somerset
TA24 7SH   (Tel. 064 383 259)
Closed December and January
£39–£42 pp b&b

A fine 17th-century hunting lodge in heart of Exmoor Forest. Most rooms have fine southerly views of River Barle, and some have four-poster beds. Mike and Sue Barns aim to create a home, not a hotel, atmosphere: there are plenty of fresh flowers in evidence, a convivial library bar and log fires. Bedrooms are characterful, and furnished to a high standard.

Generous portions served in the oak-panelled dining room. Three self-catering barn units and a bistro have recently been added to the hotel. No facilities for the disabled.
Fishing; riding; many interesting walks

STOCKBRIDGE
inn 〰️ ⁰/³ 🏠 🖐️ 🔲

The Vine, High Street, Stockbridge, Hants SO20 6HF
(Tel. 0264 810652)
Open 11am–3pm, 7pm–11pm Mon–Sat; noon–2.30pm, 7pm–10.30pm Sun
£17.50 single, £27.50 double b&b
A cosy, 16th-century high street pub, with village trophies displayed in cabinets around the bar. Ales on offer include Wadworth's 6X, Marston's Pedigree and Flowers. There is a willow tree and seven big tables in the garden, and a pretty little stream with a tiny bridge and plenty of trout. Bar food is available at lunchtimes and evenings (except on Sunday evenings), and fish dishes are a speciality. No facilities for the disabled.
Trout fishing on the River Test (permits available locally); pheasant shooting (details from Winchester tourist information); pretty river walks

STON EASTON
🏛️ 〰️ ⁶/¹⁹ 🏠₁₂ 🖐️ 🔲

Ston Easton Park, Ston Easton, nr Bath, Avon BA3 4DF
(Tel. 076 121 631)
On the A37 from Bristol to Shepton Mallet
£185–£285 per room b&b
The River Norr runs through the landscaped park grounds of this magnificently restored, Grade I listed Palladian mansion. Guests are pampered in luxurious period surroundings. Some rooms have river views, and the master bedroom has antique Chippendale furniture. The fine interiors were decorated by Jean Monro in 18th-century style. For those who want total seclusion, and a slightly less formal atmosphere, there is an

isolated riverside cottage that has two suites. The hotel dining room, with four tables looking out on to the river, is open to non-residents; a jacket and tie should be worn for dinner (set dinner £29.50). A Victorian kitchen garden provides flowers, vegetables and herbs for the hotel. Picnic lunches are a speciality, and can be ordered, at a cost of £16.50 per person, by both residents and non-residents. You must give at least three hours' notice when ordering, and then you can take the wicker baskets and a blanket off into the park for as long as you fancy. No facilities for the disabled.

On-site croquet and hot-air ballooning; nearby golf and shooting (clay and game); walks; trout fishing; tennis court

TESTCOMBE

The Mayfly, Testcombe, Stockbridge, Hants
(Tel. 0264 860283)
Between the A303 and the A30, Stockbridge to Andover
Open 11am–11pm Mon–Sat; noon–2.30pm, 7pm–10.30pm Sun

A delightful and peaceful place on the banks of the River Test. There are nine tables outside beside the road bridge (not too busy) and the small weir. A small clear stream runs past the other side of the pub and there are about 18 more tables along the river and stream banks. The Victorian-style lounge on the river bank would also be a fine place to pass a summer evening. A selection of guest ales are on offer at the bar, and the food – available from noon to 2pm, and 4pm to 9pm – merits a mention in Lord Lichfield's *Courvoisier's Book of the Best*. No facilities for the disabled.

Fishing (must have permit, £50–£80 a day per rod) and walking along Test Way (just over bridge)

TOPSHAM

The Bridge Inn, Topsham, Exeter, Devon
(Tel. 0392 87 3862)
Two and a half miles from M5 junction 30; take A376 for
Exmouth from Topsham
Open noon–2pm, 6pm–10.30pm
A 16th-century maltings above the River Clyst, the inn is a
fascinating and eccentric place to visit, and a must for Real Ale
freaks. It has been scheduled as an historic and ancient
monument. Two of the four bars overlook the river, and there
is an area of grass by the water. There are 16 real ales on offer,
basic bar food is available at lunchtime, and visitors are
guaranteed a warm reception by the entire Cheffers clan.
Winners of the *Consumer Guide* award 'National Cellarman of
the Year' in 1989. No facilities for the disabled.
*Walks; salmon fishing on River Exe (check ahead on licence
requirements); sailing and sea fishing can be arranged at Exmouth,
five miles away*

TORQUAY

Livermead Cliff Hotel, Seafront, Torquay, Devon TQ2 6RQ
(Tel. 0803 299 666)
From Torquay, head for Livermead; the hotel is hard to miss
£40–£46.50 pp b&b; £51.50–£57 dinner and b&b
A family owned hotel right on the seafront, with direct access
to the shore and the sea wall. From the elongated terrace in
front of the hotel, there are excellent views of bay. The
restaurant seats 120, and most of the tables have a sea view (set
lunch costs £7.50). Snacks are available in sea-facing lounge.
Small pets can be accommodated by arrangement, for a charge
(£4.50 a day). It is worth noting that this hotel often has rooms
available, even at short notice. According to the manager,
people seem to assume they'll always be full. No facilities for
the disabled, though the staff are very helpful.
Heated outdoor swimming pool; walks to Cockington and into

Torquay; waterskiing and windsurfing nearby (ask at hotel); jetskis and paragliding; fishing from hotel garden and steps (bring equipment); beach adjacent

TORQUAY

The Osborne Hotel, Meadfoot Beach, Torquay TQ1 2LL
(Tel. 0803 213 311)
East of Torquay harbour; call for detailed directions
£49–£69 pp b&b (Suites cost £12 extra per person)
The hotel is in a Grade II listed Regency-style crescent out of sight of Torquay, with large, well-decorated suites and a terrace overlooking sea. The rest of the crescent comprises 46 timeshare apartments run by the hotel. Five and a half acres of private gardens sweep down to Meadfoot Beach. There are two restaurants which seat 45 people each; in each, seven tables have a sea view. A four-course dinner costs £19.50. Sporty guests will find plenty to keep them busy: there are heated swimming pools indoors and out, a games room, a snooker room, a health club, a putting green, and an all-weather tennis court. Some rooms are accessible by ramp and lift, but there are no special facilities for the disabled.
Beach (two minutes' walk); cliff walks; waterskiing and jetskiing in Torbay (ask at hotel); fishing can be arranged

TOTNES

The Waterman's Arms, Bow Bridge, Totnes, Devon
TQ9 7EG   (Tel. 080423 214)
On the Tuckenham road from Totnes
Open 11am–3pm, 6pm–11pm Mon–Sat; noon–2.30pm, 7pm–10.30pm Sun
A snug yet extensive pub, which has grown out of an old smithy, in a beautiful setting by Bow Bridge. The decor includes old guns, copper ornaments and brasses, and there are new stained-glass panels above the bar, which overlooks the road and the river. The dining room seats 64, and there is an

extra family room, which seats 50 people. There is seating for another 80 people in the waterside garden. Bar specialities include Palmers beer and fish dishes. No facilities for the disabled.

Fishing (salmon and trout, bring equipment); beach five miles away

TREBARWITH STRAND

🏠 🏠 🐟 ▭

The Port William, Trebarwith Strand, Tintagel, Cornwall
PL34 0HB   (Tel. 0840 770230)
Open 11am–11pm Mon–Sat Easter–November (and noon–
3pm, 6pm–11pm Mon–Sat November–Easter); noon–
2.30pm, 7pm–10.30pm Sun
The pub is cosy within, though not beautiful on the outside, and in a marvellous setting, on cliffs overlooking the beach at Trebarwith Strand. Formerly, the building was a harbour-master's house, office and stables. There are good sea views from the bar, and the main attraction is the splendid front terrace, on the clifftop. St Austell ales, guest beers, and the local cider (in summer) are worth noting. There is an extensive menu of bar snacks (£1.20–£3.50), and main meals are served in the evening (£6–£8). Well-behaved pets are allowed into the bar if they are on leads. Children are allowed in the family areas. There is one self-catering holiday flat available for rent, which has two bedrooms overlooking the sea. Book well in advance, as it is very popular. No facilities for the disabled, though the landlords welcome disabled visitors and will make every effort to help them.

Trebarwith Strand swimming beach is half a minute away (has lifeguards in summer); surfing on beach; fishing from end of the drive; sea fishing trips from Boscastle (ask landlords); coastal path walks

TREBARWITH STRAND

🏠 2/3 🏠 🐟 ▭

The Old Millfloor, Trebarwith Strand, Tintagel, Cornwall
PL34 0HA   (Tel. 0840 770234)
Open for dinner all year; accommodation closed late

November to late March
£14.50 pp b&b
A converted mill dating from the 16th century, half a mile before Trebarwith Strand, and down a steep hill. There are ten acres of grounds, with the millstream winding through the pretty garden and right past the house. The dining room – from which you can hear, but not see, the stream, seats 14 people. Non-residents are welcome for dinner (£10.50; no lunch). The dining room is not licensed, so bring your own wine. No facilities for the disabled.
Sandy beach at Trebarwith Strand (half a mile away); walks on coastal path (to Boscastle and St Juliet), and to beach on path through grounds; golf at Rock; riding (four miles away); surfing at Trebarwith Strand beach, where the Surf Shop hires out equipment

UMBERLEIGH

🏠 ²/₆ 🏠₁₄ 🚫 🎴

Rising Sun, Umberleigh, North Devon EX37 9DU
(Tel. 0769 60447)
On the A377 Barnstaple to Exeter
Open 11am–2.30pm, 6pm–11pm Mon–Sat; noon–3pm, 7pm–10.30pm Sun
£36.50 single, £47.50 double
A pleasant and historic inn near the River Taw (a good salmon and seatrout river). An ideal place for fishermen, with a rod room and three and a half miles of private fishing. The river views are not particularly impressive, but the rooms are extremely comfortable. The residents' lounge is bedecked with angling souvenirs, and the front patio area overlooks the river. No facilities for the disabled. The pub is changing hands soon, so some details may change.
Fishing (season is 1 March to 30 September); riverside walks

VERYAN

🏠 ²⁶/₄₀ 🏠 🎴 🎴

The Nare Hotel, Carne Beach, Veryan, Truro, Cornwall
TR2 5PF   (Tel. 0872 501279)

£51–£69 pp b&b

A fine hotel in a very peaceful location, overlooking well-tended gardens and a safe sandy beach. The rooms are tastefully decorated; the result is an elegant, yet home-like interior; many rooms have a balcony or a patio from which to enjoy the views. A courtesy car is provided, to fetch guests from Truro railway station 12 miles away. Men are advised that jackets and ties are recommended attire in the evenings. The restaurant seats 80 (all tables have a sea view), and serves light lunches and dinner (set dinner £18.50). Dogs, but no other pets, are accepted. There is an all-weather tennis court at the hotel, together with swimming pool, paddling pool, games room, sauna, and solarium. No facilities for the disabled.

Coastal path walks; watersports along beach; hotel has windsurfers, and one sports boat for waterskiing; complimentary golf at Truro (10 miles away)

WAREHAM

The Old Granary, The Quay, Wareham, Dorset BH20 4LP
(Tel. 0929 552 010)
On the A351 from Poole to Swanage
£18.50–£33 pp b&b

An attractive converted grain warehouse which is at least 200 years old, in a picturesque setting on the banks of River Frome, overlooking the Purbeck hills. The rooms are comfortable and unpretentious, with cottagey decor, and local prints on the walls. There are two restaurants (open from 9am to 9pm) which seat 65 altogether: both are homely and relaxing, with delicious home-made food (set lunch £7.95, set dinner £11.95). Half of the restaurant tables have views of the river. Weather permitting, the riverside terrace serves food all day, from morning coffee, via cream teas, to dinner. Private moorings are available for use by guests. There is wheelchair access to the ground floor and the lavatories, though no specific facilities for the disabled.

Walks; watersports in Poole Harbour; fishing; beaches (6 miles away); riding; swimming pool; squash; badminton; boat hire (100 yards away)

WEST BEXINGTON

The Manor Hotel, Beach Road, West Bexington, Dorset
DT2 9DF   (Tel. 0308 897 785)
On coast road between West Bay and Weymouth
£29.95 pp b&b, £46.95 dinner and b&b
A small and very comfortable hotel, with Jacobean oak panelling in the hall, and two lounges for residents. The original building was the Ancient Manor House of Bessington, which merited a mention in the Domesday book. This has been interestingly and thoughtfully developed: a pine conservatory extension of the bar fits in surprisingly well, and has good sea views. The original stone-lined cellar is now a bar, and there is an extensive bar menu, and the restaurant (no water views) seats 64 people for more serious meals. No facilities for the disabled.
Boating; sea fishing; golf; riding; shooting; walks; beach

WESTON-SUPER-MARE

The Royal Pier Hotel, Birnbeck Road, Weston-super-Mare,
Avon BS23 2EJ   (Tel. 0934 626 644)
£42–£65 pp b&b
A ten-minute walk from the town centre, this large, seafront hotel stands on a headland and enjoys good views across Weston Bay to Wales. Public rooms and bedrooms have recently been redecorated in comforting tones of peach, green and brown. Over half the bedrooms overlook the water, which recedes quite a distance at low tide. The lounge and two bars look out to sea, as do all the tables in the 80-cover restaurant. Five-course dinners cost £12.50, and full lunches are available. Snacks and simple, hearty meals are served in the bar. There are two games rooms, a library suitable for conferences and a large car park. Rooms are accessible by lift,

but there are no special facilities for the disabled.
Walks; fishing trips can be arranged; beach; two golf courses in Weston; nearby watersports, tennis courts and riding facilities

WEYMOUTH
inn ¹/₆ 🏠 🐾 ▭

The Smugglers Inn, Osmington Mills, Wareham, Preston, nr Weymouth, Dorset DT3 6HF   (Tel. 0305 833 125)
One mile from the A353, clearly signposted
Open 11am–2.30pm, 6pm–11pm Mon–Sat (11am–11pm July and August); noon–3pm, 7pm–10.30pm Sun
£27.50 single, £47.50 twin, £50 double b&b
An attractive pub, set in a hollow on the Dorset coastal path, with a bubbling stream and clifftop views, 50 yards from the beach where Constable painted 'Weymouth Bay'. There has been an inn here since the 13th century; four and a half acres of grounds extend to the high tide mark. Refurbishments a few years ago have in no way detracted from the Smugglers' immense character. Real ales are served at the bar. The restaurant seats 80 (no water views), and provides the famous Osmington Bay lobsters (£14–£24 for a whole one). The restaurant is open from noon to 2pm and 7pm to 9.30pm; bar snacks available from 11.30am to 2.30pm, and 6.30pm to 9.30pm). No facilites for the disabled.
Coastal and inland walks; jetskiing, waterskiing, windsurfing (all at Weymouth); yachting (in Kingstead); coarse, beach and sea angling; Weymouth and Preston beaches, Ringstead Bay and Osmington Bay

WEYMOUTH
🍽 🏠 🐾 ▭

The Sea Cow Restaurant, 7 Custom House Quay, Weymouth, Dorset DT4 9BE   (Tel. 0305 783524)
On the harbourside in Weymouth
Open noon–2pm, 7.30pm–10.15pm; closed Sunday evenings September–June
On the harbourside, five minutes' walk from ferry terminal, the restaurant is made up of four rooms, each with a different

character. Altogether, there is seating for 120 people, and most of the tables are open to harbour views. The ground-floor rooms offer evening meals and, in summer (June to September) one room is open from 10am for coffee and light lunches. The first floor offers a cold-buffet-and-carvery lunch. Much of the fish comes straight from quay, and the menu also has varied and extensive meat dishes. The restaurant has held the Routiers Casserole Award for three years running, and the chef, Terry Woolcock, is a member of the British Team of Chefs. A very hospitable place. No specific facilities for the disabled, though the doorways are wide, the restaurant is all on one level, and the lavatories are large enough for wheelchair access.

Beach; coastal walks; watersports; fishing; Deep Sea Adventure Museum

WINKTON

Fisherman's Haunt Hotel, Salisbury Road, Winkton, Christchurch, Dorset BH23 7AS   (Tel. 0202 477283)
On the B3347
£24 pp b&b, £50 double b&b (four-posters £54)
An attractive 17th-century hotel with good gardens and extensive parking; very popular for its food, the restaurant can get very busy. The restaurant and conservatory seat 80, and offer excellent traditional English fare and unspectacular water views. There are two four-poster beds, and the hotel is a popular place for weddings. Despite the name, the hotel is not particularly geared up for fishermen: the location is better suited to walkers, and guests who want to fish must make their arrangements in Christchurch. If you do happen to find fishermen staying, they have probably dropped by for the food. One room is designed to accommodate wheelchairs.

Walks; beach and watersports in Bournemouth and Christchurch (15 minutes by car)

WOOLACOMBE

🏨 7/10 ♒ 🏠7 ⬦ 💳

The Little Beach Hotel, The Esplanade, Woolacombe, Devon
EX34 7DJ   (Tel. 0271 870 398)
Open March to October
£32–£39 pp dinner and b&b
Small, family-run and on the seafront, the Little Beach is a
solid Edwardian house built of local slate and stone. Newly
refurbished, rooms are comfortable and bright, with good
decor; the three seafront rooms share a balcony. The spacious
dining room seats 22 people, and all tables look out over the
beach. Non-residents can enjoy the 'imaginative home
cooking', but must book in advance. A five-course dinner
costs £11.50. Altogether, good value: you won't find hidden
extras working their way mysteriously on to your bill. The
hotel has a small antique shop, open to residents only. Popular
for spring mini-breaks (March to May). No facilities for the
disabled.
Three miles of golden-sand beach 500 yards from hotel; walks on
coastal path and in surrounding National Trust land – the hotel staff
are happy to provide maps and ideas for itineraries; clay pigeon
shooting can be arranged; surfing and windsurfing; fishing from beach
and surrounding rocks

WOOLACOMBE

🏨 24/26 ♒ 🏠 ⬦ 💳

The Watersmeet Hotel, Mortehoe, Woolacombe, North
Devon EX34 7EB   (Tel. 0271 870 333)
£40–£65 pp dinner and b&b
A medium-sized hotel by a small cove on the headland at
Mortehoe, with fabulous views, especially from the new
octagonal Pavilion restaurant (50 places; all tables have an
excellent view of the sea). The food is particularly good; in
1989, the chefs won second and third places in Roux Brothers'
Chefs Scholarship. The rooms are very comfortable indeed –
each has individual designer decor – and the whole place is
peaceful and not ostentatious. Bridge and painting weekends

are a speciality. Pets can be accommodated by arrangement.
There is one ground-floor suite, which is popular with disabled
visitors.

*Walks on Devon coastal path; windsurfing and surfing; river, lake,
and sea fishing (boats from local harbour); secluded, semi-private
beach in front of hotel; golf (championship course at Saunton), clay
pigeon shooting; painting holidays*

WOOLACOMBE

🏨 ~~39/59~~ 🐑 🚫 🎴

Woolacombe Bay Hotel, South Street, Woolacombe, Devon
EX34 7BN   (Tel. 0271 870 388)
Closed January
£40–£80 pp dinner and b&b

Oldest and grandest of Woolacombe's hotels: a rambling
Victorian building standing in grounds that sweep down to the
sea. There is a splendid air of fading grandeur to the place, and
many original features give a pleasant feel to public rooms,
though the bedrooms can be fairly utilitarian, and the views are
not exceptional. The dining room seats 140 (non-residents are
welcome), with about 20 tables overlooking the sea. The hotel
is famous for its seven-course dinners; these and the full
English breakfasts are included in the room price, and many
guests find they cannot manage lunch as well. Those that can
might visit Maxwell's bistro, within the hotel. Diversions for
guests include a sauna, spa bath, squash courts, solarium,
fitness room, tennis, croquet, swingball, short-mat bowling, a
snooker room, and indoor and outdoor swimming pools. No
facilities for the disabled, though there is a ramp that gives
wheelchair access to the restaurant, and hotel has a lift to three
floors.

*Walks; sea fishing from Ilfracombe can be arranged; the main three-
mile beach, and other smaller beaches, are set between the National
Trust headlands of Morte Point and Baggy Point; the* Frolica, *the
hotel boat (a 40-foot Swordsman), can take guests on day trips to
Lundy Island (home to many puffins and seals, £40 pp), or up and
down the coast. The crew are members of a sub-aqua club, and can take
people diving in the protected area off Lundy*

Scotland

Telegraph GUIDE

SCOTLAND

PENTLAND FIRTH

Stroma

THURSO

WICK

Helmsdale

Golspie

Tain

Buckie

Banff

Bridge of Marnoch

Delnies

INVERNESS

Bunchrew

MORAY FIRTH

N O R

DINGWALL

Lairg

Kinlochewe

Scourie

Lochinver

Achiltibuie

Ullapool

Dundonnell

Shieldaig

Plockton

KYLE OF LOCHALSH

Skye

THE MINCH

A T L A N T I C   O C E A N

Whitebridge

Fort Augustus

Glenbiel

H I G H L A N D

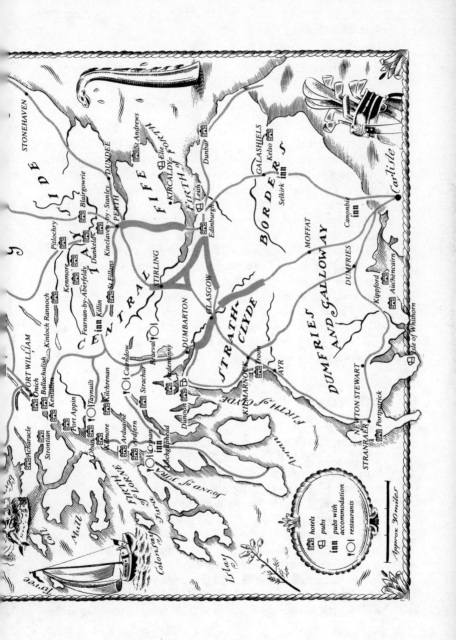

ABERDEEN

Ardoe House Hotel, Blairs, South Deeside Road, Aberdeen
AB1 5YP   (Tel. 0224 867 355)
From Old Bridge of Dee, head west along South Deeside
Road, then follow signs to hotel
£55–£100 b&b
This baronial-style country house hotel, built in 1878, looks on
to the River Dee, though it has little to do with the river apart
from the panoramic views. Five minutes by car from the city
centre, the hotel has turrets and heraldic inscriptions; open
hearth fires, and stunning wood carving in the hall and the
lounge lend a country-house feel. The atmosphere is business-
like, and there is piped music. This is a better place for a
conference than a family holiday: seventy per cent of the hotel's
guests are there for business rather than pleasure. The dining
room is open for breakfast, lunch and dinner, and non-
residents are welcome; vegetarian and special diets are catered
for. There are good views from the ballroom, which is a
popular venue for wedding receptions. The dining room is on
one level, and there is disabled access to the bar.
Walks; fishing; pétanque; putting

ABERDEEN

The Silver Darling Restaurant, Pocra Quay, Footdee,
Aberdeen AB2 1DQ   (Tel. 0224 576 229)
From the city centre, follow Beach Boulevard, turn right at
beach and drive towards lighthouse and Pocra Quay
Open noon–2.30pm, 7pm–10pm Mon–Sat; 7pm–10pm Sun
(closed winter Sundays)
Although minutes from city centre, this lovely restaurant, set
in a picturesque fishing village dotted with tiny cottages, feels
much further away from the real world. The menu focuses on
fish (in common parlance, a silver darling is a herring), much
of it cooked on the wood barbecue, and the fresh pastries are
well worth sampling. There is seating for 30 people, and the

three window tables offer the best sea views. The restaurant is an attractive shape, with pretty decor: the watercolours and Victorian prints on the walls are for sale (prices start at £17). There is a wide door, a ramp, and a lavatory for disabled visitors. *Walks; watersports; fishing; beach*

ACHILTIBUIE

7/12 8

Summer Isles Hotel, Achiltibuie, by Ullapool, Ross-shire IV26 2YG   (Tel. 085 482 282)
Turn left off the A835 10 miles north of Ullapool; it's then 15 miles to Achiltibuie
Open April to October
£51–£75 per room b&b
Fifteen miles of single-track road lead to this remote hotel with spectacular views out over the Summer Isles. It is certainly well off the beaten track: Lucy Irvine, sister of the proprietor, wrote *Castaway* here. The interior is spacious, the decor warm and comfortable, and the large windows make the most of the views, though the Hydroponicum, an indoor garden building on the shore 200 yards from the house, is less than beautiful. There is a snug bar; the restaurant seats 26 people, with six sea-facing window tables – a five-course dinner costs £27.50. Vegetarians should give advance notice. All of the tables in the restaurant face the sea. Dogs can be accommodated by arrangement. No facilities for the disabled.
Mountain-range walks; fresh water and sea fishing (equipment not supplied); boating around islands; bird watching; sandy beaches

ACHARACLE

4/4

Glencripesdale House, Loch Sunart, Acharacle, Argyll PA36 4JH   (Tel. 096 785 263 – this is a radio telephone, so keep trying)
Detailed directions (which are crucial) are sent to guests when a booking is made
Open March to October, Christmas and New Year

£56 full board pp
A modernized 18th-century farmhouse 200 yards from the shores of Loch Sunart, in a remote spot at the end of a nine-mile track from the main road, which takes an hour to drive. No other buildings are visible from the house, and there is no mains electricity supply. The views across Loch Sunart, backed by the Ardnamurchan mountains, are magnificent. Inside, the hotel is neat and modern yet comfortable, with ornaments and the odd antique that add character. The general atmosphere tends to be formal, but this must vary, depending on your co-guests: you will escape the world here but not the other refugees. (The proprietors consider that any air of formality comes entirely from the visitors: they just want guests to enjoy themselves.) The food and wine are very fine: there are three puddings every night, and guests are encouraged to 'do the hat-trick'. Dogs are not allowed into the house. No facilities for the disabled.
Conducted trips around the loch in an inflatable boat; hotel fishing dinghy and two windsurfers (bring own wetsuit); scuba diving (limited equipment, e.g. cylinders available); walking

ARDENTINNY

The Ardentinny Hotel, Loch Long, nr Dunoon, Argyll PA23 8TR   (Tel. 036 981 209)
Twelve miles north of Dunoon on the A880
Accommodation closed November–March; food available all year
£23–£35 b&b
From its perch on a Loch Long promontory, this white 18th-century droving inn enjoys brilliant views up and down the loch. It is popular with Clyde yachtsmen, and there are private moorings for boats. The Argyll Forest Park surrounds the hotel. The bedrooms are straightforward and practical, and most of them have loch views. An unfussy and friendly place, where the waterside gardens are regularly full at lunchtime. The restaurant seats 65 people (set dinner £17.50). There are lavatories for the disabled, but no bedrooms.

Fifty miles of forest walks; garden walks; fishing; sailing; boating; sandy beach (one mile away)

ARDFERN

2/9

The Galley of Lorne Hotel, Ardfern, by Lochgilphead, Argyll
PA31 8QN   (Tel. 08525 284)
On the B8002, signposted off the A816 Lochgilphead to Oban
£20–£30 pp b&b
An attractive, informal hotel, right on Loch Craignish. There are big navigation lamps in the panelled bar, where food is served up in generous portions. The bistro area has a piano and a dance floor, though apparently these are only called into action for Hogmanay. The restaurant offers two window tables, Loch Craignish king prawns and Scottish cheeses: an à la carte dinner will set you back £14. The entire hotel – motel-style bedrooms and bathrooms included – is on one floor, and so should not present a problem for disabled visitors.
Waterskiing; windsurfing; trout and sea fishing; boat trips; clay pigeon shooting; riding

ARDUAINE

25/26

The Loch Melfort Hotel, Arduaine, by Oban, Argyll
PA34 4XG   (Tel. 085 22 233)
Signposted off the A816, 19 miles south of Oban
Closed January and February
£42.50 pp b&b
Set in 30 acres of rolling pasture and woodland, the hotel faces south across Asknish Bay, with magnificent views of Shuna, Scarba and Jura: it is no idle boast that they possess the finest location on the West Coast. There are mooring facilities and showers for passing yachtsmen. The chartroom bar opens out on to a waterside terrace and has a pair of tremendous mounted marine glasses for spotting seals in the bay. All rooms but one look out to sea; the six rooms in the old part of the hotel are particularly attractive, but those in the modern extension are

utilitarian, though saved by the splendid views. Fifteen tables enjoy views from restaurant's huge windows; the set dinner costs from £19.50. The hotel is renowned for its shellfish, which are kept in their own pots at the end of jetty. It also has a well-stocked library. There is a portable ramp and four ground-floor rooms for the disabled.

Riding; sailing; windsurfing; canoeing; waterskiing; fishing on hill lochs, river and sea; garden walks (Arduaine Gardens are next to the hotel); small sandy beach

ARISAIG

Arisaig House, Beasdale, by Arisaig, Inverness-shire
PH39 4NR　(Tel. 06875 622)
On the A830 at Beasdale, three miles south-east of Arisaig
Open from Easter to early November
£95–£120 pp dinner and b&b

Giant Sequoia and Wellingtonia line the drive of this stone mansion overlooking the loch. Built in 1864 and completely refitted in the 1930s, the hotel has now been sensitively modernized, with fine wallpapers which run through the beautiful bedrooms: each room is named after a different loch, and nearly all of them look out over the loch. The atmosphere is one of spacious, solid luxury (the hotel is a Relais et Châteaux, member, with attendant high standards), and the large windows make for a light interior. Four tables in the dining room look out to the loch. There are 20 acres of grounds. It is a 10-minute walk down to the sea, through private woods, so the views are long range, but excellent because the house is so well situated. No facilities for the disabled.

Croquet; golf; fishing; climbing; walks; sailing at Arisaig; beach

ARISAIG

The Old Library Lodge and Restaurant, Arisaig, Inverness-shire PH39 4NH　(Tel. 06875 651)
On the A830 in Arisaig village, 10 miles before Mallaig

Open from April to October
£28 pp b&b
This 200-year-old converted barn, in an area famous for its links with the Jacobite Rebellion, has good views of Loch Nan Ceall and the Inner Hebrides. The village street – which is also the main road to Skye – runs between the hotel and the sea. The sea-view bedrooms are slightly cramped; the rooms in the modern extension at the rear are larger, but have no view of the water. The residents' lounge is homely; the highlight of the hotel is its charming bistro-style restaurant. This seats 28 people: there is one table in the window, and several outside. Cooking is modern and British, with a strong emphasis on local fish; Alan Broadhurst, the chef, was a former navy diver, who has now turned passionate cook. The set dinner menu costs £12.50; the à la carte menu costs between £15 and £18; light lunches are also available. No facilities for the disabled.
Walks; visits to Skye, Rhum, Eigg and Muck; boat trips and fishing on Loch Morar; spectacular beach three miles away was used as a Local Hero *location; golf (three miles away)*

ARISAIG

· The Arisaig Hotel, Arisaig, Inverness-shire PH39 4NH (Tel. 06875 210)
In Arisaig village, 10 miles before Mallaig on the A830
£31–£41 pp b&b
This comfortably old-fashioned hotel was an early Jacobite inn. Now modernized, its rooms have recently been upgraded; there are good open fires and fine views of the island of Eigg across the road and the marina. The bar is cosy and has over 100 malt whiskies on offer. The restaurant offers good home cooking, with the emphasis on fresh local fish; a full dinner costs £21.50. One unusual attraction of the locality is a cave where Bonnie Prince Charlie once stayed. No facilities for the disabled.
Fishing and boating can be arranged; walks; sandy beach and golf (three miles away); cruising to the islands

AUCHENCAIRN

🏨 7/13 ⚓ ◁ ▭

The Balcary Bay Hotel, Auchencairn, nr Castle Douglas,
Kirkcudbrightshire DG7 1QZ   (Tel. 055 664 217/311)
Village is on the A711 between Kirkcudbright and Dalbeattie.
Hotel is signposted on shore road, two miles out of village
Open from March to November
£36–£42 pp b&b, £50–£56 pp dinner and b&b
Originally built as a country house for a firm of smugglers in
1625, the hotel nestles in a secluded spot right on Balcary Bay.
The area is well off the main tourist trail to the Highlands.
There are three acres of gardens and super views across the bay
to Heston Island (which can be reached on foot at low tide).
Inside, the hotel has been discreetly modernized, with an open
fire in the reception on chilly evenings. The interior, with its
utility furniture, is not especially easy on the eye, but the
bedrooms are light and airy, and the public rooms comfortable. The restaurant seats 50 people; most tables have a water
view, and there is one table in a bay window (set dinner
£16.25). No facilities for the disabled.
*Walks; hotel can arrange fishing; eight miles to golf; sailing and
windsurfing (bring equipment); rocky beaches; riding nearby*

BALLACHULISH

🏨 17/30 ⚓ ◁ ▭

The Ballachulish Hotel, Ballachulish, Argyll PA39 4JY
(Tel. 08552 606)
On the A828 Oban to Fort William road
£48.50 pp b&b
This listed Scottish Baronial building on Loch Linnhe retains
its grand character despite modernizations; the site was
formerly a ferry port for crossing the loch. By night, it is
floodlit; inside, the reception rooms are gracious, with high
ceilings. Large gothic-arched windows look across the road on
to Loch Linnhe and up to the main road bridge. The cheery
bedrooms are furnished in country style, with pine furniture
and floral prints. The restaurant has room for 70, with seven

window tables that have the best views of the loch. Light lunches are served all day, and the set dinner costs £16.50. No facilities for the disabled.

Hotel can arrange mountain hikes; canoeing; sailing; windsurfing; fishing; cruising on the loch; walks

BANCHORY

🏨 8/14 🛏8 ✕ 💳

Invery House, Bridge of Feugh, Banchory, Kincardineshire AB3 3NJ
(Tel. 03302 4782)
Just past Bridge of Feugh, on the B974 (off the A93 at Banchory)
Closed for first three weeks of January
£90–£125 pp b&b April to September; October to March dinner and b&b for the same price

This attractive hotel sits at the end of a lovely drive, on the west bank of the River Feugh in 47 acres of grounds. Carefully restored in 1910, the decor pays meticulous attention to detail. Everything matches, and the bedrooms are exceptionally comfortable: even the pickiest perfectionist should be happy here. Books, magazines, whisky, ice and glasses are provided in the rooms, as well as fine bathrobes, towels and luxury bath oils. The restaurant seats 34, and six of the tables overlook the river: a five-course dinner costs £29.50, and the menu changes daily. The wine cellar is well stocked, with over 500 wines. There are kennelling facilities for dogs within the hotel grounds. There is a lavatory for disabled visitors, but no specially adapted bedrooms.

Billiard room; tennis; croquet; putting; one mile salmon and trout fishing in hotel grounds (free); fishing on the Dee (£65 a day); walks; gliding; riding; pony trekking; 20 golf courses within 20 miles (£6 winter, £12–£14 summer)

BANCHORY

🏨 14/23 🛏 ◁ 💳

Banchory Lodge Hotel, Banchory, Kincardineshire AB3 3HS
(Tel. 03302 2625)

On the A93, 18 miles west of Aberdeen
Closed 12 December to 25 January
£58.50 single, £96.50 double dinner and b&b. No charge for
children if they are sharing parents' room
Richly wooded grounds surround this secluded Georgian
country house. The interior is comfortably furnished in
period style, with open log fires in lounge and bar. Both
lounges enjoy beautiful views over the River Dee. Altogether, the hotel is very comfortable, and completely
unstuffy, and the staff are very friendly. Three of the
bedrooms have four-poster beds. The restaurant has room for
80, and all tables overlook the water. Non-residents are
welcome: a three-course lunch costs £10.50; a four-course
dinner costs £21.50, and the menu is strong on local fish.
There are facilities for holding private dinner parties at the
hotel. Additional attractions inside the hotel include a pool
table and sauna. At Bridge of Feugh, nearby, you can see
salmon leaping upstream. The hotel was awarded an RAC
Blue Ribbon in 1990 (the only one in Scotland). There are no
facilities for the disabled.
*Bowling; golf; tennis; waterskiing; pony trekking; gliding; salmon
and sea trout fishing on a one-and-a-half-mile stretch of River Dee
(five rods, book in advance); forest walks and nature trails*

BANFF

Banff Links Hotel, Swordanes, Banff AB4 2JJ
(Tel. 02612 2414)
Signposted off the A98, between Banff and Portsoy
£35 pp b&b
Close to the beach, the hotel looks out to sea across the Moray
Firth. New owners offer friendly hospitality, which adds to
the warm decor to create a 'country inn' atmosphere. All tables
in the 50seat restaurant have good sea views, if you ignore the
caravan site to the left of the hotel. Lunches, high teas, bar
suppers and à la carte dinners are served; there is live
entertainment for dinner guests at weekends, and a disco
area by the bar. Our researcher was impressed, though a

subsequent visitor found service and food sub-standard. Bedrooms currently being renovated.
Children's playground; walks; 12 golf courses within a 20-minute drive (golfing packages available); windsurfing on beach; rod fishing

BLAIRGOWRIE

🏨 ≈ 15/29 🏠 ✍ 🛏

Kinloch House Hotel, by Blairgowrie, Perthshire PH10 6SG (Tel. 025 084 237)
On the A923 between Blairgowrie and Dunkeld, about three miles from Blairgowrie
Closed for three days over Christmas
£63 single, £120 double, suite £150 dinner and b&b
A fine 19th-century hotel overlooking the water 400 yards from the loch, set off by a rhododendron-lined drive and grazing Highland cattle. Dunsinane Hill (of *Macbeth*) is also in view. Indoors, features include splendid oak panelling, a stained-glass skylight and a conservatory with ornamental pool and tropical plants. Six of the bedrooms have four-poster beds. Mr Shentall offers a choice of 130 malt whiskies at the bar and serves dinner clad in a kilt. The restaurant seats 55, with a view over the ornamental pool. Light and full lunches cost from £2.50 to £12.50. Four-course dinner £19.50 (men are advised to wear a jackt and tie). The menu is long and well regarded, with game and seafood specialities. Guests can buy jars of home-made bramble jelly, marmalade and jam as souvenirs of their visit (£1.50–£2.75). There are four rooms on ground floor for disabled guests.
Fishing nearby; golf (there are nearly 40 courses within a little more than an hour's drive from the hotel, including the championship courses of Carnoustie, St Andrews, and Rosemount); shooting (there are arrangements with local estates for driven and rough shooting)

BRAEVAL

🍽 🏠 12 🚭 🛏

Braeval Old Mill, Braeval, by Aberfoyle, Stirling FK8 3UY (Tel. 087 72 711)

On the A81, one mile from Aberfoyle (ask for detailed
directions when booking)
Closed on Mon, last two weeks of February, one week in May,
and first two weeks of November
This 18th-century flax and corn mill has been completely
renovated, though its waterwheel still runs on a trickle, and the
floor is flagged with grey stone. Creative seafood dishes and
local game feature on a menu combining classic French and
Scottish cuisine, cooked by Nick Nairn. The fixed-price three-
course dinner, with four choices at each course, costs £27.50; the
set lunch costs £17.50. During July and August, visitors should
plan to book a month in advance for Saturday evenings – the
restaurant is that popular. Accolades include winning the
Scottish Field/Bollinger 'Newcomers 87/88' award; Scottish
Field/Carlton 'Best Restaurant' 1988/9, and a Michelin red 'M'.
No cigar or pipe smoking in restaurant. Bed and breakfast
accommodation is available locally (from £15 pp). Wide
doorways allow wheelchair access, and there is a lavatory for
disabled visitors.
Trout fishing at Lake Menteith, £20 per session

BRIDGE OF MARNOCH

The Old Manse of Marnoch, Bridge of Marnoch, Huntly,
Aberdeenshire AB54 5RS   (Tel. 0466 780873)
On the B9117 less than a mile off the A97, hotel well
signposted
£16.50–£36 pp b&b
With the River Deveron at its edge and Crombie Burn running
through, the five-acre garden is a main feature of this spacious
Georgian house. Most of the rooms enjoy the pretty view, and
there are many antiquities that the Carters have collected from
the Middle East. The bedrooms, which are comfortable and
cheery, are equipped with china teacups, pots, and fresh milk,
and all sorts of items that might have been left out of a hastily
packed sponge bag, such as cotton wool, razors, a sewing kit,
aspirins and nail files. Even more impressive than the high
degree of comfort is the friendliness of the owners. The dining

room table overlooks the water and seats up to 12 guests, who all eat together. The bread is home made, the vegetables are organic, grown in a walled kitchen garden, and a three-course dinner costs £12.50. In the morning, the tables groan with bountiful Scottish breakfasts. Packed lunches can be made for guests for £4.50. The hotel has a herb nursery, with 80–90 aromatic and culinary varieties of herb for sale. The home-made jams are also for sale. No facilities for the disabled.

Walks; salmon and sea trout fishing (February to October), licence £15–£20 per day; pony trekking, £3 per hour; stalking and shooting arranged; five-day cookery courses in winter

BUCKIE

IOI 🎣 8 ⌘ ▭

The Old Monastery Restaurant, Drybridge, nr Buckie, Banffshire AB5 2JB   (Tel. 0542 32660)
Turn off the A98 at Buckie junction on to Drybridge road.
Follow road for 2½ miles (do not turn right into Drybridge village)
Closed Sun, Mon; last three weeks of January; and first two weeks of November

The cloisters of the old monastery have been turned into a bar; the chapel has become the restaurant, overlooking the mountains of Sutherland and the Moray Firth. The cooking is mainly Scottish and inspired by the fresh local supplies, with a little French influence: a hint of the Auld Alliance. The Grays are charming and friendly, very proud of their high standards, but keen to keep the atmosphere in the restaurant easy and relaxed – they say they take pleasure in continuing the tradition of hospitality for which monks were always known. There are binoculars on the windowsills through which to take a peek at the marvellous view, and beautiful original Benedictine stencils in the chapel. The restaurant can seat 45 people; three inside tables and two outside have good water views. If you are planning to visit on a Saturday night, you will be well advised to book three weeks in advance. Guide dogs are allowed into the restaurant. Bed and breakfast accommodation is available locally, prices from £12. No facilities for the disabled.

Harbour and fishing tours available; walks; sailing; river (£10–£25 a day) and sea fishing (£12.50 a day); beach (three miles away); riding; skiing nearby in winter

BUNCHREW

🏠 5/11 🏘 ⬦ ▭

Bunchrew House Hotel, Highland, Bunchrew, Inverness
IV3 6TA   (Tel. 0463 234 917)
£65–£85 single, £85–£110 double suite b&b
The Beauly Firth borders the lovely fifteen acres of landscaped gardens of this 17th-century Baronial house. The house, with its turrets and castellated front, was built by Simon Fraser, the eighth Lord Lovat, and portraits of the Fraser family, going back to 1655, adorn the dining room, the lounge and the cocktail bar. Inside, it is spacious and peaceful, with dark oak panelling, good sofas and the open fire in the lounge all adding to the atmosphere of calm comfort. The owners, Alan and Patsy Wilson, extend a warm welcome to guests, and bedrooms are well equipped, right down to the baskets of fruit and complimentary sherries. There are two dining rooms, seating 120 people altogether, with seven tables overlooking the water. A three-course lunch costs £9.50; a four-course dinner costs £21.50. The award-winning chef combines classic Scottish cuisine with French influences. Conferences and business functions can be accommodated in the Mackenzie Room. There are lavatories for disabled visitors, but no specially adapted rooms. *Walks in 18 acres of grounds; croquet; shooting (wild game, deer); sailing; free salmon fishing on tidal firth; shingle beach; championship golf, swimming, riding, ice-skating and tennis can all be arranged*

CAIRNDOW

🍴 🏘 ⬦ ▭

Loch Fyne Oyster Bar, Clachan Farm, Cairndow, Argyll
PA26 8BH   (Tel. 04996 217/264)
On the A83 10 miles out of Inveraray at the head of Loch Fyne
Open 9am–9pm April to October; 9am–6pm winter
Converted from a cow shed, this bright and down-to-earth

restaurant, with white walls and larch-wood fittings, has seating for 80 with five window tables overlooking Loch Fyne. Tables outside the restaurant can seat an additional 30 people. The menu features the same wide range of Loch Fyne produce which is being packed in the back rooms and sent worldwide. One aim here is to restore oysters to their 'affordable snack' status of last century: at present they are £7.20 a dozen. Champagne to accompany them is £23.50 per bottle; if you prefer wine, the house white is £4.95 a bottle, or there is an extensive choice of bottled beers. Smoke-house and seafood shop on premises. There is a ramp and lavatories for the disabled.
Sea fishing; hill walking; boating on loch; wildlife park and castle in Inveraray; Pinetum in Cairndow with the tallest tree in Britain

CANONBIE

inn   4/6   🏔   🍴   🔲

Riverside Inn, Canonbie DG14 0UX   (Tel. 03873 71295)
Just off the A7 between Langholm and Carlisle
Open 11am–2.30pm, 6.30pm–11pm; closed Sunday lunch
£30 pp b&b
A road separates this attractive inn from the nearby River Esk. The bar is furnished with a curious mixture of Singer sewing machine tables, old chairs and stuffed animals, which is nonetheless attractive. There is one bar, with Yates Bitter and real ale on offer. Bar lunches are available between noon and 2pm. The set dinner costs £18.50. The meals are highly praised – food is described as English with French influence, with puddings 'like Granny used to make' – and the breakfasts are said to be exceptional. Vegetarians can be catered for if advance notice is given. The bedrooms are especially bright and comfortable-looking, with little finishing touches that make guests feel at home. There are some rooms available in the cottage annexe, with a garden that runs down to the river. There is one ground-floor room with only one step up to it, and the proprietors say they have coped with visitors in wheelchairs before now.
Walks (Hadrian's Wall not far); hotel can arrange fishing; riding; golf (four courses within 30 miles)

CRINAN

IOI 🏠 🐟 💳

Lock 16 Restaurant, at the Crinan Hotel, Crinan, by
Lochgilphead, Argyll PA31 8SR　　(Tel. 054683 261)
From Lochgilphead, take A816, then A841 to Crinan
Dinner promptly at 8pm; lunch by request only. Restaurant
closed Sunday and Monday

In a fine vantage point on the roof of the Crinan Hotel, this
popular restaurant has a prized reputation for fresh seafood,
which is off-loaded from the loch 50 yards from the hotel and
prepared by chef/proprietor Nicholas Ryan (dinner £35).
Decor is unfussy and spartan, and there is seating for 20 at the
large windows looking on to the loch. No pushchairs in the
restaurant. There are lifts and lavatories for disabled visitors.
The hotel has 22 rooms, all with good loch views (£42.50–
£47.50 pp b&b) and another restaurant on the ground floor
serving dishes other than seafood. Fifty yards away, on the
quayside of the Crinan Canal, is the renowned Crinan coffee
shop: two low rooms, formerly the stables for the barge
horses, which are separated from the water by a pathway.
There are benches outside, overlooking the boats and the lock
apparatus, and cakes, quiches and open sandwiches are served
every day from 9am to 5pm.
Walks; waterskiing; windsurfing; fishing; beach (200 yards away)

DELNIES

🏨 ♒7/14 🏠 🦢 💳

The Carnach House Hotel, Delnies, Nairn IV12 5NT
(Tel. 0667 52094)
Two miles west of Nairn on the A96
£36.50–£39.50 b&b

To be completely honest, Carnach House is not directly on the
water: the Moray Firth is half a mile away, but there is nothing
between it and the hotel apart from the A96: on a clear day, you
can see for 55 miles. The view across the sea, Ben Clibrek and
the Suters of Cromerty is splendid. This fine stone house, built
in 1914, is set in eight acres of lawns and woods; the bar has

tables overlooking the Firth, and a fine selection of malt whiskies. Decor is simple but adequate; the rooms are well equipped with alarm radios, sewing kits and shoe cleaning kits. No facilities for the disabled.

Watersports; fishing; beach; walks; riding; croquet; historic castles nearby

DUNBAR

🏨 6/14 🛏️ 🐕 💳

The Bayswell Hotel, Bayswell Park, Dunbar EH42 1AE
(Tel. 0368 62225)
Off the A1 to Dunbar
£40 single, £54 double pp b&b

A friendly and comfortable seafront hotel, where you are quite likely to find local pensioners discussing politics in the bar at 11am. Built of red sandstone, and set high up on the cliff, the hotel has private access to the beach; the public rooms have fine views to the Bass Rock, May Island, Dunbar Harbour and the ancient ruins of Dunbar Castle. Three sides of the bistro restaurant have windows overlooking the rugged and exciting beach. The main restaurant seats 60; six tables have a water view. Lunch and dinner available; all main courses cost less than £12, and food is described as British/Italian. Carvery on Sunday from £5.50; dinner dances are held every Saturday night. There is one downstairs bedroom with a wide bathroom door, and the bistro is on the ground floor.

Walks; watersports; fishing (trout £12 a day, equipment for hire); long sandy beach nearby; golf (there are 14 golf courses nearby, including Muirfield, the 1992 Championship course); pony trekking (£5 an hour); bowling; putting

DUNDONNELL

🏨 13/24 🛏️ 🐕 💳

The Dundonnell Hotel, Dundonnell, by Garve, Ross–shire
IV23 2QS   (Tel. 085 483 234)
On the A832 from Ullapool to Gairloch
£28.50–£33.50 pp b&b

An old coaching inn for travellers in Wester Ross, now modernized and family run, sheltering beneath the massive mountain range of An Teallach, with views down Little Loch Broom. The building is separated from the loch only by the main road and a small filling station. The interior is modern, the decor plush: all the rooms look very comfortable and well equipped. The restaurant seats 70, with 10 window tables (dinner costs £16.50). Vegetarians can be catered for if they give advance notice. There is a special flat for disabled guests.
Mountain walks; bird watching; fishing can be arranged (hill lochs only, bring equipment); windsurfing (bring equipment); beach (12 miles away); golf (25 miles away); Inverewe Gardens (25 miles away).

DUNKELD

The Taybank Hotel, Dunkeld, Perthshire PH8 0AQ
(Tel. 03502 340)
Twelve miles from Pitlochry on the A984
£30 for a double room
This small hotel, the best part of 200 years old, is set in beautiful surroundings: the pine-covered hills of what one might be tempted to call Macbeth Country (Burnham Wood is nearby). The accommodation is basic (no *en suite* bathrooms, no telephones or televisions in bedrooms) but excellent value. There is a good pub garden, with picnic tables on the bank of the River Tay, and views of the hills, the bridge and the pretty town of Dunkeld. Bar food available (scampi and burgers £2.20–£4.40); lunch noon–2pm; supper 6pm–8pm between Easter and October. No facilities for the disabled.
Trout fishing; tennis and golf nearby; Scottish horse museum, tea rooms and antique shops in Dunkeld; Highland games nearby in August

DUNOON

inn ~3/3~ 🏠 ❌ 💳

The Coylet Inn, by Dunoon, Loch Eck, Argyll PA23 8SG
(Tel. 036984 426)
On the A815, east side of Loch Eck, north of Dunoon
Open 11am–2.30pm, 5pm–11pm weekdays; until midnight
Fri and Sat; noon–2.30pm, 6.30pm–11pm Sun
£16.50 pp b&b
Black and white, low-slung, 18th-century coaching inn on
shores of Loch Eck, surrounded by Argyll Forest Park. The
interior is very attractive and cosy, with open log fires; the
downstairs rooms are pleasantly furnished in traditional inn
style. Bedrooms are pretty, small, and simple, and all have a
fine view of the tree-lined shores of the loch. The bar serves
McEwans 80/-, and Youngers No. 3 and bar snacks (no
children allowed in the bar). The restaurant seats 30 people,
and there is room for 40 more at tables in the garden, looking
over the loch. Dinner costs £13. No facilities for the disabled.
Walks; inn has six boats with motors for hire and fishing permits

DUNOON

🏨 ~5/12~ 🏠 ⬇ 💳

The Enmore Hotel, Marine Parade, Dunoon, Argyll
PA23 8HH   (Tel. 0369 2230/2148)
On the A815 on the outskirts of Dunoon, half a mile from
Hunters Quay ferry terminal
Closed Christmas and New Year
£37–£53 pp b&b
A Victorian building with a fair view of the Clyde estuary,
separated by the road from the seafront. There is always
something going on on the water; the passing craft vary from
cruisers to yachts. Decor is sumptuous, with gilt reproduction
furniture, soft lighting, and some startling colour schemes.
The bedrooms are luxuriously appointed, and the beds are
something of a speciality: there are three four-posters, one
canopied bed, and one queen-size heated water bed. The
bathrooms have similarly indulgent touches, with canopied

silk ceilings (two have whirlpool baths), and golden swan-shaped tap fittings. The hotel restaurant seats 40 people, with two window tables that have the best view of the estuary: dinner costs £18, and the food is Scottish/French. There are two international standard squash courts, and the hotel grounds include a private shingle beach across the road.

Walks; hotel can arrange pony trekking and fishing; private shingle beach; sandy beach (five miles away); three golf courses in Dunoon; trips to the isles of Arran and Bute

EDINBURGH

The Hilton National, Bells Mills, Belford Road, Edinburgh EH4 3DG   (Tel. 031 332 2545)
Off Queensferry Road, close to city centre
£70–£110 pp b&b
Built around a 19th-century grain mill, the hotel stands on the edge of the Water of Leith and is within easy reach of all Edinburgh's attractions. Only steps away, a pleasant walkway follows the Water through the town centre; kingfishers and other waterfowl add to the scenery. The comfortable, functional bedrooms and public rooms have modern decor, though windows in river-facing bedrooms do not make the most of the view. A sociable pub occupies what was once the mill, and serves snacks all day. The 110-cover restaurant has 20 water-view tables; a four-course dinner costs £15, lunch is £12. There is a self-contained meeting and conference centre. Pets are allowed in guests' rooms only. Public rooms and some bedrooms have wheelchair access.

Walks; visits to the castle; theatres; shops; art galleries

ELIE

The Ship Inn, The Toft, Elie, Fife   (Tel. 0333 330 346)
Follow signs to harbour
Open 11am–midnight, Mon–Sat; 12.30pm–2.30pm, 6.30pm–

11pm Sun; outside bar open 11am–11pm during July and August; closed at Christmas

In an old seaside village, this small, white 18th-century fishing pub has a strong nautical atmosphere. Heavy beams, wood panelling and high-backed leather seats give the bar a cosy, welcoming feel. On sunny days, the best spot for a drink is the beach-facing beer garden, where there are barbecues every lunchtime and evening in summer. The bar serves Belhaven real ale and basic food (rolls and soup). The new landlord is busy making various improvements. Children are allowed into some areas of the pub. Bed and breakfast accommodation available nearby. There are no facilities for the disabled.

Excellent walks along beach, cliffs and golf course; watersports; rod fishing; golf (£15 a day); tennis; putting green; nine-hole junior golf course

FEARNAN-BY-ABERFELDY

Tigh-an-Loan, Fearnan-by-Aberfeldy, Tayside PH15 2PF
(Tel. 08873 249)
£30 pp dinner and b&b

Across the road from the shores of Loch Tay, this solid stone house is well run by the friendly proprietors. The bedrooms are comfortable and not over-modernized; some have fine loch views. There are four tables overlooking the water in the 30-cover restaurant, and non-residents are welcome. A four-course, traditional Scottish dinner costs £11. There is a fine selection of malts on offer at the bar, and bar meals are available at lunch and in the evenings and can be enjoyed at picnic tables in the garden.

Hill and forest walks; watersports; beach; golf (three courses nearby); fishing on Loch Tay (hotel has rights)

FORT AUGUSTUS

Inchnacardoch Lodge Hotel, by Fort Augustus, Inverness-shire PH32 4BL (Tel. 0320 6258)

On the A82 half a mile north of village
Open from April to December
£40–£75 b&b for two
With its rugged old architecture, beaming local faces and
distinct lack of rush, the area feels lost in time, especially in low
season. The hotel was once Lord Lovat's hunting lodge, and
retains its period flavour with antiques and generously proportioned rooms. The village is situated at the southern end of
Loch Ness, where it meets the Caledonian Canal. Most bedrooms have good views of Loch Ness; there is an old brass bed
in one, and the attic rooms are quite pretty. The restaurant
seats 40, with 12 tables overlooking the water. A three-course
dinner costs £17.50. The lounge and bar have loch views, and
snacks are served at lunchtime. There are no facilities for the
disabled.

*Golf (nine-hole course, £4 a day); walks; watersports can be arranged
at waterpark (eight miles away); fishing (£3 a day); rowing on loch*

FORT AUGUSTUS

The Lock Inn, Canalside, Fort Augustus, Inverness-shire
PH32 4BL   (Tel. 0320 6302)
A friendly local pub, the Lock Inn is right on the Caledonian
Locks and has delightful canal views. Loch Ness comes up to
the edge of this wee village, so there is plenty of scope for
thirst-building walks along the loch or towpath. McEwan's
Export and Younger's Tartan Special round out the selection
of beers, and for those after stiffer refreshment, there are no
fewer than 30 whiskies on offer. Full cooked bar meals have an
excellent repution and feature fresh local haddock, salmon, and
meat (from the butcher next door). These are served in
summer only and cost from £2.50 to £5. The pub is on the
ground floor, and doorways are wide enough to accommodate
wheelchairs, but there are no special facilities for the disabled.
Children are allowed in for meals only.

*Forest, lochside and towpath walks; salmon and trout fishing (permits
available locally); watersports at South Laggan Water Park (20 miles
away)*

GLENSHIEL

🏘 9/12 ⚓ 📶 ▭

Kintail Lodge, Glenshiel, by Kyle of Lochalsh, Ross-shire
IV40 8HL (Tel. 059 981 275)
On the A87, at the head of Loch Duich, near Kyle of Lochalsh
Closed over Christmas and New Year
£36–£46 pp dinner and b&b
This former shooting lodge is right on the shores of Loch
Duich, at the foot of the Five Sisters of Kintail. A large
National Trust property borders the four acres of hotel
grounds, and there are plenty of mountain and lowland walks
nearby. Views across the loch and up to the Five Sisters
combine with the rough shooting lodge atmosphere to make
this a fine Highland retreat. Bedrooms vary from classic old
lodge-style to modern, and a new sun lounge affords
wonderful loch views. There is seating for 30 in the restaurant;
three window tables overlook the loch. Dinner costs £15 for
non-residents. Lunches are served in the loch-view public bar.
Well-behaved pets can be accommodated by arrangement, but
are not allowed into public rooms. No facilities for the
disabled.
*Mountain or lowland walks, advice centre nearby; hotel can arrange
fishing with sufficient notice (bring equipment), and canoeing; four
acres of walled garden; sandy beach and watersports (10 miles away)*

GOLSPIE

🏘 3/8 ⚓ 📶 ▭

The Golf Links Hotel, Golspie, Sutherland KW12 6TT
(Tel. 04083 3408)
£20–£23 pp b&b
Adjacent to the Golspie golf course, this small hotel looks out
to Ben Baraggie at the rear and to Dornoch Firth at the front.
The sunny residents' lounge has lively decor and good views of
the sea, which is just across the road. Bedrooms and public
rooms have a comfortable, relaxed feel; three self-catering
chalets are open from Easter to early autumn. Lunches are
available in the bar, and the 48–cover restaurant serves set

dinners for £12. Nearby are the fairy-tale towers of Dunrobin Castle, seat of the earls and dukes of Sutherland since the 13th century. The Royal Dornoch golf course is within striking distance, as is the Loch Fleet Bird Sanctuary. Chalet rooms are accessible by wheelchair, but there are no special facilities for the disabled.

Good walks (beach, golf course); fishing (free to £12 a day); bird watching; beach; golf (£9–£17 a day)

HELMSDALE

Navidale House, Helmsdale, Sutherland KW8 6JS
(Tel. 04312 258)
Just after Helmsdale on the A9
£19.50–£30 pp b&b, also two garden chalets
This pretty houe is perched right on the clifftop, with excellent sea views over Moray Firth and the Ord of Caithness. Built as a hunting lodge for the Duke of Sutherland in 1830s, it is set in six acres of woodland and garden which ramble down to the foreshore; there is a path to the beach. The restaurant seats 47 people and has 10 tables overlooking the water. A set dinner costs £17.50. Smoking is not allowed anywhere in the hotel. There is a ground-floor annexe, but no special facilities for the disabled.

Walks; watersports; salmon fishing at £13–£18 a day (there are only 12 rods, so book well in advance and bring equipment); beach; golf (local £9 a day, Royal courses nearby); squash and tennis courts nearby; Dunrobin Castle also nearby; gold panning in Balle an Or, scene of 1869 Kildonan gold strike (11 miles away)

ISLE OF WHITHORN

The Steam Packet, Isle of Whithorn, Dumfries and Galloway DG8 8LL   (Tel. 09885 334)
At the end of the A747, on the Wigtown peninsula
Bar open: 11am–11pm Mon–Sat; noon–11pm Sun (January to March 11am–2.30pm, 5.30pm–11pm Mon–Sat; noon–

2.30pm, 5.30pm–11pm Sun)
£20 pp b &b
The most southerly pub in Scotland, the Steam Packet is set on a lovely natural harbour bustling with fishermen, yachtsmen and a colourful variety of boats. The bar has a cosy feel with a picture window and wood-burning stove, and is popular with both visitors and locals. Reasonably priced snacks are available at lunch and in the evening; garden tables are the perfect spot for a meal if the weather is fair. The dining room seats 60, with 12 tables overlooking the water, and a big model steamship hangs from one of the walls. Cooking features fresh seafood (scallops and lobsters are landed at the harbour), and a full dinner costs £10.50. *En suite* bedrooms are simple but comfortable; three enjoy pretty harbour views, and two look out over the garden. Vast Scottish breakfasts, not for the faint hearted, include potato scones, haggis and kippers. The ground-floor bar and dining room are accessible to wheelchairs, but there are no special facilities for the disabled.
Inn can arange fishing (even for shark); boat trips from harbour; St Ninian's Church behind the inn; golf (six miles away)

KELSO

20/32

Ednam House Hotel, Kelso, Roxburghshire
(Tel. 0573 24168)
£35–£72 pp dinner and b&b
Built in 1761, and considered the finest Georgian building in Roxburghshire, the house overlooks the River Tweed and the Junction Pool with the River Teviot. The atmosphere is relaxed yet opulent, and surrounds guests with gracious country house hospitality. Three acres of gardens and a generous stretch of river frontage offer plenty of scope for pleasant strolls. All lounges, both bars and the beautiful old function room overlook the Tweed. The restaurant serves bar lunches Monday to Saturday and a more elaborate spread on Sunday (the four-course Sunday lunch costs about £15); the river is in view from all tables. A treat for anyone, Ednam House is especially recommended for the serious fisherman.

There are no facilities for the disabled.
Fishing: salmon and trout (£1.50 a day); tennis, golf, swimming and riding all nearby; many walks

KENMORE

🏘 10/38 🏕 🔶 ▭

The Kenmore Hotel, The Square, Kenmore, by Aberfeldy, Perthshire PH15 2NU   (Tel. 08873 205)
On the A827 and Loch Tay, six miles from Aberfeldy
£35–£45 per room
This lovely hotel dates back to 1572 and claims to be the oldest inn in Scotland, and Robbie Burns once graced one of the walls with a graffiti'd poem. With a good position beside the River Tay, it is situated in a pretty village with a (private) castle. The hotel has a tennis court, and a par 69 18-hole golf course in the castle grounds. The bar-lounge is charmingly rustic, with an old stone-and-beam bar. The bedrooms with verandas over Loch Tay are particularly attractive, and all have bathrooms *en suite*. The restaurant seats 80, with 12 tables overlooking the water. Fish and game feature prominently on the menu; a three-course dinner costs £18.50. Pets are allowed in the annexe only. There is easy access to ground-floor rooms, but no special facilities for the disabled.
Walks; windsurfing; jetskiing; two miles of private fishing (£10–£15 a day); beach on Loch Tay; glacial museum

KENTALLEN

🏘 3/13 🏕 🔶 ▭

Ardsheal House, Kentallen, Appin, Argyll   (Tel. 063174 22)
Off the A828 (Oban from Fort William); clearly signposted from road
Open April to November
£58–£80 pp dinner and b&b
An ancient pile of a hotel, found at the end of a one-mile-long private drive that winds along beside Loch Linnhe. From its superb elevated position in Stevenson's *Kidnapped* country, the hotel's view, especially from the tower, is unparalleled. Nine

hundred acres of private woodland, gardens and shore front surround the stone and granite mansion, which was built in 1545, sacked in the 1745 uprisings, and rebuilt in 1760. The estate does not belong to the hotel, but they have access through it, down to their own pebbled beach. The bedrooms are well furnished with antiques in an old-fahioned style with some boisterous wallpapers. There is an oak-panelled reception lounge, a cosy bar, and an open fire on an old stone hearth in the reception area. The dining room, which has a conservatory extension, seats 45 people; dinner costs £29.50. No facilities for the disabled.

Billiards room and tennis court at hotel; fishing can be arranged (bring equipment); riding; walks in Glencoe and surrounding area; private shore-front pebble beach

KENTALLEN

10/12

The Holly Tree Hotel, Kentallen, Appin, Argyll PA38 4BY (Tel. 063174 292)
On the A828, 15 miles south of Fort William
Open early March to end of October; also Christmas and New Year (quite often, the hotel is actually open when it is meant to be closed, so it is worth ringing up to find out)
£44–£63 dinner and b&b
A former turn-of-the-century railway station overlooking Loch Linnhe and mountains of Ardgour, this hotel has been cleverly converted, with close attention to Glasgow art nouveau detail. The Railway Bar, for instance, used to house the station's tea room. The dining room (no smoking in here) has picture windows and seating for 50 people, and has recently been revamped. It now has a split-level floor this season, which makes the most of the wonderful view over the floodlit garden, former railway pier and out over Loch Linnhe. The bedrooms are spacious, with solid modern furniture and stylish fabrics, and give a particularly strong impression of being on the water. There is a strong family atmosphere about the hotel, with the Robertsons' children and personal possessions everywhere. The hotel grounds run for a mile down the

disused railway. Dogs can be accommodated by special arrangement only; they are not allowed into the public rooms. Two of the ground-floor rooms have special bathrooms for disabled visitors.

Walks; hotel can arrange riding, fishing, sailing, boat trips and canoeing

KILCHRENAN

🏨 5/14 🏠 8 ⬙ ▭

Ardanaiseig, Kilchrenan, by Taynuilt, Argyll PA35 1HE (Tel. 08663 333)

Leave the A85 at Taynuilt, take the B845 to Kilchrenan, then follow signs to Ardanaiseig (three miles)

Open from end of April to October

£68–£96 dinner pp b&b

A Scottish Baronial style house, dating from 1834, set in 32 acres of woodland garden beside Loch Awe. The gardens are beautifully kept, and boast a collection of rare shrubs. Modernizations have, of course, been carried out, but these are most discreet, and do not in any way interfere with the civilized elegance of the place. There are plenty of large windows and log fires, and the bedrooms are stylish, though not plush. The view down across the fine lawn and out over loch is exceptionally good. The restaurant seats 30 people, with two window tables (dinner £28.50). Vegetarians can be catered for, with advance notice. Diversions for guests inside the hotel include a billiard room. The hotel has recently changed hands, but no dramatic changes are planned. Dogs can be accommodated by prior arrangement only. No facilities for the disabled.

Three boats (engines for hire); fishing (rods supplied); tennis; croquet; clay pigeon shooting (guns supplied)

KILCHRENAN

🏨 13/15 🏠 ⬙ ▭

Taychreggan Hotel, Kilchrenan, by Taynuilt, Argyll PA35 (Tel. 08663 211)

Signposted from the A85 just east of Taynuilt

Open March to October
£55–£72 dinner and b&b
Situated right on waterfront, the Taychreggan hotel looks out along Loch Awe – the longest fresh-water loch in Scotland – in 25 acres of its own grounds. Originally an old drovers' inn, it now has modern extensions and an attractive suntrap of a courtyard where guests can eat in the summer. Most of the bedrooms are identical except for their pleasantly differing colour schemes, and the whole place looks generally comfortable and relaxed. The bar is airy, and well populated with stuffed birds and fish. There are five window tables by the picture windows in the restaurant, and these have the best view of the loch. Dinner costs £25.50. Vegetarians can be catered for, with advance notice. No facilities for the disabled.
Hotel can arrange fishing, boats, windsurfing (boards and wetsuits available), shooting, riding, and croquet; swimming from hotel lawn

KILLIN
inn

The Clachaig Hotel, Falls of Dochart, Gray Street, Killin, Perthshire   (Tel. 05672 270)
On the A827
£17 pp b&b; self-catering chalet £275 per week
A listed, rambling, 18th-century inn, which incorporates an even older smithy, the Clachaig hotel is also known as the Salmon Lie because of its excellent angling location. There are beautiful views of the Falls of Dochart and the bridge. This is McNab country, so history positively drips from the walls. The bar has a wide range of malt whiskies, and an original fireplace with log fire, and a pool table. There is no residents' lounge, so the hotel may not be suitable for people who like somewhere other than their bedrooms where they can read in peace and quiet. The dining room seats 32 people, with two water-view tables. If you feel like a lighter meal, try the salad restaurant. The hotel has won a 'bar meal of the year' award for Scotland. Pets can be accommodated for a charge of £2 for the first night, and £1 for subsequent nights. There is a lavatory for disabled visitors.

Walks, hiking, canoeing, waterskiing, sailing, salmon and trout fishing, £30 per day for salmon fishing trips on Loch Tay (equipment can be hired); salmon fishing beat on Loch Tay; fishing packages can be arranged; nine-hole village golf course, £5 a day

KILMORE

Glenfeochan House, Kilmore, by Oban, Argyll PA34 4QR
(Tel. 063177 273)
Five miles south of Oban on the A816
Open March to October
£95–£110 per room b&b
A listed, turreted and recently restored Victorian sandstone building, with beautiful ornate plaster work on high ceilings, and a finely carved American-pine staircase. The hotel is situated half a mile from Loch Feochan, and is surrounded by 350 acres of land, which includes a stretch of shore. The five-acre garden is full of rare specimen trees, rhododendrons (they're on the Gulf Stream), and often, deer – it is open to the public. This is very much a private house with paying guests, all of whom eat together at the Babers' dining-room table (dinner costs £25, and is for residents only). The bedrooms are large and decorated in a plain, sensible, old-fashioned style, and the views from them are splendid, with mountains and trees as well as the loch. Pets can be accommodated, but only by prior arrangement. No facilities of the disabled.
Hotel can arrange clay pigeon shooting, riding, sailing, windsurfing and fishing (salmon and sea trout on rivers and loch); golf (three miles away); walks; bird watching; loch-bathing

KINCLAVEN BY STANLEY

Ballathie House, Kinclaven by Stanley, Perthshire PH1 4QN
(Tel. 025083 268)
Off the A9 two miles north of Perth
Closed last two weeks of February
£64–£85 pp dinner and b&b

A Baronial mansion built in 1850, now comprehensively refurbished and set in its own estate overlooking the River Tay, up an impressive private drive. It is more like a private house than a hotel, with log fires in original marble fireplaces in the public rooms, and lovely grounds full of rhododendrons. The decor is tasteful, with draped beds and turreted bathrooms, and there are fresh flowers and Victorian dressing table sets in each room. The light and airy Sportsman's Lodge annexe sleeps an additional 11 people and is separate from house so that guests can come and go at all hours without disturbing the night porter. The dining room seats 80 people, and most of the tables have good views of the river. Children and pets can be accommodated, by prior arrangement only. There are two rooms for disabled visitors on the ground floor, with large bathrooms.

Walks; prime salmon fishing on River Tay (salmon fishing holiday packages available for Ballathie Water, book one year in advance); trout fishing on loch and river; clay pigeon shooting; golf; Scone Palace and Glamis Castle nearby

KINCRAIG

The Boathouse Restaurant, Kincraig, Inverness-shire
(Tel. 05404 272)
Once in Kincraig, follow signs to Loch Insh Watersports
Closed late October to 27 December
The restaurant is housed in a log cabin above a stone boathouse, with seats on the balcony that give a grandstand view of Loch Insh, and the windsurfers and waterskiers down below. There is seating for 35; all tables share the view. The restaurant serves pâté, ham and soup at lunch; cakes and toasted sandwiches at high tea; three-course dinners cost £7.50. Fondue nights, with *glühwein* on tap, are held every Wednesday from February to April. The restaurant doubles as a gift/craft shop, selling tempting jams and presents. Visitors can find accommodation at Insh Hall (also overlooking Loch Insh, and is next to Aviemore; same telephone number), a converted community hall with two to six bunks per room and two self-

catering kitchens, television room and keep-fit gym. The place has an alpine feel, and offers good value packages for skiing or watersports (telephone for further details). Log chalets are also available for rent, which might make a good base for a family (telephone restaurant for details). There is a ramp into the restaurant for visitors in wheelchairs, and one six-person chalet is suitable for the disabled.

Canoeing, sailing and windsurfing hire and instruction May to October; close to Aviemore; artificial ski slope hire and instruction all year; downhill and cross-country hire and instruction December to April; walks; fishing; beach on site

KINLOCHBERVIE

6/14

Kinlochbervie Hotel, by Lairg, Sutherland IV27 4RP
(Tel. 097 182 275)
£73–£95 twin/double b&b; garden annexe £23 pp
A modern family hotel overlooking Kinlochbervie harbour and Loch Clash, with unbeatable panoramic views from the lounge of sunsets over the Atlantic. The rooms have large windows with views of either the working harbour or the sea. The highlight of the day is going down to the fish market to watch the buyers arranging orders with Billingsgate on their portable telephones: a marvellous blend of the old and the new. From the lounge, you can watch the seals following the fishing boats out to sea. Five miles up the road there is the most beautiful white sandy beach; wild and wonderful. The public bar has a choice of 180 malt whiskies and a pool table, and is used by local skippers and fishermen. Bar meals are available. Occasionally, you can find a travelling Ceilidh band playing there. The restaurant seats 40, and 12 tables have sea views. Fish is, obviously, a speciality; a four-course dinner costs £25. No specific disabled facilities, though the annexe has wheel-chair access.

Walking; mountaineering; golf; sailing; river/loch/sea fishing (hotel offers fly fishing on lochs, £1–£15 a day); pony trekking; beach; trips to Handa Island Bird Reserve, Cape Wrath lighthouse, etc.

KINLOCH RANNOCH

The Loch Rannoch Hotel, Kinloch Rannoch, by Pitlochry
PH16 5PS   (Tel. 08822 201)
One mile from Kinloch Rannoch
£30–£46 pp dinner and b&b (also self-catering lodges, see
below)

The hotel is a fine, late-19th-century building in a lochside
setting, with a good atmosphere and friendly staff. Visitors can
be fetched from Pitlochry station, 20 miles away (£10 charge,
which includes the return journey). The restaurant seats 65; all
tables have a view of the loch, and the set dinner costs £11.75.
Bar meals are available in the pub lounge and the grill room,
and guests can be provided with packed lunches. This is an
excellent place for an active holiday in beautiful surroundings.
There are full indoor leisure facilities (indoor swimming
pool, multi-gym, sauna, solarium, spa bath, squash, snooker,
exercise trail, games room), and windsurfers, bicycles, rowing
boats, and an adventure playground outside. Eighty-five self-
catering lodges, rented off time-share owners, are available for
rent. These are large and airy, with big windows and balconies
facing the water, sleep between four and eight people, and cost
£250 a week. Three-quarters of the lodges have their own
saunas. The scenery along the road between the motorway and
the hotel (a 20-mile drive) is truly spectacular, though the road
can become clogged with traffic in summer. Some of the
lodges would be suitable for the disabled.

From forest walks to mountain climbs; on site sailing, windsurfing,
white-water rafting, canoeing (no motorized watersports, to preserve
peace of the loch); loch (fly and spinner) and river fishing; beach; dry-
slope skiing, mountain biking; ski trips to resorts; clay pigeon
shooting; pony trekking; motobikes; war games; pottery classes; trips
to distilleries; golf can be arranged

KIPPFORD

The Anchor Hotel, Kippford, Dalbeattie, Kirkcudbright
DG5 4LN   (Tel. 055662 205)
Off the A710 south of Dalbeattie
Open 10.30am–midnight from April to October; 10.30am–
2.30pm, 6pm–11pm November to March
Despite its name, the Anchor has no accommodation, but
don't let that put you off. The pub, separated from the busy
yacht harbour by the village street, has three bars; the lounge
bar and the Anchor bar overlook the water, and the former,
with Dalbeattie granite walls, is a little more formal than the
latter. All the bars serve local beers, and are beautifully
panelled, including the ceilings. There is an open fire, and
interesting ornaments, pictures, and a collection of jugs in the
main bar. Children can be despatched to the games room, to
play pool or video games, or watch MTV. Excellent, home-
cooked meals are served in the lounge bar from noon to 2pm,
and 6pm to 9pm – main courses cost about £4. No specific
facilities for the disabled, though there are no stairs into the
bar, and the doorways are wide enough to admit wheelchairs.
Sailing can be arranged; walks

LAIRG

The Sutherland Arms Hotel, Lairg, Sutherland IV27 4AT
(Tel. 0549 2291)
Open Easter to mid-October
£48 single, £78 double b&b
Originally a 17th-century coaching inn on the shores of Loch
Shin; the main part of the hotel was built in 1850. The
bedrooms have proper old windows, and there are good views
from all reception and dining rooms. There are two bars, one
of which overlooks the loch, and there is a waterside garden.
Bar meals are available at lunchtime, and a four-course dinner
in the restaurant costs £16.50. There are also six self-catering
cottages available for rent; each of these sleeps between two

and eight people and costs £170–£260 a week. No facilities for
the disabled.
*Walks; golf; pony trekking; trout and salmon fishing (the hotel
arranges special fishing holiday packages); grouse shooting and
stalking can also be arranged*

LEITH
🍴 🏠5 🐾 🖃

The Waterfront Wine Bar, 1c Dock Place, Leith EH6 6LU
(Tel. 031 554 7427)
At the back of Dock Place, off Commercial Street
Open 11am–midnight. Closed Sunday dinner; 25 and 26
December; 1 and 2 January
The wine bar is housed in a 17th-century listed building which
used to be the lock keeper's office, on the historic dockside, by
a swingbridge. The bar and restaurant have been created out of
hatch covers off fishing boats, with old lamps and the original
panelled ceiling. There are excellent waterside seats in the
Victorian-style conservatory and on the floating platform
(book well in advance of your visit for these); altogether, they
can accommodate 190 people. The clientele ranges from
businessmen to students, via tourists and passers-by. Cuisine is
national and international; the menu changes twice daily, and a
three-course meal costs from £10. Guide dogs are allowed in.
They stock more than 100 wines, and won a Scottish wine bar
of the year award in 1989. There is a lavatory for disabled
visitors, and there are no steps into the restaurant.
*Start/finish of Water of Leith river walkway through Edinburgh;
beach (one and a half miles away)*

LOCHGILPHEAD
🍴 🏠14 🐾 🖃

The Tayvallich Inn, by Lochgilphead, Argyll PA31 8PR
(Tel. 05467 282)
On the B8025, off the A816, 10 miles south of Kilmartin
Open 11am–11pm; closed 2.30pm–6.30pm November to
March

A low modern building in a picturesque village, separated from the waterfront by the village street. You'll need to make a lengthy detour from the main road to visit the inn, but it's worth it. The inn has lightwood furnishings and fittings inside, and opens on to a water-view beer garden, from which you can admire the boats gathered in the bay. The restaurant seats 36 people; there are three tables by the window inside, and five outside in the garden. The house speciality is seafood (including oysters, mussels and scallops), which is brought straight into the village from the sea. Bar meals cost from £5; a full dinner costs £15. The landlord is adding a conservatory sun lounge on to the patio area at the inn; this should be finished by summer 1991. The inn is all on one level, but there are no special facilities for the disabled.

Walks; watersports; fishing; darts; sailing

LOCHINVER

Inver Lodge Hotel, Lochinver, Sutherland IV27 4LU
(Tel. 05714 496)
Drive down waterfront and take second left after village hall in Lochinver
Open April to mid-November
£44–£75 pp b&b
A modern hotel, built two years ago, and set high above a small fishing village, looking over Loch Inver and across the Minches to the Isle of Lewis. The hotel is well designed, and all the bedrooms, decorated with pretty chintzes, have splendid views across the village to the loch, with a backdrop of wild, craggy mountains. The restaurant has the same view, and seats 60 people (the set dinner costs £21); bar meals are also available. There is a sauna, a solarium and a billiard room for when guests do not feel like venturing outside. No facilities for the disabled.

Walks (Ardvreck Castle and Inverpolly Nature Reserve nearby; Smoo Cave on north coast; Fas a Chual Aluinn Falls nearby; salmon and trout fishing (hotel has rights for 10 rods on nearby Inver, Oykel and Kirkaig rivers, and also 10 rods for loch fishing; bring equipment); beach

OBAN

🏠 7/11 🛏10 ◇ ▭

The Manor House Hotel, Gallanach Road, Oban, Argyll
(Tel. 063162 087)
Half a mile from Oban town centre; follow signs to ferry
terminal
£55–£80 dinner and b&b
On the outskirts of town, this small late-Georgian house has
fine views over the harbour and Oban Bay. The bedrooms are
beautiful; prettily decorated, and with fine views. The
reception and bar area are less easy on the eye, with flocked
walls and patterned fitted carpets, but the dining room, with its
dark green walls and fine panelling, and the lounge, with a log
fire, help to achieve the private house atmosphere. The dining
room seats 30 people (no bay views), and the set dinner costs
£17.50. No pets in public rooms. No facilities for the disabled.
A wide range of activities can be arranged: ask at hotel; ferry to Mull
(terminal 200 yards away)

OBAN

🏠 18/18 🛏 ◇ ▭

The Knipoch Hotel, Oban PA34 4QT   (Tel. 08526 251)
On the A816, six miles south of Oban
£55 pp b&b
Once the local tax collector's residence, and since extended,
this ochre-coloured Georgian house enjoys lovely views of
Loch Feochan. A road separates the hotel from the water and a
pebbly beach. Interior features include pine floors, Persian rugs
and dark wood furniture. The bedrooms are functional yet
comfortable, and all are identical save for their colour schemes:
upstairs is done in 'old rose', while downstairs is mustard/
ochre, and all have dark wood furniture and overlook the loch.
The 44-seat restaurant occupies three separate rooms, with a
total of four tables in the window. Home-smoked salmon and
halibut (both wild) highlight the dinners, as does an endless
wine list. Five courses cost £33. Mr Craig offers a selection of
over 50 single malts, the oldest of which date back to before the

Second World War. A measure of vintage 1936 runs to between £14 and £15, while a shot of '38 will set you back £31. There are no facilities for the disabled.
Hotel can arrange waterskiing, windsurfing, riding, sailing and fishing; swimming from the beach; good walks

ONICH

The Allt-nan-Ros Hotel, Onich, by Fort William, Inverness-shire PH33 6RY   (Tel. 08553 210)
Open April to November
On the A82, 10 miles south of Fort William
£54.50–£60.50 pp dinner and b&b
This attractive Victorian shooting lodge enjoys panoramic views of Loch Linnhe (across the main road), and the rooms are geared to make the most of these. A stream winds through its four acres of garden down to the water's edge. Guests can relax in front of an open fire in the lounge. The spacious bedrooms are comfortably furnished with dark wood, and several have bay windows. The restaurant seats 50 people (non-residents are welcome), and thirteen of the tables have loch views. The set dinner costs £17.50. On a fine summer's evening, you can enjoy the views from the hotel's terraced lawns. There is a ramp at the front door, and two ground-floor rooms are suitable for the disabled.
Hotel can arrange riding; golf; waterskiing; windsurfing (wetsuits and boards can be hired); yachting; scuba diving (equipment can be hired); speed boats; cruises; stalking; fishing (some rods available)

ONICH

The Lodge on the Loch, Onich, nr Fort William PH33 6RY
(Tel. 08553 237)
On the A82, five miles north of Glencoe and 10 miles south of Fort William
Open March to November, Christmas and New Year
£55 pp dinner and b&b

From its five-acre gardens the lodge looks over the road and Loch Linnhe to Argyll and the Morvern mountains. A recently refurbished, modern interior sets it apart from most other Highland hotels. Sponged walls and pastel colours work well, and the bar, in tones of heather and soft blue with a tented silk ceiling, is certainly unique. Soft fabrics and more pastel colours highlight reception rooms and new wing bedrooms, while bedrooms in the old wing retain their traditional flavour. The bay windows in the drawing rooms and dining room open out to striking loch views. The restaurant seats 50, with four window tables (non-residents welcome; set dinner £16). Guests can make use of the hotel's private moorings. There is a ground-floor room for disabled visitors, and a disabled lavatory.

Watersports and fishing nearby (ask for details); spring and autumn watercolour painting courses

PITLOCHRY

30/37

The Green Park Hotel, Clunie Bridge Road, Pitlochry,
Perthshire PH16 5JY   (Tel. 0796 3248)
Off the A9, Pitlochry turning
Open 1 April to 28 October
£27.50–£35 pp b&b
The gardens of this 18th-century country house hotel run down to the banks of Loch Faskally. It is quiet and peaceful inside, with original panelling and tapestries in public rooms; the bedrooms are large and comfortable. There are spectacular loch views from the sun lounge. The restaurant has seating for 100 people, and 28 of the tables overlook the water. A four-course dinner costs £15.50. Bar meals are served at lunch and dinner, and can be taken outside and eaten on the lawns during the summer. The hotel would make a good base for touring, as it is situated just off the main road to the Highlands and the West Coast, and it is popular with visitors to the Pitlochry Festival Theatre (this is daily rep, so you can see six plays in a week, if you're up to it). Ground-floor rooms available which are suitable for the disabled.

Putting on hotel lawns; table tennis; bar billiards; children's play area; walks; watersports; trout and salmon fishing on loch (free, bring own equipment); Pitlochry Festival Theatre (3 May to late September)

PITLOCHRY

3/12

The Killiecrankie Hotel, by Pitlochry, Perthshire PH16 5LG (Tel. 0796 3220)
Well signposted off the A9 between Pitlochry and Blair Atholl
Open February to November
£37.75 pp b&b

Though not directly on the water, the hotel has exceptional views over the River Garry, and stands in lovely surroundings, overlooking the historic Pass of Killiecrankie and the RSPB nature reserve opposite. A cheery sun room and the cosy, pine-furnished bedrooms add to the charm of this rambling country house (the bedrooms have recently been revamped, so now all have *en suite* bathroom, television and direct dial telephone). The dining room seats 34 people, and five tables have river views. The hotel has a particularly good reputation for food; the cooking features fresh local fish and meats, and the five-course set dinner costs £20.75 (non-residents are welcome). Bar meals are available at lunch and supper. Four ground-floor bedrooms, and only two steps at the front of the hotel, though there are no specific facilities for disabled visitors.

RSPB reserve immediately across river; golf; shooting; Pitlochry Festival Theatre; walks; watersports on Loch Tay; trout and salmon fishing can be arranged

PLOCKTON

2/2

Plockton Hotel, 41 Harbour Street, Plockton, Ross-shire
IV52 8TN   (Tel. 059 984 274)
Off the A890
£17.50 pp b&b

In a tiny village where the cows roam free, this pretty, low stone house looks out to Black Rock Island; by a quirk of geography, it is on the West Coast, but faces due east. Its waterside beer garden across the street has been known to disappear at high tide, and a solitary palm tree attests to the presence of the Gulf Stream. The atmosphere is outstandingly friendly and comfortable; the rooms are homely, and the large yet cosy bar is carpeted in tartan. The bar food is memorable – prawns are a speciality here – and there are plenty of games (such as shove ha'penny and dominoes) with which to while away an evening. Other attractions include the village sailing regatta, held in late July/early August. No facilities for the disabled.

Hotel has a canoe; motor boats and windsurfers for hire in the village; seal-spotting trips (money back if no seal spotted); coral beach within walking distance

PORT APPIN

The Airds Hotel, Port Appin, Appin, Argyll PA38 4DF
(Tel. 063 173 236)
Off the A828, south of Fort William, 25 miles north of Oban
Open March to January
£91 pp dinner and b&b
This extended cottage, formerly a ferry inn, dates back 300 years and has views past a little lighthouse to Loch Linnhe. Its gardens, across the village street, nearly touch the shore. The bedrooms are superb: large and well decorated in an old-fashioned style, with pretty wallpapers and plain, fitted carpets. Useful extras include electric blankets. The public rooms are comfortable, made cosy by the open fires, and the tasteful paraphernalia of books and ornaments. The dining room (for dinner only) seats 36 people; there are 14 tables, and all have good views of the loch. The set dinner costs £32, and, by all accounts, is something to write home about. No facilities for the disabled.

Walks; hotel can arrange windsurfing, jetskiing, boating and fishing; shingle beach nearby

PORTPATRICK

🏠 ♒ 5/12 🐎 ⬧ ▭

The Crown Hotel, North Crescent, Portpatrick, Stranraer
DG9 8SX   (Tel. 077681 261)
On the A77, south of Stranraer
£30 single, £56 double b&b
Separated from the harbour by the village street, the hotel has
good views past a disused lighthouse and west across the Irish
Channel. Some of the comfortable bedrooms look across to
Northern Ireland. The bars are cosy and traditionally furnished;
two of the three have water views. The tile-floored restaurant
seats 60 people and opens out through a conservatory into the
sheltered back garden. On summer evenings, you can make
the most of the waterside ambience by taking your drinks out
to the seats in front of the hotel. Lunch and dinner cost from
£6.95. No facilities for the disabled.
*Hotel can arrange fishing, shooting and pony trekking; golf and tennis
in Portpatrick*

PORTPATRICK

🏠 ♒ 5/10 🐎 ⬧ ▭

Knockinaam Lodge, Portpatrick, Wigtownshire DT9 9AD
(Tel. 077681 471)
Off the A77 between Stranraer and Portpatrick, signposted
from the main road
Open March to January
£70–£85 pp dinner and b&b
Once the site of a secret Churchill–Eisenhower meeting, this
secluded Victorian house is bordered on two sides by cliffs and
on one by sea. The fine lawns run down to a reasonably sandy
beach. The decor pays close attention to detail and features
antique clocks and rich wood panelling and beautiful wallpapers. There are log fires in the comfortable sitting rooms,
and a good country house atmosphere. Some of the bedrooms
(inevitably, there is one dubbed 'Churchill') have views to
Ireland. The restaurant seats 26 and has two window tables; the
four-course dinners are renowned. Vegetarians should give the
chef advance notice. No facilities for the disabled.

Hotel can arrange fishing and croquet; golf (three miles away); garden visiting; walking

ST ANDREWS

19/50

Rusacks Hotel, Pilmour Links, St Andrews, Fife KY16 9JQ.
(Tel. 0334 74321)
On the A91 towards Cupar
£80–£225 per room
This carefully refurbished Victorian hotel has a superb position, overlooking the fairways of the famous Old Course, the Royal and Ancient club house, and beyond these, the curve of the beach and the sea. The reception rooms are large, with fine high ceilings; decor is consistently smart, and the walls are adorned with Scottish paintings. The sun lounge has excellent views of the sea and hills; it is also a perfect spot for watching the golf Opens. There is a snug basement bar with a good deal of tartan in the furnishings, and a solarium and sauna. The restaurant seats 64 (no water views), and a three-course dinner will cost you between £21 and £30. All of the staff, whatever their level of responsibility, are quite astonishingly polite, efficient and helpful. There is a lavatory for disabled visitors, but no specially adapted rooms.
Walks; watersports; sand yachting; riding (£4 an hour); fishing (sea trout, £10 a day); beach

ST FILLANS

9/12

The Four Seasons Hotel, St Fillans PH6 2NF
(Tel. 076 485 333)
Closed January and February
On the A85 towards Crianlarich
£24–£38.50 pp b&b
A pleasant hotel, in an idyllic loch-side situation, with exceptionally good views from the terrace and picture windows. There is a warm family atmosphere to the place; the bedrooms are pretty, and the ones at the front of the house

share the splendid views across Loch Earn to the mountains beyond. The restaurant seats 60 and specializes in fresh game and seafood; all tables overlook the loch. The public rooms are simply decorated, but comfortable, and there is a library to provide reading matter for a quiet afternoon inside. The bar and coffee shop enjoy good water views. Snacks are available all day in the bar; teas in the coffee shop; packed lunches can be made up for guests planning a day out. Service, provided by various members of the Scott family, is enthusiastic and welcoming. There is disabled access to the hotel, but no specific facilities for the disabled.

Riding; watersports centre; private jetty; sailing club nearby; fishing; golf (there are five courses nearby); walks

SCOURIE

The Eddrachilles Hotel, Badcall Bay, Scourie, Sutherland
IV2 4TH   (Tel. 0971 2080)
Signposted from the A894
Open 1 March to 31 October
£27–£32 pp b&b

At the head of island-studded Badcall Bay, this 18th-century church manse is surrounded by a 320-acre estate. It really is miles from anywhere, and an extremely good hideaway. You would be pushed to find a more peaceful location, and it is very popular with bird watchers and fell walkers. Visitors can admire the seals and dolphins in the bay, but there isn't an immense amount for children to do, so it is not perhaps the best place for a family holiday. A large sunny conservatory opens out to lovely views of the loch and hills, and watercolours by local artists decorate the walls. There are no fewer than 90 malt whiskies on offer in the bar, and snacks are available at lunchtime. The restaurant has stone walls and flagstoned floors, log fires and loch views. A three-course dinner costs from £9.25; packed lunches cost £3.40. There are some ground-floor rooms, but no specific facilities for disabled visitors.

Fell walks; fishing (£3 a day); bird watching; boat hire (£15 a day)

SELKIRK

inn ᵃ²/⁵

Tibbie Shiel's Inn, St Mary's Loch, Selkirk TD7 5NE
(Tel. 0750 42231)
On the A74, 20 miles from Selkirk
Closed Mondays, and November to Easter
£15 pp b&b
This isolated old inn enjoys a striking position on the isthmus
between St Mary's Loch and Loch of the Lowes. It was named
after Isabella Shiel, who after her husband's death in 1824
supported herself by taking in lodgers. The inn became a
popular place to stay among the rich and famous, as well as
among the shooting fraternity: there is an impressive roster of
famous guests, including Sir Walter Scott, Wordsworth,
Carlyle and Gladstone. The cosy bar and the adjacent small
dining room occupy the original late-18th-century cottage; the
whole place is still tiny, and there are only six bedrooms. The
dining room overlooks the loch and offers full Scottish high
teas. The main courses at dinner cost between £6.95 and £9.50.
Snacks are served in the bar from noon to 8.30pm. Back-
packers can camp for a mere pound (per person, per night); a
bolstering breakfast costs £3.50. There is one ground floor
room with a large bathroom available for disabled visitors.
Walks (Southern Upland Way passes the front door); sailing;
windsurfing; loch fishing (£4 a day, equipment not provided); stony
beach

SHIELDAIG

ᵃ⁷/¹²

Tigh an Eilean Hotel, Shieldaig, by Strathcarron, Ross-shire
IV54 8XN   (Tel. 05205 251)
Off the A896, 17 miles from Kinlochewe, 43 miles from Garve
Open April to October
£25.50 pp b&b
The hotel enjoys an extremely beautiful location, at the centre
of a tiny unspoilt village, with only the village road separating
it from Loch Shieldaig. The excellent views stretch over the

water, past the Isle of Pines (which is less than a mile away), across Loch Torridon, to the Isle of Skye. The decor in both the original 17th-century building and the modern extension is charming, with pretty wallpapers and attractive chairs and prints. The restaurant is open for dinner and seats 26 people; there are three window tables, and the set dinner costs £14. No facilities for the disabled.

Hotel can arrange fishing (book in advance); golf (15 miles away); diving and windsurfing (no equipment supplied); boat hire in village; spectacular drive over Applecross peninsula, the 2000-foot pass of Bealach na Bo

SPEAN BRIDGE

The Letterfinlay Lodge Hotel, Spean Bridge, Inverness-shire
PH34 4DZ   (Tel. 039 781 622)
On the A82, seven miles north of Spean Bridge
Closed November to March
£30 pp b&b
The grounds of this country house run down through rhododendrons to a jetty and Loch Lochy. The bedrooms are simply decorated and unfussy; each is named after the colour on its walls, and the public rooms have wood panelling. The whole aura of the place is practical, friendly and down-to-earth. The hotel is a popular stop-off point for families and for visitors cruising the lochs and Caledonian Canal. Banknotes 'gifted' by appreciative customers decorate the walls, and one glass wall gives marvellous views of the loch. Bar lunches are served in a sun lounge overlooking the loch. The dining room seats 60 people and a four-course dinner will cost you £14. There is a caravan area next to the hotel. Packed lunches can be supplied. No facilities for the disabled.

Walks; waterskiing; fishing (salmon £100 a week, trout free)

STRACHUR

inn 15/19

The Creggans Inn, Strachur, Argyllshire PA27 8BX
(Tel. 036986 279)
Take the A83 or A815 from Dunoon car ferry to Strachur, near
Inveraray
£50 pp b&b
An attractive, 17th-century Highland inn, set among magnificent scenery, and separated from Loch Fyne only by the main
road. There has been extensive modernization, but this has
been tastefully done. The bedrooms are beautifully decorated
in a traditional style. One of the two cosy bars overlooks the
loch; both have open log fires and serve the inn's own malt,
Old MacPhunn. The Victorian-style restaurant has a wide-
ranging reputation, and the six window tables enjoy the best
loch views. The hotel has its own beach on the loch, and there
is an outstanding woodland walk devised for guests through
the Macleans' own estate behind the hotel. There are two
ground-floor rooms with large bathrooms for disabled
visitors.
*Private beach; woodland walks on estate; hotel can arrange pony
trekking, fishing, shooting and boating; golf (18 miles away)*

STRONTIAN

5/9

Kilcamb Lodge Hotel, Strontian, Argyll PH36 4HY
(Tel. 0967 2257)
Open April to October
Village on the A884, driveway signposted at bridge
£50 dinner and b&b
Set apart from the village, this small hotel was formerly an
18th-century dower house, and has large stained glass
windows in the hall. The pretty interior falters in lounge but is
saved by huge windows that look across 100 yards of grass to
Loch Sunart and the massive mountains beyond. The hotel has
30 acres on this beautiful Ardnamurchan peninsula and half a
mile of loch front. All the bedrooms are prettily decorated; the

comfortable if utilitarian furniture is gradually being replaced by owner John Bradbury, who makes his own. The restaurant seats 25; the one window table has the best view. The set dinner costs £19. No facilities for the disabled.
Walking; riding, fishing and boating can be arranged

TAIN

🏚 ³/₁₁ 🏠 ◁ ▭

Morangie House, Morangie Road, Tain, Ross-shire IV19 1PY (Tel. 0862 2281)
Follow Morangie Road from town centre
£30–£60 per room b&b
This fine Victorian mansion was built in 1903 and, although modernized, retains its period character. There is a good view of the Dornoch Firth from the bar and some of the bedrooms, despite the new supermarket and petrol station that have sprung up at the end of the drive. Fine Victorian stained-glass windows light the hallway and many of the public rooms. The bedrooms are spacious and individually decorated, and are thoughtfully supplied with sherry, mints and biscuits. One double room has a brass bed, and one has a four-poster. The restaurant seats 50 (no water view). The menu is built around salmon, venison and game in season, and the food is widely recommended. Service is excellent: in 1990 the hotel won second place in an Ashley Courtenay exceptional service competition, and an RAC award for hospitality and service. No facilities for the disabled.
Walks; fishing; beach; golf; sports centre five miles away

TAYNUILT

🍽 🏠 🚫 ▭

Shore Cottage, Taynuilt, Argyll PA35 1JQ   (Tel. 08662 654)
One mile from village along the side of Loch Etive; small sign on main road
Open from one week before Easter to mid October, 10am–6pm; closed every Wednesday
This 200-year-old white cottage was built as a meal store for

the iron foundry nearby (the iron ore for the furnace came by boat to the old pier in front of the cottage). Through the blue front door, the charming Mrs Lily McNaught and her extensive family serve coffee, tea, snacks and light lunches in her own home. Everything is home made, from the hearty soups to the daily-baked bread and cakes. Prices are very reasonable. There are blue-checked tablecloths and bone china; the cottage seats 36, and the views are of Ben Cruachan and the mountains beside Loch Etive rather than of the loch itself. Diners can also look out to the cottage's lovely garden. The tea room and lavatories are on the ground floor, though there are no special facilities for the disabled.

Seal-spotting and boat trips up Loch Etive (queue at pier half a mile from Shore Cottage); craft work for sale in cottage

TROON

The Marine Highland Hotel, Troon, Ayrshire KA10 6HE (Tel. 0292 314 444)
On the Royal Troon golf course on the outskirts of Troon, just north of Prestwick on the A77
£80–£125 pp b&b
This four-star hotel overlooks the 18th fairway of the Royal Troon Championship Golf Course, with breathtaking views across the Firth of Clyde to the Isle of Arran. The large picture windows and other traditional features of the house have been retained amid the trappings of first-class luxury. The stylish bedrooms are well appointed and will suit either the well-heeled tourist or the businessman. The dining room is splendid, and has a brasserie for lively, continental-style eating. There is seating for 150 and 10 tables in the window. A four-course dinner costs £18.95. Facilities include a conference and banqueting centre, heated pool, squash courts, gymnasium, solaria, spa bath, saunas, snooker room and beauty room. There is one bedroom designed for use by the disabled, and there are also disabled facilities in the conference and leisure centres.

Walks; boating and windsurfing at Troon Marina; beach; fishing 3 miles away

ULLAPOOL

The Altnaharrie Inn, Ullapool, Wester Ross IV26 2SS
(Tel. 085483 230)
Ring from Ullapool and wait for private ferry (no charge) for
the one-mile crossing. Leave car in Ullapool
Closed December to March
From £95 pp dinner and b&b
Guests are fetched by ferry across the water to the peaceful old
Drovers inn and its extraordinary, perfectionist environment.
The inn is positioned right on the water, looking back to
Ullapool, and has a beautiful interior that combines antiques
with modern art and traditional Scottish decor. The dining-
room floor is of scrubbed red pine, and there are rugs and
weavings everywhere. Dinner is a set, five-course meal cooked
by Gunn Eriksen (the Norwegian wife of owner Fred Brown)
who has acquired an international reputation for her cuisine.
Her food (featured on television) and Fred's wine are both
taken very seriously. The dining room seats up to 18 people;
half the room has a water view; depending on how full the
hotel is, non-residents can sometimes be brought across for
dinner, which will cost them £40 per person. Vegetarians
should give advance notice. The Altnaharrie is a non-smoking
hotel, and there is no mains electricity. Accommodation for
pets can be arranged; children can only stay if they are old
enough to appreciate, and sit through, dinner. No facilities for
the disabled.
*Fishing can be arranged; walking (the activities are far less important
here than the food)*

WHITEBRIDGE

Knockie Lodge, Whitebridge, Inverness-shire IV1 2UP
(Tel. 04563 276)
Off the B862, on the eastern shore of Loch Ness
Open late April to late October
£68 single, £110–£170 double dinner and b&b

Another of Lord Lovat's old hunting lodges, built in 1798 and set above Loch Nan Lann. An immensely peaceful place: there are no signs of civilization in sight, and no televisions in the hotel, partly to maintain the peace and quiet, and partly to keep the conversation flowing. The hotel has been beautifully done up, and is perfect for people who want tranquillity, beautiful walks or a high-class touring base. Far more like a grand country house than a hotel, it has recently been declared the best country house hotel in Scotland in the Caithness Glass/ Taste of Scotland Awards 1990. The hotel is particularly popular with Americans, who cannot believe that such a quiet and remote place exists. Given the high standards of the food and service and the general atmosphere, the prices seem par for the course. An additional attraction is the full-size, three-ton billiard table in a room with panoramic views. The dining room (open for dinner only) seats 23 people, and half the tables have a view of the loch. Open bar – guests sign for what they drink. Teas and packed lunches available. Pets can be accommodated by special arrangement only. No facilities for the disabled.

Walks; sailing; fishing (free, hotel owns three boats); stalking £250 a stag (book in March for October)

London, the South-east and the Isle of Wight

LONDON

WESTMINST[...]

CHISWICK

CHELSEA

BARNES

1 The City Barge, Strand-on-the-Green , Chiswick, W4
2 The River Café, Thames Wharf Studios, Rainville Road, W6
3 The Ship Inn, 41 Jews Road, SW18
4 The Battersea Barge, Nine Elms Lane, SW8
5 The Elephant on the River, 129 Grosvenor Road, SW1
6 Tattershall Castle, Kings Reach, Victoria Embankment, SW1
7 The Review Restaurant, Royal Festival Hall, SE1
8 The Wine Barge, Wilfred Sailing Barge, Victoria Embankment, WC2
9 The Gourmet Pizza Company, Gabriel's Wharf, 56 Upper Ground, SE1
10 Doggett's Coat and Badge, 1 Blackfriars Bridge, SE1
11 Le Quai, 1 Broken Wharf, EC4

London Thames-side

THE CITY BARGE

Strand-on-the-Green, Chiswick, London W4
(Tel. 081-994 2148)
Open 11am–11pm Mon–Sat; noon–3pm, 7pm–10.30pm Sun
This 15th-century riverside pub was named after the state
barge of the Lord Mayor of London, which used to be moored
nearby. It is very close to the river, and is a wonderful spot to
watch the end of the Boat Race from. There are two bars, one
of which, the Old Bar, still has many old features, such as an
ancient fireplace, which is raised above the stone floor as a
protection against flooding, and worn oak beams. There is a
beer garden outside which seats 120 with good river views, and
a conservatory. The pub does bar meals, with home-made
steak and kidney pie, pizzas, and so on, for between £3 and £5.
No facilities for the disabled.

CITY

SOUTHWARK

Approx 2 miles

TTERSEA

GREENWICH

THE BULL'S HEAD

Strand-on-the-Green, Chiswick, London W4 3PQ
(Tel. 081-994 1204)
By Kew Bridge railway bridge
Open 11am–3pm, 5pm–11pm Mon–Fri; 11am–11pm Sat;
noon–3pm, 7pm–10.30pm Sun
Half a mile from Kew Gardens, this busy pub has three bars
overlooking the river. Built in 1642 (Cromwell used it as his
headquarters for a time), it is very pretty outside, with white
walls, dark timbers and bright flowers, and there are seats
along the towpath. There are three bars, all of which overlook
the river, and a conservatory. The beers on offer include
Ruddles Best and Country, Websters, Budweiser, and
Holsten, and they do a good range of bar food: particularly
popular for Sunday lunch. No facilities for the disabled.

THE BULL'S HEAD INN

373 Lonsdale Road, London SW13 9PY   (Tel. 081-876 5241)
Open 11am-11pm Mon-Sat; noon-3pm, 7pm-10.30pm Sun
This old pub, originally recorded in 1700 but rebuilt in 1845, stands close to Barnes Bridge, and its balconies provide a prime viewing position for the Boat Race. Unfortunately the Thames Flood Wall obscures the views from the bars, but most of the visitors are there for the jazz – for which the pub is famous – rather than the view. There are top-class jazz acts every night, and lunchtime big band sessions. There is a carvery in the saloon bar, and another restaurant in the original stable buildings which is open in the evenings and Sunday lunchtimes, and specializes in steaks, fish and the like. The restaurant does not have a river view. The pub serves Youngs beers. No facilities for the disabled.

THE DOVE

19 Upper Mall, Hammersmith, London W6 9TA
(Tel. 081-748 5405)
Open 11am-11pm Mon-Sat; noon-3pm, 7pm-10.30pm Sun
This old-fashioned riverside pub, which dates back to 1796, is in the *Guinness Book of Records* for having the smallest bar in the world – only 4 feet 2 inches by 7 feet 10 inches (and they once got 27 rugby players in it at the same time!). It also has many historical connections; Nell Gwyn and King Charles II drank here, and *Rule Britannia* was written in an upstairs room. There are great river views from a small terrace, and from the beer garden. Bar food is available, prices from £2.50 to £5. There is a pleasant atmosphere in all the low-ceilinged bars, and there are no jukeboxes or fruit-machines to intrude upon the old-fashioned feel of the place. No facilities for the disabled.

THE RIVER CAFÉ

Thames Wharf Studios, Rainville Road, Hammersmith,
London W6 9HA   (Tel. 071-381 8824)
Open 12.30pm–3pm, 7.30pm–9.30pm Mon–Fri; closed Sat,
Sun, and two weeks in August

This restaurant, in a Thames-side studio converted by its
owner, architect Richard Rogers, has swiftly become one of
the most fashionable places to eat in London. While Rogers'
idiosyncratic and controversial style is doubtless part of the
attraction here, the main draw for visitors is the cooking, done
by Rose Grey and Rogers' wife Ruth. The food is regional
Italian – the recipes are chiefly from Tuscany – and revolves
around ingredients high in flavour, such as mozzarella, plum
tomatoes, polenta, black olives, virgin olive oil, peppers, red
onions and broccoli. The restaurant is very popular with
people who like vibrant and tasty food in a simpler style than
has prevailed in recent years. A three-course meal costs about
£36 per person. The river views are best from the eight outside
tables, which are used when the weather is fine. Access and
lavatories for the disabled.

THE SHIP INN

41 Jews Row, London SW18 1TB   (Tel. 081-870 9667)
Open 11am–11pm Mon–Sat; noon–3pm, 7pm–10.30pm Sun

This pub, in the middle of an unattractive industrial area still
manages to be extremely popular with the upwardly mobile
youngsters of Wandsworth, Battersea and Fulham, especially
since it added its conservatory. It has two pleasant bars,
although the river views are better from the large garden. The
food is inventive and popular, tending more towards the
imaginative bar snack rather the formal meal. A three-course
meal would cost approximately £10 per person. They also have
barbecues in the summer, and in the winter they serve Young's
Winter Warmer beer, which lives up to its name. No facilities
for the disabled.

THE WATERFRONT RESTAURANT
IOI 🏠 🐾 ▭

Harbour Yard, Chelsea Harbour, London SW10
(Tel. 071-352 4619)
Open 12.30pm–3pm, 7pm–11.30pm; closed Sun evenings in
summer, and all day Sun in winter
Inside the new Chelsea Harbour complex, this chic restaurant
seats 120, with six tables in the arched windows overlooking
the smart yachts in the harbour pool below. They also have 10
tables on the outdoor terrace during the summer, which have
excellent views. The restaurant is beautifully decorated, with
paintings on the walls, as well as sculptures and plants in the
corners, and the furniture is modern and pleasant. The bar is
made out of grey marble and chrome, and is striking. The food
is northern Italian, with emphasis on seafood and fresh
vegetables, and a three-course meal costs between £20 and £30
per person. The restaurant is popular, so booking is advisable,
especially for the window tables. There is a lavatory for
disabled visitors.

THE BATTERSEA BARGE
IOI 🏠 🐾 ▭

Nine Elms Lane, Battersea, London SW8
(Tel. 071-498 0004)
Open noon–3pm, 6pm–late; closed Sundays
This barge, tucked away on the south side of the river between
Chelsea and Vauxhall Bridges is best located by looking for the
Federal Express warehouse: the barge lie in its lee. Once found,
the intrepid diner is likely to be well rewarded for his
endeavours. The Battersea Barge offers excellent English and
French bistro-style food, at very reasonable prices. A three-
course à la carte dinner costs around £15 per person, and table
d'hôte is available for £11; both of which represent extremely
good value for money, considering the quality of the food.
The views are very good across the river to Pimlico and
Chelsea, and the character of the restaurant is civilized without
being pretentious. On Sundays in the summer they have jazz

lunches on the top deck, which are popular. The eternally fascinating bulk of Battersea Power Station looms large just along the river, and if you fancy a stroll after lunch or before dinner, Battersea Park is nearby. No facilities for the disabled.

THE ELEPHANT ON THE RIVER

 lOl ⚐ ✗ ▭

129 Grosvenor Road, London SW1V 3SY
(Tel. 071-834 1621)
Open 7pm–2.30am; Closed Mon
This large restaurant, which provides dinner and dancing, also has tremendous river views from 40 of its tables. The cuisine is international and varied, and a three-course dinner costs in the region of £25 per person. They have an extensive wine list, which goes up to an astonishing £550 per bottle, if you feel like splashing out. There is a five-piece dance band which plays every night, and the place is apparently popular with actors who come to relax after performances. The restaurant is also open for Sunday lunch, which is very family-oriented, with children being especially welcome. The staff are very friendly, and there are ramps and lavatories for the disabled.

THE TATTERSHALL CASTLE

⚐ ⚐ ✗ ▭

Kings Reach, Victoria Embankment, London SW1A 2HR
(Tel. 071-839 6548)
Open 11.30am–11pm. Restaurant open noon–3.30pm,
6.30pm–10.30pm
Boasting four bars, a nightclub and a restaurant, this large converted ship on the Embankment is a lively place to have a drink on the water, with pop music playing in all areas. The restaurant serves English food, roast lunches and salads (the three-course lunch costs approximately £8), although there are no water views from the restaurant. The large deck area provides good views along the Thames. No facilities for the disabled.

RESTAURANT SHIP HISPANIOLA

IOI ⚐ ⚒ 🗂

Victoria Embankment, London WC2   (Tel. 071-839 3011)
Open noon–2.15pm, 6.15pm–10.30pm; closed Sat lunch, all day Sun

This permanently moored ship, which was originally a steamer on the Clyde, provides a pleasant, floating restaurant which can accommodate 170 people. All of the tables have a water view, and there is a promenade deck on the port side. There is another entire deck which is used for private functions. The cuisine is European with a bias towards French, and there is an extensive wine list. A three-course meal costs about £20. No facilities for the disabled.

THE REVIEW RESTAURANT

IOI ⚐ ⚒ 🗂

Level 3, Royal Festival Hall, The South Bank Centre,
London SE1   (Tel. 071-921 0800)
Open 5.30pm–10pm

This enormous, airy restaurant, designed by the Conrans, has impressive views across the Thames, especially from its eight window tables. There are high ceilings, big pillars, huge floor-to-ceiling windows, providing a feeling of quiet spaciousness rare in London. The cuisine is international, with main courses between £6–£10, and vegetarian dishes always available. It is ideally placed for concert-goers and others using the extensive cultural facilities of the South Bank Centre to relax and have a pleasant meal in elegantly modern surroundings; the view at night with the lights of the opposite bank, and the interesting new development at Charing Cross station, shining on the water should be enough to tempt anyone. Good access and facilities for the disabled.

THE SAVOY HOTEL AND RIVER RESTAURANT

🏨 ³⁶⁄₂₀₂ 🏠 ⊗ 🪪

The Strand, London WC2R 0EU   (Tel. 071-836 4343)
£150–£600 per room per day
This magnificent hotel, long the epitome of sophistication, offers marvellous river views from its Thames-side rooms, although the prices for double riverside rooms start at £260 per night. The decor throughout the hotel is stylish and varied, utilizing Art Deco and classicism to create a unique feel for each room, and no expense is spared to provide a feeling of traditional luxury. Although 70 yards from the water, the restaurant provides a fine view of the Thames, as long as you ask for a table with a view, and an ideal environment for power breakfasts (traditional English breakfast £14.50; 7am–10.30am Mon–Sat; 8.30am–10.30am Sun), sophisticated lunches and dinners (set lunch £22.50; 12.30pm–2.30pm: set dinner from £29.50; 7.30pm–11.30pm, until 10.30pm on Sundays). These window tables also give lounge lizards a grandstand view of the London Marathon in April. Lounge suit or black tie evening. Facilities for the disabled.

THE WINE BARGE

🍷 🏠 ⬦ 🪪

The Wilfred Sailing Barge, Victoria Embankment,
London WC2R 2PP   (Tel. 071-379 5496)
Open noon–midnight, Mon–Fri; only open for private
functions at weekends
This pleasant wine bar/restaurant has been created on board a 1927 Thames sailing barge, whose mast, at 100 feet, is the highest on the river. It has been sensitively converted, panelled with wood throughout, and it has a friendly atmosphere. There is seating for 60 people downstairs but it is difficult to see the water, although on deck, where there are 20 tables, the river flows past close by on both sides. They have live piano music on Tuesdays, Thursdays and Fridays. The menu is composed mainly of pasta and salads, and a three-course meal

costs about £13 per person. They also have a small bar menu. Pets allowed on deck but not in the main restaurant. No facilities for the disabled.

THE GOURMET PIZZA COMPANY

🍽 🏠 🚫 🪪

Gabriel's Wharf, 56 Upper Ground, London SE1 9PP
(Tel. 071-928 3188)
Open noon–3.30pm, 5.30pm–10.45pm
This recently opened pizza restaurant is situated at the end of an interesting little market development, overlooking the Thames to the east of Waterloo Bridge. It serves pasta and pizzas that are less conventional than usual and combines the ease of pizza eating and serving with a rather more gastronomic approach. The results are exotic with cajun prawn and chicken, camembert and chinese duck, and so are the prices (between £5 and £10 for the pizzas). There is also a wide range of vegetarian dishes. The staff are young, enthusiastic and friendly. They especially welcome children, and have children's menus, high chairs, and a magician on Sundays. Ten tables have good views of the water. No facilities for the disabled.

DOGGETT'S COAT AND BADGE

🍺 🏠 🚫 🪪

1 Blackfriars Bridge, London SE1   (Tel. 071-633 9081)
Open 11am–11pm Mon–Sat; noon–3pm, 7pm–10.30pm Sun
This pub was named after an 18th-century actor, Thomas Doggett, who made a celebrated river crossing and gave his coat and a badge to the ferryman in gratitude. Occupying four floors, it offers views of the Thames, although because of its position on Blackfriars Bridge it also offers views of London traffic. The restaurant has an à la carte menu and better views of the river and the city skyline. (A four-course lunch costs about £25 per person; the restaurant is not open in the evenings). The bars serve cask-conditioned beers, and also do salads and quiches for around £4. No facilities for the disabled.

LE QUAI

IOI ⌂ ⌀ ▭

1 Broken Wharf, London EC4V 3QQ   (Tel. 071-236 6480)
Open 7.30am–10.30am, noon–2pm, 6.30pm–9pm Mon–Fri;
closed Sat and Sun
Located halfway between Southwark Bridge and Blackfriars
Bridge on the riverside walk along the north bank, this elegant,
modern French restaurant is popular with City workers. The
decor is plush and tasteful, with scumbled walls and a black
marble bar; a wall of windows facing the river provides good
views. There is a set menu for both lunch and dinner, which
costs £29 per person. Breakfast is popular, and costs £6. The
champagne bar is open all day, and there are plans to build a
conservatory. Lavatories for the disabled.

THE FOUNDERS ARMS

⌂ ⌂ ◈ ▭

Bankside, 52 Hopton Street, London SE1
(Tel. 071-928 1899)
Open 11am–11pm Mon–Sat; noon–3pm, 7pm–10.30pm Sun
To the east of Blackfriars Bridge on the south bank, this
narrow, modern and popular pub makes the most of its
riverside position with huge floor-to-ceiling windows looking
out towards St Paul's Cathedral on the far side. It also has 20
tables outside. They serve Youngs cask-conditioned real ales,
and the restaurant, which seats 35, does steaks, salads and
seafood (a three-course meal costs between £10 and £15). Bar
snacks are also available. Sunday lunch (£11.50) is popular, so
it is worth booking. Just behind the pub is the Royal
Academy's Watercolour Gallery, and the site of Shakespeare's
Globe theatre, which is being rebuilt. No facilities for the
disabled.

THE ANCHOR BANKSIDE

34 Park Street, London SE1   (Tel. 071-407 1577)
Open 11.30am–11pm Mon–Sat; noon–3pm, 7pm–10.30pm
Sun. Restaurant open noon–3pm, 6pm–10pm Mon–Sat;
noon–2pm, 7pm–10pm Sun
The original building perished in the Great Fire of London; the
present pub, situated to the east of Southwark Bridge, has
great character, and views of the river from the upstairs bar,
the restaurant (main courses £8–£14.50), and the terrace (which
seats 200).

THE OLD THAMESIDE INN

St Mary Overy Wharf, 1 Clink Street, London Bridge,
London SE1   (Tel. 071-403 4243)
Open 11am–11pm Mon–Fri; 11am–3pm, 6pm–11pm Sat;
noon–3pm, 7pm–10.30pm Sun
In the shadow of London Bridge and just behind Southwark
Cathedral, this pub, converted out of an old warehouse, has
timber beams, brick-arched windows and fine river views
from two of its three bars and the riverside terrace (which seats
about 80 people). Also in view are the new Lloyds building, St
Paul's Cathedral and the Monument. The restaurant, also with
terrace, serves lunch and dinner (main courses £10–£14, set
lunch £14.50). Only yards away a three-masted schooner, the
Kathleen and May, is permanently docked: it is tucked neatly
between buildings, with a few feet on either side of its rigging.
The Clink – an old ecclesiastical prison destroyed in a poll-tax
riot in 1381, and now a prison museum – is just down the road.
No facilities for the disabled.

THE REGALIAN

🍽 ♿ 🚭 💳

Swan Pier, Swan Lane, London Bridge, London EC4R
(Tel. 071-623 1805)
Open 11.30am–3.30pm Mon–Fri; closed at weekends

This large boat, permanently moored west of London Bridge on the north bank, offers cuisine of a high standard which is popular with people who work close by in the City. The feeling of being on a boat is heightened by the fact that the Thames Line river boat service docks at the same pier, and the wash from these can cause the boat to rock as though in a gale. All of the tables have a river view, and there is also a bar. Set lunch is approximately £25. There are no facilities for the disabled.

QUINTESSENCE THAMESIDE

🍽 ♿ 🚭 💳

Hay's Galleria, London Bridge City, London SE1 2HD
(Tel. 071-378 0672)
Open 11am–11pm weekdays; closed weekends

This restaurant, which specializes in international dishes, is situated in the new Hay's Galleria development, on the opposite bank of the Thames from the Tower of London. The restaurant is on two floors, with good views across the river, especially from the upper level. Decor is luxurious, and the whole restaurant is extremely comfortable. The menu has lots of fish and game in season, as well as vegetarian dishes. A three-course lunch costs £15 per person. The atmosphere is smart but friendly, and the staff pride themselves on their willingness to help. HMS *Belfast*, a warship turned into a floating museum, is moored just outside and the London Dungeon is also just a few yards away. Hay's Galleria is also home to one of the most unusual pieces of sculpture in London, the huge, kinetic Navigators, which is well worth a look. No facilities for the disabled.

THE HORNIMAN AT HAY'S

Hay's Galleria, London Bridge City, London SE1 2HD
(Tel. 071-407 3611)
Open 9am–11pm Mon–Fri; 9am–6pm winter weekends
This large, multi-level pub is filled with large fern trees, dark
wood, tiles and brass in an attempt to recreate the atmosphere of
the 1830s when the eponymous Frederick Horniman used to set
out on voyages of exploration from this wharf. It has a carvery
restaurant, open for lunch only (three-course lunch £16.50), and
a hot pantry which serves quiche, shepherd's pie, curries and so
on for about £5. They have a good selection of beer, including
Boddingtons and Wadworths 6X. The river views are good,
and there are seats outside as well. No facilities for the disabled.

THE QUAYSIDE RESTAURANT

World Trade Centre, International House, 1 St Katherine's
Way, London E1 9UN   (Tel. 071-481 0972)
By Tower Bridge, on the slip road leading to the Tower Hotel
Open noon–2.30pm, 6pm–10pm; closed Sat lunch and Sun
dinner
A luxurious restaurant, with real trees (on coasters) in the hall. A
long set of rooms overlooks St Katherine's Yacht Haven, and
provides a romantic setting, with live music every evening.
Fifteen of the tables have a water view. There is also a small
terrace outside which can be used if weather permits. Cuisine is
modern and French; set meals cost from £16, à la carte also
available. Dinner dances Friday and Saturday. They also have
functions facilities.

THE TOWER THISTLE HOTEL

St Katherine's Way, London E1 9LD   (Tel. 071-481 2575)
£110–£265 per room
This huge hotel, resolutely boxlike in appearance, and an
unattractive brown colour to boot, nevertheless boasts fine

views of Tower Bridge, St Katherine's Dock and the newly refurbished warehouse frontage at Butlers Wharf on the other side of the river. The hotel is of international standard, and has a spectacular lobby with huge marble pillars and banks of mirrors. It also has a coffee shop, a bar with a nautical theme and three restaurants of varying luxury. All the bedrooms have televisions, trouser-presses and mini-bars. Room service is 24-hour. Facilities for the disabled.

THE BLUEPRINT CAFÉ

🍽 🏠 🚫 ▭

Butlers Wharf, London SE1 2YD
(Tel. 071-378 7031)
Open noon–3.30pm, 7pm–11pm Tues–Sat; noon–4.30pm Sun
On the first floor of the fascinating Design Museum, this restaurant makes the most of its wonderful position with sliding glass windows that open out on to a long riverside terrace. The views, especially along the river to nearby Tower Bridge, are splendid. There are eight tables within the restaurant next to the windows, and ten on the terrace when the weather is suitable. The restaurant is chic and bright and cheerful, and the staff are friendly and helpful. The food is inventive and Mediterranean in influence. Main courses cost between £6 and £9. Access for the disabled, but no lavatories.

THE ANGEL

🚪 🏠 🚫 ▭

101 Bermondsey Wall East, Rotherhithe, London SE16 4NB
(Tel. 071-237 3608)
Open 11am–3.30pm, 5.30pm–11pm (11am–11pm in summer) Mon–Sat; noon–3pm, 7pm–10.30pm Sun
There has been a pub on this site since the monks of Bermondsey Priory first opened a tavern here in the 15th century. In the intervening centuries, it became the haunt of smugglers. Samuel Pepys, Captain Cook and Laurel and Hardy are all reputed to have frequented it, and the walls of the pub are covered with pictures and photographs illustrating the

local history. As well as being steeped in Thames-side history, the pub also offers some of the most picturesque and classic views of Tower Bridge and the City. There is a balcony, built of wooden boards on pilings over the river which is lit by lanterns at night, and the water laps underneath at high tide. The restaurant is open for both lunch and dinner, has five window tables, and main courses cost about £12. The bar also serves food. No facilities for the disabled.

THE MAYFLOWER

117 Rotherhithe Street, London SE16 4NF
(Tel. 071-237 4088)
Open 11am–11pm Mon–Fri; 11am–4pm, 7pm–11pm Sat; noon–3pm, 7pm–10.30pm Sun

Another docklands pub steeped in history, the Mayflower is named after the ship which took the first pilgrims to America and which was moored nearby, and there are claims that some of the ship has actually been incorporated into the structure of the pub. There are many wooden beams and panels about the place which might support this theory. Another interesting and even less well known fact about the pub is that it is the only place in the British Isles, apart from the American Embassy, which is licensed to sell American postage stamps. There is a wooden jetty outside which holds 40 people, and affords excellent views across the river to Wapping. Inside, there are two bars which are dark and full of character, although the small leaded windows make viewing the river difficult. The restaurant, which has good river views, is closed on Sunday and Monday evenings. A three-course meal costs approximately £12 per person. No facilities for the disabled.

THE PROSPECT OF WHITBY

57 Wapping Wall, London E1 9SP   (Tel. 071-481 1095)
Open 11.30am–3pm, 5.30pm–11pm Mon–Sat; noon–3pm, 7pm–10.30pm Sun

This is London's oldest pub, dating back to 1520, when it was known as the 'Devil's Tavern' because of the pirates and smugglers who congregated here. Justly famous for its history, it used to be frequented by Judge Jeffreys, of the 'Bloody Assizes' fame, who used to eat his dinner while watching the hanging of convicts at the execution dock on the other side of the river. The pub is very popular with tourists, and it has an international reputation. The interior of the pub is suitably authentic, with lots of old wood, panelling, flagstones and a pewter-topped bar. It has two bars, one with good water views, a riverside terrace, a garden on the river wall and two restaurants upstairs. These serve a variety of food from an à la carte menu; a main course is between £12 and £15, and it is advisable to book. They also have live music on Thursday, Friday and Sunday nights. No facilities for the disabled.

THE BARLEY MOW

144 Narrow Street, Limehouse Basin, London E14 8DP
(Tel. 071-265 8931)
Open 11.30am–3pm, 5.30pm–11pm Mon–Sat; noon–3pm, 7pm–10.30pm Sun
This pub, recently converted out of the 200-year-old dock-master's house, commands panoramic views over a huge sweep of the river, from the Isle of Dogs to Bermondsey, due to its position at the entrance to the old Limehouse Basin dock. There are 20 tables outside, and good river views are also available from both of the bars. The house has been sensitively converted, with palm trees and comfortable cane chairs contributing to its pleasant relaxed atmosphere. The restaurant seats 30, and offers good pub food at reasonable prices. Small children should be kept under close supervision, as there is a frighteningly steep drop down the dock wall about five feet from the (fenced-in) beer gardens. Lavatories and access for the disabled.

THE GRAPES

76 Narrow Street, London E14 8BP   (Tel. 071–987 4396)
Open 11am–3pm, 5pm–11pm Mon–Sat; noon–3pm, 7pm–
10.30pm Sun
Restaurant open noon–3pm, 7pm–10.30pm; closed Sun, Sat
lunch, Mon evening
Like many Docklands watering holes, this small, dimly lit pub
has a long and colourful history. Dickens apparently used it as a
model for the 'Six Jolly Fellowship Porters' in his novel *Our
Mutual Friend*. The interior is cosy and pleasant, with a
collection of prints and pictures adorning the walls and there is
a small glassed-in snug above the river. The restaurant upstairs
is good for seafood, and you can order prawns by the pint in
the bar. There are no facilities for the disabled.

BOOTY'S

92a Narrow Street, London E14   (Tel. 071–987 8343)
Open 11am–3pm, 5pm–11pm Mon–Fri; 7pm–midnight Sat;
closed Sun
This popular wine bar enjoys extreme proximity to the river; it
is not unknown for the local river policeman to drop by and
enjoy a glass of wine on the river itself, on the deck of his
launch. The bar is popular with local office workers, and can
consequently be busy at lunchtimes. The views from the few
window tables are worth the traffic jams in Narrow Street;
make sure of your seat by booking in advance. Food is
available at lunchtimes and in the evenings; baked potatoes and
chilli, coq au vin and goulash, all home made. There are no
facilities for the disabled.

THE TRAFALGAR TAVERN

Park Row, Greenwich, London SE10   (Tel. 081–858 2437)
Open 11am–11pm Mon–Sat; noon–3pm, 7pm–10.30pm Sun.

Restaurant open 7.30pm–11pm
This large pub is situated so close to the Thames that the river laps against its brickwork, so the view from the large windows is impressively watery, as one looks across the river to Cumberland Mills. It is a very easy pub to find, because it is next door to the impressive Naval College. The pub has been open since 1827, and is famous for its annual whitebait dinners which were originally instituted by Gladstone in 1830. As pubs go, the Trafalgar Tavern is smart and comfortable, and has large and magnificent banqueting facilities for 250 people. There is also a private members' bar. The restaurant specializes in seafood, and a three-course dinner would cost around £25, and they serve a range of guest beers which change regularly. Children allowed in restaurant, but not in the pub. There are lavatories for disabled visitors.

THE YACHT

Crane Street, Greenwich, London SE10 9NP
(Tel. 071-858 0175)
Open 11am–11pm Mon–Sat (noon–3pm, 5.30pm–11pm in winter); noon–2.30pm, 7pm–10.30pm Sun
Situated halfway down a somewhat insalubrious alleyway, this pub nevertheless has good water views, especially from the four window tables in the restaurant, and the small patio. They offer traditional cask-conditioned ales, and the restaurant has a range of meals, including scampi, ploughman's lunch and baked potatoes, which are reasonably priced (last orders for meals 2.20pm and 8.10pm). The bar is circular, in the centre of the spacious room, and gives a pleasant impression of space. Ramps and lavatories for the disabled.

THE CUTTY SARK

Ballast Quay, Greenwich, London SE10 9PD
(Tel. 081-858 3146)
Open 11am–11pm Mon–Sat; noon–3pm, 7pm–10.30pm Sun

This dark and cosy pub is in a listed warehouse dating back to 1695, and derives much of its character from its different levels and its old feel. The pub is very friendly, and enjoys good river views over towards the Isle of Dogs and much of industrial east London. There are four window tables in the pub, and eight outside on the river bank. The restaurant offers good food, with a three-course dinner costing £19 per person. No facilities for the disabled.

THE GUN

27 Coldharbour, Isle of Dogs, London E14
(Tel. 071-987 1692)
Open 11am–2.30pm, 5pm–11pm Mon–Sat; noon–3pm, 7pm–10.30pm Sun
This small pub used to be popular with dockers, and still retains something of the unpretentiousness of the old days of heavy industry. In common with the other docklands pubs, it has had its fair share of history, including being the rendezvous point for assignations between Lord Nelson and Emma Hamilton. It has a fine balcony at the back of the pub which overhangs the river, and gives great views of the wharves and the Blackwall Power Station (dogs and children are allowed out here, but not in the bars). There are three bars, the best one being the middle bar which has the access to the deck. Bar snacks available. Access and lavatories for the disabled.

The South-east

ABINGDON

inn 2/3

The Old Anchor Inn, 1 St Helen's Wharf, Abingdon, Oxon
OX14 5EN   (Tel. 0235 521726)
Open 11am–11pm Mon–Sat; noon–3pm, 7pm–10.30pm Sun
£25 pp b&b

Right on the Thames, this family-run pub has been recently and tastefully refurbished: there has been a pub on the same site for more than 100 years. Jerome K. Jerome, the doyen of river travel, is said to have written *Three Men in a Boat* here. The main bar overlooks the water, and serves Morland Bitter, Morland Old Masters and Kaltenberg lager. There is a separate dining area and patio by the river, and there are mooring facilities for boats. The inn also offers bed and breakfast accommodation, with two rooms overlooking the river. The pub has a pleasant, quiet location, with little traffic, and is good for an early evening drink, a lunchtime snack or an inexpensive overnight stay. There are facilities for the disabled in the pub but no wheelchair access to the accommodation.
Walking; boat hire nearby

ABINGDON

4/26

The Upper Reaches, Thames Street, Abingdon, Oxon
OX14 3JA   (Tel. 0235 522311)
£77 single, £94 double

This pleasant, if somewhat bland member of the Trust House Forte group, was until 1968 the mill for Abingdon Abbey. The mill stream now actually runs underneath the hotel, and even turns the mill wheel, which is situated in the dining room (set dinner £17). The buildings have been converted to provide cosy public rooms and a high standard of accommodation. There are terraces outside, one of which is above the mill stream, and the Thames flows by on the other side of the hotel, where there are good views of the bridge and meadows.

THE SOUTH EAST

Telegraph

• Sheffield

NORTH SEA

• Nottingham

• Leicester

• Coventry

• Northampton

PETERBOROUGH

Wansford
Needingworth
Holywell Inn
Huntingdon Inn

CAMBRIDGE-SHIRE

Sutton

Cambridge

BEDFORD

Bedford

Old Hunstanton
Titchwell
Heacham

KING'S LYNN

Brandon Creek
Mildenhall

NORFOLK

Blakeney
Cley-Next-The-Sea
Coltishall

Horning
Norwich
Wroxham

Reedham

Great Yarmouth

LOWESTOFT

Beccles
Shouthwold

SUFFOLK

BURY ST EDMUNDS
Monk Soham
Sudbury

Otley

Aldeburgh

BOOK OF WADERS

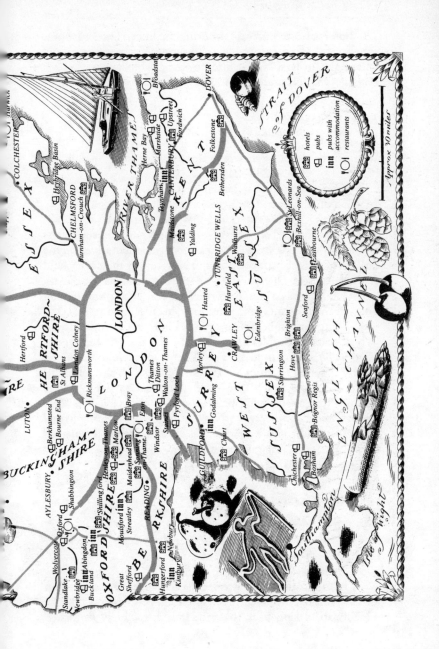

The hotels also has private mooring facilities. The bedrooms are cheerful and comfortable, with reproduction furniture and brass light fittings. No facilities for the disabled.
Walking; boat hire nearby; Unicorn Theatre in the old Abbey; fishing

ALDEBURGH

Wentworth Hotel, Wentworth Road, Aldeburgh, Suffolk
IP15 5BD   (Tel. 0728 452312)
Closed first two weeks in January
£45–£55 pp dinner and b&b
A somewhat plain exterior belies the comfort, style and dignity of this hotel on the sea front, which has been run by the same family for 70 years. The owners pride themselves on the quality of the accommodation and service that they offer, and deservedly so. The atmosphere of the hotel is extremely pleasant. There is a sunken terrace garden facing the sea, log fires, framed prints and antiques in the lounges, and a welcoming atmosphere. Most of the tables in the dining room (which seats 80 people) have a view of the sea, and the food is good. The staff would be very happy to explain about the nearby sporting facilities but should you just wish to relax and stroll along the beach, they will understand. There is one ground-floor room, with special lavatory for disabled visitors.
Sailing and sea fishing (no licence needed); Aldeburgh and Thorpeness golf courses nearby; beach; International Festival of Music at Snape Maltings every June; Havergate Island and Minsmere bird reserves (10 miles away)

ALDEBURGH

The White Lion, Market Cross Place, Aldeburgh, Suffolk
IP15 5BL   (Tel. 0728 452720)
£65–£85 double b&b
With its imposing whitewashed façade, in a prime position looking out over the sea, the White Lion is the oldest hotel in Aldeburgh, dating back to 1563. It is attractively furnished

throughout, and the rooms are light and airy. Some bedrooms have four-poster beds, and the rooms at the front have very attractive sea views. There are two residents' lounges, one of which is non-smoking, a buttery bar for light meals and a restaurant which serves good fresh food, and is open to non-residents. No facilities for the disabled.

Sailing; fishing (licence necessary for river fishing); windsurfing; waterskiing; Aldeburgh and Thorpeness golf courses nearby; International Festival of Music at Snape Maltings every June; Havergate Island and Minsmere bird reserves

BECCLES

4/13

Waveney House Hotel, Puddingmoor, Beccles, Suffolk
NR34 9PL   (Tel. 0502 712270)
£42.50 single, £55 double, £61 four-poster
In a beautiful position on the banks of the River Waveney, this grey stone hotel is only five minutes from the town centre. Parts of the building date back to 1592. The rooms, though well appointed and with modern facilities, are a little unprepossessing, and lack style. Its attractive location on the riverbank makes it a popular stopping place for boaters, who like to use the bar and the moorings, especially in the summer. The public rooms are furnished in a simple style, and the restaurant seats 60, and serves English and French food. There are no facilities for the disabled.

Municipal swimming pool nearby; boat hire (in Puddingmoor); fishing; golf course nearby

BEDFORD

53/115

Bedford Swan, The Embankment, Bedford, Bedfordshire
MK40 1RW   (Tel. 0234 46565)
£72 single, £85 double b&b
Conveniently located on the embankment near the town centre, the hotel is elegant and spacious. It has recently been refurbished inside, and offers a wide range of facilities for

guests, including a delightful indoor swimming pool and a spa bath, and two banqueting halls in addition to the restaurant. Most of the tables in the restaurant overlook the river. The rooms are spacious and tastefully decorated, and many have good views of the tranquil River Ouse running peacefully outside. There are no facilities for the disabled.

Walking; fishing (rod licences available); Woburn Abbey, Safari Park and Althorp nearby; Shuttleworth Aircraft Collection at Old Warden

BERKHAMSTEAD

The Boat, Gravel Path, Berkhamstead, Hertfordshire
(Tel. 0442 877152)
Off the A41, on Ravens Lane, east side of town
Open 11am–3pm, 5.30pm–11pm Mon–Sat; noon–3pm, 7pm–10.30pm Sun

This tastefully decorated and well-maintained new pub is thankfully free of the computerized games and fruit machines that are so often found in modern pubs. The Boat enjoys a pleasant position by the canal, and there are moorings for people arriving by river. There is a friendly atmosphere, encouraged by the landlords, and the beer, which includes Fuller's London Pride and ESB, is very well kept. Outside, there are 10 tables overlooking the canal, and in the summer there are barbecues on Friday and Saturday evenings, and Sunday lunchtimes. There are also good-value lunchtime bar snacks to be had. No facilities for the disabled.

Fishing (rod licences available in town); walks along canal to Hemel Hempstead

BETHERSDEN

Little Hodgeham, Smarden Road, Bethersden, Kent
TN26 3HE   (Tel. 0233 850323)
Off the Bethersden–Smarden road
Open mid March to 1 October

£44.50 pp dinner and b&b (£39.50 pp dinner and b&b for stays in excess of four nights)

This picture-postcard Tudor cottage has roses tumbling round the door, ancient wooden beams, antiques and leaded windows, and is over 500 years old. It is set in rose gardens and surrounded by wooded farmland in the Weald of Kent. The water comes in the shape of a large pond, known as Hodgeham Water, and large water gardens, although there is also a swimming pool. The real attraction is the atmosphere of gracious living which is due to the efforts of the proprietress, Erica Wallace. She has set high standards, and guests can be sure of enjoying the very best in luxurious gentility. Silver cutlery, bone-china coffee cups and cut glass and crystal bowls are the norm. Dinner is like a dinner party, with all guests eating at the same table. The food is chosen and prepared by Miss Wallace, and guests are asked their likes and dislikes when booking. If one is after a genteel house-party atmosphere, this is the perfect place because the level of attention and the warmth of the welcome guarantee that you will enjoy your stay. No facilities for the disabled.

Many stately homes, castles and gardens to visit nearby; walking; fishing; swimming; tennis; golf

BEXHILL-ON-SEA

The Cooden Resort, Cooden Sea Road, Cooden Beach, nr Bexhill-on-Sea, East Sussex TN39 4TT   (Tel. 04243 2281)
£62 single, £85 double

This pleasant hotel is right on the seafront, and has marvellous views of Pevensey Bay, the English Channel and Beachy Head on the horizon. The bedrooms are decorated with lightwood furniture and floral fabrics. There are two bars, one of which has good sea views, and a smart restaurant which serves a wide range of international cuisine, with set lunches costing £12.50 and set dinners £18. Ten of its tables have good views of the water. The hotel also boasts a large health and leisure club, with swimming pools, spa bath and sauna, exercise equipment and massage. They also offer banqueting and conference

facilities. Pets can be accommodated by prior arrangement. Facilities for disabled visitors include a bedroom in the annexe, ramps and lavatories.
Beach walks; health club; beauty salon; windsurfing; fishing; tennis; golf; squash

BLAKENEY

14/50

Blakeney Hotel, The Quay, Blakeney, Holt, Norfolk
NR25 7NE   (Tel. 0263 740797)
Village on the B1156
£49–£67 pp dinner and b&b
This 1920s red–brick hotel is located in enclosed gardens on the quayside, and has good views of Blakeney Point. Blakeney offers what many English seaside resorts no longer do – an unspoilt, traditional seaside setting, and the hotel complements this nicely. The emphasis of the hotel is on comfort and the staff make every effort to provide an efficient and professional service. The bedrooms vary in size and decor, but tend towards comfort and simplicity. The hotel's facilities include an indoor swimming pool, sauna, billiard room, beauty salon and games room. Twelve of the tables in the restaurant have sea views. It is idyllically peaceful in the winter. There is one ground–floor room for disabled guests.
Coastal path walks; sailing (tuition and boat hire can be arranged); fishing (trips with local boatmen, fly fishing nearby); tennis; beach; waterskiing and windsurfing (equipment not supplied); riding and golf courses nearby; bird watching

BOGNOR REGIS

23/51

Royal Norfolk Hotel, The Esplanade, Bognor Regis, West Sussex PO21 2LH   (Tel. 0243 826222)
£55 single, £70 double b&b
Built in the 1840s by the Duke of Norfolk, this Trust House Forte hotel has in its time provided accommodation for Queen Victoria, Queen Alexandra and Napoleon III. The hotel is in a

beautiful spot, has a fine Regency exterior, and enjoys lovely views across its gardens to the sea. The decor is smart, there is a good view of the water from both floors, and the staff are friendly and helpful. The rooms vary in size and comfort so make sure to ask for one of the better ones when booking. As well as the main swimming pool, there is a children's pool and games area; a baby-listening service is available on request. The restaurant seats 125 people, with seven tables looking out to sea. A set lunch will cost you £10.50, the set dinner £13.50. No facilities for the disabled.

Tennis courts at hotel; beach nearby; walks on Sussex Downs and along the waterfront; sea fishing can be arranged; sailing at Little Hampton; surfing, windsurfing and jetskiing equipment at Surf Shop opposite; golf at Goodwood; nature reserve at Selsey Bill; Goodwood Races

BOSHAM

Anchor Bleu, High Street, Bosham, West Sussex PO18 8LS
(Tel. 0243 573956)
Open 11am–2.30pm, 6pm–11pm Mon–Sat; noon–3pm, 7pm–10.30pm Sun

This 17th-century, white-painted pub (with a blue anchor) is right on the seafront: before it became an alehouse, it used to be the storehouse for the local manor. It has low ceilings and stone floors, and half of the bar looks towards sea. The tide is a major factor in life here, and the sea views depend on it to some extent. More spectacularly, the parking is also dependent upon its caprices – photographs of the foreshore car park taken in December 1989 show vehicles floating away in high water. There is a waterside-terrace and a rear garden each of which seats 30. Bar snacks are available from noon to 2pm and 7pm to 9.30pm, and Ruddles and Webster's beers are served. No facilities for the disabled.

Walking; bird watching; Chichester harbour and boats nearby; beach at Selsey and Whitterings (15-minute drive away); fishing at Selsey

BOURNE END

Three Horseshoes, Winkwell, Bourne End, Hertfordshire
(Tel. 0442 862585)
In Winkwell hamlet, off the A41
Open 11am–2.30pm, 6pm–11pm Mon–Sat; noon–3pm, 7pm–
10.30pm Sun
Standing on a swing bridge in a quiet glade by the canal, the
Three Horseshoes has been in business since 1535. Pretty and
white painted outside, with baskets of hanging flowers, this is
everyone's idea of 'Ye Olde Worlde Pub'. The atmosphere is
highly traditional with dark wood-beamed ceilings, gleaming
brass and inglenook fireplaces in both the Tack Room and the
aptly named Snug bars. Nestling right on the water's edge, this
appealing pub also offers plenty of seating on the canalside
terraced courtyard. Both bars overlook the canal to some
extent and serve tempting lunchtime snacks with a variety of
sandwiches, cold meat or seafood platters and a choice of two
hot dishes per day for around £4. Children are welcome to visit
the courtyard terrace, but are not admitted to the interior bars.
Several moorings are available beside the pub for those boating
along the canal. The pub is not suitable for the disabled.
*Walking; boating nearby; canoeing and fishing (rod licence necessary)
in Hemel Hempstead*

BRANDON CREEK

The Ship, Brandon Creek, Downham Market, Norfolk
PE38 0PP   (Tel. 035376 228)
On the main A10 where the two rivers Great Ouse and Little
Ouse meet
Open 11am–11pm Mon–Sat in summer (11am–3pm, 7pm–
11pm Mon–Sat in winter); noon–3pm, 7pm–10.30pm Sun
This pub is unusually situated in that it occupies the point of
confluence of the Great Ouse and the Little Ouse – the Great
Ouse flows behind the pub, and the Little Ouse in front, so this
pub is very definitely on the water – front and back! It is very

convenient for people arriving by water, as there are extensive moorings for boats. There are tables outside, and a riverside patio which offers plenty of seating during warmer weather. The interior is extremely spacious – part of it used to be a forge, and the bar is over 100 feet long. The restaurant offers good-value food and river views, and bar snacks are also available. This is a friendly and comfortable pub, with a nice warm atmosphere. They often change the range of ales, including Ruddles, Greene King and Webster's. Because of its location, it can get busy. There are special disabled entrances and lavatory facilities. *Walking; fishing (rod licence needed)*

BRAY

🍽️ 🏠12 🍴 💳

Waterside Inn, Ferry Road, Bray-on-Thames, Berkshire
SL6 2AT   (Tel. 0628 20691)
Open noon–2pm Wed–Sun; 7pm–10pm Tues–Sun.
Closed 26 December–15 February, Sun dinner October–Easter
This highly polished Thames-side restaurant is renowned for the quality of its cuisine, a well as the size of the bill at the end of the meal. It is beautifully situated on the river, and half the tables inside have excellent views; the floral arrangements are fabulous. There is also a pretty terrace outside for pre-dinner drinks or after-dinner coffee. The chef, Michel Roux, is so well known that booking is absolutely essential; if sheer quality of food is important to you then this is a very good place to come. The set lunch, at £26, is excellent value for money; the set dinner costs £53. They have valet parking and a large and attentive staff, and facilities for disabled visitors.
Walking; fishing; windsurfing at Bray marina (five minutes away); restaurant has one boat for hire, and there are plenty available locally

BRAY

🏠 20/25 🏠 🍴 💳

Monkey Island Hotel, Bray-on-Thames, Maidenhead,
Berkshire SL6 2EE   (Tel. 0628 23400)

Exit 8/9 from the M4, take Old Mill Lane from Bray across the M4

£105–£155 per room

Originally an 18th-century hunting lodge, the hotel is set on a pretty, small island in the Thames and is accessible only by footbridge. The name originated not from any exotic pets kept here, but because of the local monks who fished from the banks of the island. These days, peacocks, swans and wildfowl wander through the garden. Inside, the hotel is highly civilized and elegant, and most of the rooms have lovely river views. The Marlborough restaurant, perched on the narrowest tip of the island, has seating for 100 and all tables look upstream; gentlemen are required to wear a jacket and tie. The food, at breakfast as well as dinner, has received high praise. The River Room (a good place for weddings, dinners or seminars) is actually suspended over the Thames.

Plenty of walks; windsurfing in Bray marina; residents can fish from island

BRIGHTON (HOVE)

The Alexandra Hotel, 42 Brunswick Terrace, Brighton, Sussex BN3 1HA   (Tel. 0273 202722)

£66 single, £88 double b&b

This elegant Regency hotel has recently been restored, and its Grade I listed façade looks out over Hove esplanade to the sea. The interior decor continues the Regency feel, and the public rooms are stylish and comfortable. The bedrooms are simply decorated and well equipped, and some of the larger suites have seafront balconies. The restaurant is on the lower ground floor and consequently has no sea views, but serves good food nonetheless, with the set dinner costing £13. The pleasant and spacious bar has good sea views. There is a small health club with sauna, spa bath, solarium and exercise machine. They also offer banqueting and conference facilities. Pets can be accommodated by prior arrangement. No facilities for the disabled.

Beach; windsurfing; tennis; golf; Royal Pavilion

BRIGHTON

The Hospitality Inn, King's Road, Brighton, Sussex
BN1 2GS   (Tel. 0273 206700)
£110–£130 single, £135–£160 double b&b
A monstrous five-star structure that defies description but is
most striking to look at. The entrance atrium so big and high it
reduces the large restaurant at its front to insignificance. There
is a luxurious variety of real plant life in this atrium, including
full grown trees, and there is a piano and acres of space for
lounging. The whole effect is very pleasant and restful, even
when there are dozens of people coming and going. Service is
excellent – and friendly. The spacious rooms and huge suites
are tastefully decorated (bedrooms with a sea view are more
expensive than others). The Promenade restaurant seats 110
people, and offers tremendous views out to sea; there is
another, smaller restaurant which can seat an additional 48
people. Babysitting can be arranged. There are good facilities
for the disabled.
*Indoor pool; gym; solarium; sauna; walks along the beach;
watersports nearby; fishing by arrangement*

BROADSTAIRS

Mad Chef's Bistro, The Harbour, Broadstairs, Kent
CT10 1EU   (Tel. 0843 69304)
Open 11am–2pm; 6pm–10pm all week (except 6pm–11pm
Sat); closed Christmas and Boxing Day and when the sea
floods the kitchen
With good views across Viking Bay, and Bleak House just
behind, the surroundings alone deserve a visit, without the
attractions of this interesting restaurant. Inside, the bistro has
pleasant nautical decor: the odd anchor lying tastefully on the
hearth, nets hung from the ceiling, and other seafaring knick-
knacks. The three window tables have the best views, though
the water is visible from most of the 70 places. The restaurant
boasts extensive seafood and vegetarian menus: the set lunch

costs £6.50. There is a bar at the back which has Warsteiner and Labatt's on tap. It is worth keeping an eye out for the genuinely eccentric, eponymous Mad Chef: do not be too surprised if he rushes up and begins to consume your food or wine during your meal. There are no facilities for the disabled.

Deep sea, harbour and beach fishing; Viking Bay beach (20 yards away); walks along coast to Ramsgate, Margate and Sandwich; jetski and canoe rental in Kingsgate; windsurfing in Kingsgate (no equipment supplied)

BUCKLAND

The Trout Inn, Tadpole Bridge, Buckland, Faringdon, Oxon (Tel. 036787 382)
On the Bampton to Buckland road, four miles north east of Faringdon
Open 11.30am–2.30pm, 6pm–11pm Mon–Sat; noon–3pm, 7pm–10.30pm Sun

This Thames-side pub has been here, in this out of the way spot, since 1888. It exploits its river position by offering customers free mooring, and there is a mile and a half of fishing owned by the pub, for which day tickets are available. It has a pretty exterior, and the small bar has a flagstone floor and plants dotted around it. There is a variety of bar snacks and meals available, from steaks to sandwiches, at reasonable prices. Outside is a garden with pleasant, if not outstanding, views downstream. There is a hut that sells soft drinks and crisps, and in the summer they have barbecues. There is also an on-site caravan available for hire. The pub is a free house, and the beers available include Gibbs Mew Salisbury and Chudley, Wiltshire Keg and Archers bitter. Children are allowed into the eating areas and the garden. There are no facilites for the disabled.

Fishing; walking.

BURNHAM-ON-CROUCH

8/11

Ye Olde White Harte Hotel, The Quay,
Burnham-on-Crouch, Essex CM0 8AS   (Tel. 0621 782106)
£30 single, £49.50 double b&b
This 400-year-old inn is very popular with the sailing
fraternity; situated on the River Crouch, it has its own private
jetty. The bars have a strong nautical feel, with wooden floors,
high-beamed ceilings, collections of old brass and sea pictures,
and good views of the yachts on the estuary outside. Beers on
offer include Tolly Cobbold and Adnams ales, and the
landlord eschews jukeboxes and video games. The bedrooms
have recently been refurbished, and have pale-coloured soft
furnishings contrasting with the original beamwork. The
bedrooms are simple but very comfortable, and have character,
and some have good water views. The restaurant seats 50; set
lunch £8, set dinner £9. No facilities for the disabled.
Walking; yachting; golf and riding nearby

CAMBRIDGE

33/88

Arundel House Hotel, 53 Chesterton Road, Cambridge
CB4 3AN   (Tel. 0223 67701)
£27–£47 single, £39–£65 double b&b
Five minutes from the city centre, the hotel overlooks the
River Cam and Jesus Green; in the summer, you can pick up a
punt from just outside the front door. The building consists of
a row of large, 19th-century terraced houses, and is decorated
in soft colours. The bedrooms at the front have a view of the
river and the green. The overall atmosphere is pleasant, and the
staff are welcoming. The restaurant has a reputation for
serving up some of the best food in the area, and offers healthy
options menus, children's menus and vegetarian menus, as
well as regularly winning prizes for the exemplary cleanliness
of the kitchen, among other things. Prices are also extremely
reasonable, with the table d'hôte lunch costing £7.50, and the
dinner £12.50. Unfortunately, none of the tables have a view of

the river. The large hotel car park is a bonus, as parking in Cambridge can be difficult. There are 14 ground-floor rooms which may be suitable for disabled visitors.

Walking; punting; fishing nearby (hotel has details)

CAMBRIDGE

The Boathouse, Chesterton Road, Cambridge CB4 3AX
(Tel. 0223 460905)
Open 11am–11pm Mon–Sat; noon–3pm, 7pm–10.30pm Sun
With commanding views over the River Cam and Jesus Green, the pub gets very busy on fine summer days. A deck and waterside lawn provide ample outside seating for a drink or a bite in the sunshine. The bar is pleasant, with bookshelves, and rowing paraphernalia on the walls, and large windows giving good views over the garden and the river. The clientele is predominantly young. The publican is more than happy to explain how to arrange punting and fishing: all you have to do is ask. There is live jazz on Sunday evenings. A side counter serves good bar meals (from baked potatoes to steaks, including six daily specials); beers on offer include Greene King Abbot and Flowers IPA. There is a reasonably sized car park (always handy in Cambridge). No facilities for the disabled.

Walking; punting; boating; fishing nearby

CHAPPEL

The Swan, Wakes Colne, Chappel, Colchester, Essex
CO6 2DD   (Tel. 0787 222353)
Just off the A604, visible from road
Open 11am–3pm, 6pm–11pm Tue–Sat; noon–3pm, 7pm–10.30pm Sun
The Swan is very conveniently located just off the main road, and set among rolling fields. There is plenty of seating outside, both in the courtyard, with its tubs of flowers and French street signs, and in the pretty garden, which has picnic tables going

down to the River Colne. In contrast, the interior, with its oak timbers, low beams and huge open fireplace, gives one the impression of what the pub might have been like 500 years ago when it was originally built. The pub has a friendly and enjoyable atmosphere. The glass-sided restaurant serves a range of grills and fish dishes and so forth, and a three-course lunch costs around £16 per person. Bar snacks are also available. It is a free house, and serves Greene King ales, and Mauldon's bitter. Just below the garden is an extremely impressive Victorian viaduct.

Colne Valley Steam Railway Museum is 300 yards away; walking

CHICHESTER

Crown and Anchor, Dell Quay, Chichester, West Sussex
PO20 7EB   (Tel. 0243 781712)
Open 11am–3pm, 6pm–11pm Mon–Sat in summer (11.30am–
2.30pm, 7pm–11pm Mon–Sat in winter); noon–2.30pm,
7.30pm–10.30pm Sun
This former hostelry on Chichester harbour dates back to the reign of Henry VIII. The dark-beamed 'wet bar' has a big fireplace, a Ring-the-Bull game (a ring hangs down from the ceiling on a six-foot wire, which is swung from any direction to hook it on to the peg in the bull's nose on the wall), and a wood floor for wet yachtsmen and dogs. Ships' lanterns, old copper kettles and funnels hang on the walls. There is also a larger, carpeted dry bar, which is more couth but less attractive. The waterside garden has seating for 150 people. Beers include Ruddles, Webster's, Watney's, Holsten, Foster's and Carlsberg, and bar snacks are available from noon to 2pm, and 7pm to 9.30pm. The restaurant has a huge window overlooking Dell Quay and the sea, and an extensive range of fresh fish on the menu. Children are welcome in the restaurant, but not in the pub. There are no facilities for the disabled.

Four-mile walk from Chichester Yacht Basin to Fishbourne; boat launch at nearby yacht club; windsurfing at Chichester marina; beach (not sandy); fishing from quay

CHURT

3/53

The Frensham Pond Hotel, Churt, Farnham, Surrey
GU10 2QB   (Tel. 025125 5161)
£66 per room
The Frensham Pond Hotel, as its name implies, overlooks the beautiful man-made expanse of water known as Frensham Pond. This was built by local monks in 1770, and enhances this already beautiful area. During the Second World War it had to be drained because it presented too much of a landmark to passing German bombers. Now, however, peace and tranquillity are the hallmarks of this hotel. The bedrooms are modern, spacious and well appointed, and pleasantly decorated. The well-regarded restaurant has 12 tables with good water views, and the quality of the food is high. The staff are young, friendly and helpful. The hotel has very good leisure facilities, including a plunge pool, spa bath, gymnasium, two squash courts, sauna and solarium. There are ground-floor suites and special lavatories for the disabled.
Walking (much National Trust land nearby); golf; tennis; riding; bird watching

CLEY-NEXT-THE-SEA

2/4

Cley Windmill Guesthouse, Cley-next-the-Sea, Holt, Norfolk NR25 7NN   (Tel. 0263 740209)
Once in Cley, follow the signs for the windmill
£21–£25 pp b&b
Charming and unusual, the Guesthouse, converted out of an 18th-century windmill, occupies an imposing position on the edge of the salt marshes. The sea is a little way off, but the views are nonetheless spectacular and panoramic. A fine balcony runs the whole way round the mill from one of the rooms, and gives superb views over the marshes and Blakeney harbour. At the top there are observation and information rooms, complete with telescope. The bedrooms are named after the role they used to serve when the mill was operational:

the Stone Room, the Wheat Chamber and so forth. The delicious set dinner (for residents only) costs £14; bring your own wine. There are also two self-catering units available, created out of old mill warehouse buildings. An idyllic venue for getting away from it all, but busy in summertime. No facilities for the disabled.

Walking; sailing; windsurfing; fishing; golf; pebble beach nearby

COLTISHALL

Norfolk Mead Hotel, Church Street, Coltishall, Norfolk
NR12 7DN   (Tel. 0603 737531)
Six miles north of Norwich on the B1150
£49–£59 single, £65–£85 double b&b
Norfolk has always seemed rather starved of good restaurants and country hotels, but here is one of the exceptions. The gravel drive leads up to the wisteria-covered hotel which stands alone in beautiful grounds removed from the main road. The accommodation and dining facilities are elegant and tastefully decorated in coordinating pastel colours and floral designs. The dining room is open for dinner only (7pm to 9pm), except for lunch on Sundays (noon to 2pm), and is open to non-residents. The tables have good views over the lawns down to the River Bure. The food is modern, enticing, and of an extremely high standard. There are no facilities for the disabled.

Lake stocked with carp in the hotel grounds; swimming pool; 20 minutes from the coast; fishing for residents (no licence needed for lake, rod licence required for river); interesting walks; lots of antique shops in the village

DEDHAM

Le Talbooth, Gun Hill, Dedham, Essex CO7 6HP
(Tel. 0206 323150)
Off the B1029 (call for specific directions)
Open noon–2pm, 7pm–9pm

This exclusive country restaurant is extremely well known for the quality of its food and the professionalism of its staff. Situated in the heart of John Constable country, it looks down over picturesque gardens to the River Stour – a view of great charm. The impressive, half-timbered Tudor building dates from 1520; inside, it is elegant and comfortable. There is seating for 75 people, and all of the tables have very good views of the river. The menu is firmly haute cuisine, and displays much culinary style and imagination. Gourmets on a budget should note the set lunch, which, at £18 per person, represents good value for money. The wine list is also extremely good, and deserves investigation. No facilities for the disabled.

EASTBOURNE

79/114

Cavendish Hotel, Grand Parade, Eastbourne, East Sussex
BN21 4DH   (Tel. 0323 410222)
£70 single, £115 double, executive suite £220
A magnificent, 19th-century hotel, even more splendid than its brochure's pictures suggest. The large and highly luxurious first-floor rooms, with their high ceilings and friezes, are as nothing compared to the suites, which are hugely vast and comfortable. A large reception hall leads into the Marine restaurant, the Coronet bar and sun lounge (which is slightly noisy, as traffic passes right in front). The mezzanine, overlooking hall, has tables set for writing. The restaurant seats 350; 10 alcove window tables and many others have water views. The set dinner costs £16; traditional Sunday lunch costs £10. Traditional afternoon teas are served in the sun lounge. There are lifts to all floors, ramps from the car park to the hotel, and some specially adapted rooms for disabled guests.
Beach; sea fishing can be arranged; speedboats from pier and waterskiing; sailing club; windsurfing nearby; golf; tennis holidays can be arranged; walks along South Downs; Beachy Head at the end of the seafront

EASTBOURNE

🏨 47/93 ≋ 🐕 ✍ 💳

Langham Hotel, Royal Parade, Eastbourne, East Sussex
BN22 7AH   (Tel. 0323 31451)
£26–£34 pp dinner and b&b

A two-star hotel in an ideal location, closer to the sea than most
of its big brothers in Eastbourne, with a sea-facing terrace
running the length of it that seats about 150. The Langham has
been a family hotel since 1913; the rooms are bright and
cheerful, and reasonably sized. The restaurant offers a good
choice of food at low prices – a three-course lunch costs £6, the
table d'hôte dinner costs about £9. There are eight tables by the
window, and a fair number of the 160 places have a sea view. In
the upstairs bar, there is live music one night a week, and in the
wine-cellar bar there are dances four nights a week through the
summer season (May to September).

Hotel has membership of the Ball Park where guests can use the
spa bath, sauna, snooker and gym for free, and pay court fees for other
activities; nearby Treasure Island children's activity centre; Blue Flag
beach, sandy at low tide; sailing club nearby (with tuition); fishing
(beach and deep sea); windsurfing; jetskiing; tennis; bowling
packages; three golf courses in Eastbourne; Beachy Head and South
Downs Way walks

EASTBOURNE

🏨 58/108 ≋ 🐕 ✍ 💳

Queen's Hotel, Marine Parade, Eastbourne, East Sussex
BN21 3DY   (Tel. 0323 22822)
£80 single, £65 pp double

In a good position just east of the pier, the hotel was built in
1880 and still retains its original size and shape. The period
decor is tasteful, and the sea view from the sea-facing rooms
and the bar terrace is splendid. Rooms at the front on the first
and second floors have balconies which get the sun most of the
day. The dining room has no sea view, but is of an impressive
size (gentlemen are advised that they should wear a jacket and
tie for dinner); dinner dances are held here on Saturday nights

in the summer. Lunch and dinner both have a choice of basic hot dishes or cold buffet. Vegetarians can choose from a separate menu that offers daily choices (though choices have to be made in the morning). No facilities for the disabled, but there are two lifts, large rooms and helpful staff.

Watersports; fishing; golf; riding (10 minutes' drive); the hotel has membership of the Ball Park (see Langham Hotel above for details)

EASTBOURNE

The Wish Tower Hotel, King Edward's Parade, Eastbourne, East Sussex BN21 4EB   (Tel. 0323 22676)
£75 single, £95 double b&b
This attractive whitewashed promenade hotel takes its name from the 'Wish Tower', a Martello tower which was built as a coastal fortification against the threat of Napoleonic invasion. The bar and lounge have splendid views across the esplanade and the beach beyond. The bedrooms are generous in size with sofas and coffee tables to allow guests to relax in private. The King Edward restaurant serves dinner (£13.50) which is a wide-ranging menu incorporating locally caught seafood, a roast, cold buffet, a vegetarian option and a children's selection. Sunday lunch (£8.95) is also served in the restaurant and bar meals are available every day. The hotel has use of the facilities at the Ball Park sports club, which is now recognized as one of Britain's major tennis holiday centres. No specific disabled facilities but there is a lift and wide doors.

Beach; sailing club; sports club; watersports; golf; theatre

EDENBRIDGE

Honour's Mill, 87 High Street, Edenbridge, Kent TN8 5AU (Tel. 0732 866757)
Easy to find, 15 minutes off the M25
Open 12.15pm–2pm, 7.15pm–10pm; closed lunchtime on Sat, evening on Sun, all day Mon
This mill, beside the River Eden, dates from 1750, and was

grinding corn until it was flooded in 1968. The mill wheel is still in the centre of the building, in the area which is now the bar. Upstairs, the restaurant seats 38 people in a room with an attractive high ceiling and low beams, and looks east across the mill pond. The cooking is described as regional and modern French. The set lunch cost £19.75; the set dinner £29.95, and Sunday lunch is £21.50, all including service, coffee and petits fours. The menu changes twice a year but there are daily specials for each course. The wine list that accompanies the meal is equally impressive. No facilities for the disabled.

Walks around Hever Castle; watersports and fishing nearby; sailing and fishing (15 minutes' drive)

ETON

🍴 ⌂ ✗ ▭

The House on the Bridge Restaurant, 71 High Street, Eton, Berkshire SL4 6AA   (Tel. 0753 866836)
At end of Eton High Street, on Windsor bridge
Open noon–2.30pm, 6pm–11pm Mon–Sat; noon–2.30pm, 6pm–10.30pm Sun
Situated on Windsor bridge, near Eton College's old boat houses, the restaurant looks over the River Thames at the towering ramparts of Windsor Castle. There is a good, multi-level lounge for pre-meal drinks, and the restaurant, spread over three levels, is tastefully decorated and seats 80 people, with extensive river views from all tables. The riverside gardens and verandas enhance the setting. Cuisine is international; a meal from the à la carte menu costs about £30 per person; the set lunch about £20. There are no facilities for disabled visitors – they would be better off at the Montmorency, sister restaurant to the House on the Bridge, which is on the opposite side of the river and has wheelchair access. This is a modern restaurant, specializing in fish, and featuring a vast, Dali-esque mural. Main courses here cost about £10.

Walking; Windsor Castle and its parks; boat trips; rowing; fishing nearby

FOLKESTONE

Burlington Hotel, Earl's Avenue, Folkestone, Kent
CT20 2HR   (Tel. 0303 55301)
£43–£50 single, £33 pp double b&b

Built in the 1890s for the Earl of Radnor, this impressive Victorian hotel has a comfortable and relaxed atmosphere, and splendid views of Folkestone and the Channel from many rooms, though a building in front of it obscures some of the views. The rooms are light and airy, decorated with patterned carpets and fitted cupboards, some with terraces looking out to the Channel. The Bay Tree restaurant serves lunch (£7.95) and dinner (£13.65), and offers a typical hotel menu with an extensive list of 57 wines, and advice on which would go well with each type of dish. An attractive place to stay as a base to discover the coast and the cathedral city of Canterbury. Not suitable for the disabled.

Walking; fishing; beach (two minutes away); watersports at Hythe Lake; boat hire in Folkestone; golf at four championship courses

FORDWICH

The George and Dragon Hotel, King Street, Fordwich,
Canterbury, Kent   (Tel. 0227 710661)
Off the A28, the Canterbury to Margate road
£20 single, £35–£40 double b&b

First licensed to sell ales in 1562, the George and Dragon hotel was once little more than a riverside ale house. It has, of course, undergone many changes and modernizations, yet it successfully retains an authentic and historic atmosphere. Nestling on the banks of the river Stour, the hotel offers adequate and well-equipped bedrooms and warm, traditional public areas. The Beefeater Steak House restaurant opens to non-residents and is decorated in cheerful, rustic style. Menus cover steak, fish, chicken, gammon and lamb dishes accompanied by crisp salads or vegetables with three-course meals in the region of £10 to £15 (open 6pm–10.30pm Mon–Thurs; 6pm–11pm Fri;

noon–10.30pm Sun). In the bar area, the hotel also serves a good selection of bar food from £1.50 to £4 (6.30pm–10.30pm Mon–Sat; noon–3pm, 7pm–10.30pm Sun) plus a range of beers, wines, spirits and liqueur coffees to suit every taste. Additional facilities include private parking for a maximum of 70 vehicles and riverview gardens with seating for over 40 guests during the summer.
Walking; fishing

GODALMING

inn ≈ 6/20 ⌂ ◁ ▭

The Inn on the Lake, Ockford Road, Godalming GU7 1RH
(Tel. 0483 415575)
On the A3100, just south of Godalming town
£80–£90 per room b&b
A Tudor inn, showing few signs of age save for the occasional crooked floorboard, set in two acres of gardens overlooking the lake. The bedrooms are comfortable and individually furnished (all have double beds); one has a four-poster, and six have private spa baths. There is a pleasant bar with Flowers, Boddingtons, Brakspear's, the occasional guest beer and bar meals on offer; this opens on to a comfortable lounge. The restaurant seats 80 people; about eight of the tables have a view of the lake, and within the restaurant there is a fish pond with exotic Japanese koi carp. The set dinners cost £15.50 and £18.50, and there is also an à la carte menu. Dinner dances are held once a month. No facilities for the disabled.
Walking; West Surrey golf course nearby; Winkworth Arboretum

GREAT SHEFFORD

▭ ⌂ ✗ ▭

The Swan, Great Shefford, nr Newbury, Berkshire RG16 7DS
(Tel. 048839 271)
Two miles from the M4, on the A338 towards Wantage
Open 11am–3pm, 6pm–11pm Mon–Sat; 12pm–3pm, 7pm–10.30pm Sun

A large, roadside Courage pub with the river running alongside the lounge bar and patio area. One bar has a view of the river, if you get there early enough to get in. It's a popular and noisy pub, decorated with racing memorabilia and photographs, and tends to be full of racing folk from the Lambourn area all gossiping furiously – keep your ears open for tips. The large patio terrace/barbecue area overlooks the water, with a service bar. Together with the large garden room, the restaurant (open until midnight) seats about 70 people, and there is space for plenty more outside. The bar serves a good many spirits but only about three bitters; a wide range of bar food is also available. Children are welcome in the eating areas only. The doors are wide enough to admit wheelchairs, but there are no specific disabled facilities.

GREAT YARMOUTH

Carlton Hotel, Marine Parade, Great Yarmouth, Norfolk
NR30 3JE   (Tel. 0493 855234)
On the sea front
£49 single, £69 double, £130 executive suite
To compensate for the amusement arcades and the garish seafront, the Carlton Hotel has gone up-market and has recently been gutted and re-vamped. Now, it offers comfort and good facilities in very good taste. The decor is elegant and tasteful, and in keeping with the style of the Victorian building. It has always been the best hotel in Great Yarmouth, but this recent refurbishment certainly confirms its position at the top of ladder. Simpson's restaurant, within the hotel, is open to non-residents and seats 150 people, with six window tables. Penny's café-bar is open all day, serving coffees and snacks. No facilities for the disabled.

Walking; indoor/outdoor watersports across the road; sea and fresh water fishing can be arranged; beach nearby; winter season entertainment

HARTFIELD

Bolebroke Watermill, Edenbridge Road, Hartfield, nr East
Grinstead, East Sussex TN7 4JP   (Tel. 0892 770425)
One mile north of Hartfield on the B2026
Open April–November
£20 pp b&b
The watermill merited a mention in the Domesday Book, and
all possible original features have been retained and restored,
including the steep, narrow stairs, the corn-bin bathrooms, the
mill stones and the drive wheels in the sitting room (Note: this
makes it unsuitable for small children and elderly or disabled
people). There are two new rooms this year in the Millers
Barn: the Honeymooners' Hayloft complete with a view of the
pond, and a twin-bedded room downstairs. The atmosphere is
delightfully rustic, and the surroundings are idyllic: there is a
willow-fringed mill pond with Muscovy ducks, and six and a
half acres of grounds in which guests can wander through
streams, pasture and woodland. The residents-only dining
room (reached by descending through a hatch) seats 12, with
no water views. On Saturday nights, a dinner party can be
arranged for a minimum of six people (£17.50 per person);
during the rest of the week, Mrs Cooper offers a 'Taste of
Sussex' supper tray – a light, four-course supper of local
produce served on a wicker tray (£10 per person). No smoking
anywhere.
Walks in Ashdown Forest, including the three-hour Winnie-the-
Pooh Trail; Wellie-walk from the Watermill (follow the wellies in
the trees); fishing locally (five-minute drive); riding can be arranged

HARWICH

Pier at Harwich, The Quay, Harwich, Essex CO12 3HH
(Tel. 0255 241212)
Open noon–2pm, 6pm–9.30pm Sun–Fri; 6pm–10pm Sat
A well-known restaurant which caters for both simple and
sophisticated tastes: dishes range from elaborate seafood to fish

and chips. There is seating for 100 people; half the tables look
out at the water. There is some accommodation: the six rooms
(single from £50, double from £60 b&b) are attractively
decorated with quality soft furnishings and offer a very good
view over the quay, the sea and the Suffolk coast across the
estuary. No facilities for the disabled.
Boat trips nearby

HAXTED

¶ 101 ⚐ ⊗ ▭

Haxted Mill Restaurant, Haxted Road, Haxted,
nr Edenbridge, Kent TN8 6PU   (Tel. 0732 862914)
Signposted from the B2029
Open noon–2pm, 7pm–11pm Tues–Sat; noon–2pm Sun.
Closed Mon and Sat lunchtimes in winter
A relaxing and unpretentious restaurant, with a beamed
ceiling, whitewashed walls and fresh flowers, recently converted from the mill barn. The creative menu focuses on
seafood, and there is a good view of the mill stream from five
first-floor and five ground-floor window tables. The outdoor
terrace has tables with cloths, flowers and candles, and makes a
wonderfully romantic spot on a warm summer evening. There
is water on three sides of the terrace; the stream rushing
through the sluice makes a lovely sound. The mill itself, which
is nothing to do with the restaurant, is 400 years old, and opens
at weekends (from noon to 5pm) from Easter to until 31 May,
then daily (from noon to 5pm) from June to September.
Dinner and drinks cost about £35 to £40 per person; bistro
lunch and drinks is about £10, or if you are happy with a
ploughman's and a glass of wine, you'll leave with change
from a fiver. No specific facilities for the disabled, though half
the restaurant and the terrace and lavatories are all on the same
level.
*Walking; club fishing; Lingfield race course (one and a half miles
away)*

HEACHAM

🍴 ♿ ⬙ 🛏

Miller's Cottage Tea Room, Caley Mill, Heacham, Norfolk
PE31 7JE   (Tel. 0485 70384)
On the A149
Open 10am–5pm
A sweet-smelling position for a light lunch or cream tea as
Miller's Cottage is attached to the only working lavender farm
in England. The building is an old 19th-century corn mill
which still retains its rustic charm. Customers can sit in the
patio filled with flowers or enjoy the sight of the river from
tables in the well-kept garden. As well as the noted pastries and
gateaux, home-made soups and sandwiches are on offer. The
adjoining gift shop has a country theme, selling lavender
products and plants among other attractive presents. Local bed
and breakfast accommodation is available. Children are only
allowed into gift shop. Concrete ramp and disabled lavatories
are on site.
Walking; gift shop

HENLEY-ON-THAMES

🏨 18/26 ♿ ⬙ 🛏

Red Lion Hotel, Hart Street, Henley-on-Thames, Oxon
(Tel. 0491 572161)
Next to Henley bridge
£35–£68 single, £82–£95 double; breakfast £5–£7
The Red Lion has been a stopping point for travellers on the old
London road since the 16th century. Historians believe that it
was built in 1531 to accommodate the craftsmen and their
apprentices who constructed the parish church of St Mary the
Virgin. It is situated next to the bridge over the Thames in the
middle of the town. Most of the bedrooms are 17th century,
and some afford views of the finish of the Henley Royal
Regatta. One bedroom is 16th century, furnished in keeping
with the period, and boasts a fine four-poster bed. The first
guest of note whose visit was recorded was Charles I, who
stayed in the hotel in 1632; the original coat of arms has been

preserved in one of the rooms. The Regency-style restaurant has pretty striped high-backed chairs and a view of the water. The cuisine is of the traditional English style, and a three-course à la carte meal costs about £20. No disabled facilities.
Boating; rowing; fishing; walking; Henley Royal Regatta (first week of July)

HERNE BAY

Bun Penny, 46 Central Parade, Sea Front, Herne Bay, Kent (Tel. 0227 374252)
Open 11am–11pm Mon–Sat; noon–3pm, 7pm–10.30pm Sun
The pub is named after a coin which was issued in the early years of Queen Victoria's reign which had the Queen's head wearing a bun rather than straight hair as figured on later mints. Recently renovated, this traditional pub boasts high ceilings, an airy atmosphere, and a selection of real ales including Shepherd Neame, Bishop's Finger and Master Brew. Two of the three bars overlook the water, as does the large garden, which is just across the road from the sea. A wide selection of bar meals – sandwiches, sausage, egg and chips and steaks, all very good value – are available from noon to 2pm, and 8pm to 10pm. No disabled facilities but helpful staff.
Beach walks; watersports (no equipment supplied); Victorian penny showers

HERTFORD

The Old Barge, 2 The Folly, Hertford, Hertfordshire
SG14 1QD   (Tel. 0992 581871)
Call for directions
Open 11am–2.30pm, 6pm–11pm Mon–Sat; noon–3pm, 7pm–10.30pm Sun
Situated on the edge of the canal, which is known as the River Lee, the Old Barge is a comfortably renovated traditional pub. It is close to the town centre and is popular with the locals. The interior is uncomplicated and typical of this type of

establishment with old beams and antiquities, though it has a slightly sombre air about it. The beers that are on offer include well kept Benskin's, Tetley's and Abbot's. The restaurant has three tables overlooking the canal and serves lunch (from noon to 2pm), and dinner (from 6pm to 9.30 pm) with an extensive menu, daily specials and a wide selection for vegetarians. A main course in the evening would cost approximately £6. Other appealing factors include the pub's fishing rights (licence obtained in the town), and mooring facilities. No disabled facilities, though the pub is all on one level.
Fishing; museums nearby

HEYBRIDGE BASIN

Old Ship, Lock Hill, Heybridge Basin, Malden, Essex
CN9 7RX   (Tel. 0621 854150)
Follow signs from Heybridge to Heybridge Basin, then to the end of the track
Open 11am–11pm Mon–Sat in summer (11am–3pm, 6pm–11pm Mon–Sat in winter); noon–3pm, 7pm–10.30pm Sun
Built in 1798 as the lock keeper's cottage, the Old Ship sits beside the lock gates where the Chelmer river and canal meet the Blackwater estuary. The basin is used to lock boats in that are travelling to and from the sea to stop them getting stuck in the mud when the tide goes out. A very popular pub with sailing enthusiasts; the Old Ship welcomes visitors with a choice of quality beers and bar snacks. Benskin's Best, Burton ale and Adnams are served by the new landlord. Food is available day and evening; warming, home-made soups and stews in the winter and light salads and cold meats in the summer. Children are not allowed in the pub but a new play area outside is being built. This should be an interesting place in 1991 as it will be the millennium of the Battle of Malden, and many Viking reconstructions are planned. In keeping with this historical interest, the pub hopes to set up a weekly folk scene. No disabled facilities.
Sailing (moorings in front of pub); walking

HOLYWELL
inn

The Olde Ferry Boat Inn, Holywell St Ives, Huntingdon,
Cambridgeshire PE17 3TG   (Tel. 0480 63227)
Signposted off the main road through Needingworth
£39.50–£47.50 single, £47.50–£65 double b&b
Reputedly the oldest inn in Britain, dating back to AD 560,
featured in the *Guinness Book of Records*. It is said to be haunted
by a ghost called Juliet, though no one has seen her recently.
The setting is rural and peaceful, on the banks of the River
Ouse, with views a long way down river. Under new
management, the accommodation has recently been attractively and comfortably refurbished. The main pub areas have a
cosy atmosphere, with four open fires, timber and panelled
walls and welcoming sitting areas. The restaurant seats 50 and
is open for Saturday dinner and Sunday lunch (£10) and bar
meals are served daily. These involve home-made specialities
such as the 'Norfolk Sizzler' (a curried turkey pancake), Stilton
pâté and smoked chicken in lemon mayonnaise. The clientele
are a mixture of locals, business people and tourists. There are
no facilities for the disabled, though the main reception rooms
have wide doors and are on one level.
Walking; fishing (with permission); St Ives market Mon and Fri;
Cambridge (20 minutes away)

HORLEY

Ye Olde Six Bells, Church Road, Horley, Surrey RH6 8AD
(Tel. 0293 782209)
Three miles from the M23, Junction 9
Open 11am–11pm, Mon–Fri; 11am–3pm, 6.30pm–11pm Sat;
noon–3pm, 7pm–10.30pm Sun
Ye Olde Six Bells has been an inn since the 13th century, but its
history goes further back than that, to AD 827. A 1000-year-old
beam still holds the building together. The garden runs down
to the banks of the River Mole, and the pub enjoys good views
of the water from the conservatory and the bench tables

The River House Restaurant, which overlooks the Exe estuary: Lympstone, Devon

The Royal Oak, on the harbour: Langstone, Hampshire

The Warehouse Oyster Bar and Restaurant, on the quayside: Poole, Dorset

Eddrachilles Hotel: Badcall Bay, Scourie

The Waterfront Wine Bar, on the new dockside: Leith

The Altnaharrie Inn, on its own island – the launch collects guests: Ullapool

The Green Park Hotel, seen across Loch Faskally: Pitlochry

The Portmeirion Hotel, looking across the Traeth Bach estuary: Portmeirion, Gwynedd

The Butt and Oyster Pub at Pin Mill: near Ipswich, Suffolk

The Trout Inn: Wolvercote, Oxfordshire

Black Jack's Mill — the canal runs under the restaurant: Rickmansworth, Middlesex

St Michael's Manor House: St Albans, Hertfordshire

New Hall Hotel, with lily-fringed moat: Sutton Coldfield, West Midlands

The Old Manse Hotel: Bourton-on-the-Water, Gloucestershire

The Pump House, in front of the magnificent Port of Liverpool building: Albert Dock, Liverpool

Waterton Park Hotel, on its own island: Wakefield, West Yorkshire

Kirkby Fleetham Hall: Northallerton, North Yorkshire

The Watermill Coffee Shop, housed in a 17th-century mill: Caldbeck, Cumbria

outside. The restaurant, on an upper level under the heavily beamed roof, is self service, offering home-cooked food at £6.55 for a main course. Booking is advisable for the evening. The pub decoration is traditional with an open fire and tiled floor. Bass and Charrington IPA are on hand pump; fruit machine, darts and dominoes are to be found to entertain the customers who tend to be young. Children are allowed in the conservatory area but not in the bar. No disabled facilities.
Fishing; walking

HORNING

Petersfield House, Lower Street, Horning, Norfolk NR12 8PF
(Tel. 0692 630741)
Easy to locate alongside the River Bure
£53 single, £66 double b&b
Petersfield House is a 1920s building in two acres of landscaped gardens, in the village of Horning, on the banks of the River Bure. The accommodation is comfortable, with period decoration in peaceful colours. The restaurant does not overlook the water but has pretty views of the garden. The set dinner costs from £13 with a choice of six starters and main courses and three sweets that change daily. The cuisine is English and an à la carte menu is also available. The hotel is a popular retreat for business people, older guests and families in the summer. Those arriving in boats can take advantage of the hotel's private moorings. The landscaped gardens and picturesque river setting mean that you would never be short of a pleasant stroll. The main hotel areas are all on one floor, and there are three rooms on the ground floor which can be used by disabled guests although they are not especially equipped.
Walking; sailing; fishing; day launch hire (about £6 per hour/£35 a day, by prior arrangement)

HOVE

16/45

Sackville Hotel, 189 Kingsway, Hove, East Sussex BN3 4GU
(Tel. 0273 736292)
On the sea front
£55 single, £70–£90 double b&b
Built as four private houses in 1904 and turned into an hotel in
1930, the Sackville still retains many of its original features. Set
back from the seafront, the views are of the bowling greens and
the beaches. The bedrooms are individually designed with
both antique and modern furnishings, and some of the
balconies share the same sweeping sea views as the reception
areas. The Camelot suite features a four-poster bed and several
other rooms have seating areas. Oak panelling lines the walls of
the lounge and bar. The dining room seats 80, and 11 tables
enjoy a view of the sea. The menu is English with the accent on
local fresh produce, including seafood. The set price for the
table d'hôte is from £8.75 for two courses for both lunch and
dinner. Light meals and snacks are served in the sun lounge
which faces south and captures the best of the sun all year
around. The hotel's private parking is a very useful added
bonus in this busy seaside resort. A babysitting facility allows
parents time off to enjoy their holiday. No disabled facilities.
Watersports; fishing; walking; golf; cricket; tennis; bowling green;
swimming pool and health centre nearby

HUNGERFORD

7/9

Marshgate Cottage, Marsh Lane, Hungerford, Berkshire
RG17 0QX   (Tel. 0488 682 307)
From High Street, down Church Street for half a mile, turn
right into Marsh Lane
£23.50–£33 single, £33–£45.50 double b&b
Set on the marshes of the Kennet and Avon canal and a regular
host to ornate barges, pleasure boats, swans and ducks,
Marshgate Cottage offers friendly family accommodation.

The buildings have been developed to form a south-facing courtyard around a 350-year-old thatched cottage. (This original building is older than the canal, and was used as a pest house in the 1640 plague). Accommodation is tasteful and modern. Goats, dogs and cats wander about, but you can't bring your own pets. The main road is far enough away not to be too noisy, ditto the railway behind. The family room has the best access to garden. There is a dining room (dinner only), which seats 22 residents, and most tables have a view of the canal; the food is 'English', and the menu changes every fortnight or according to the season (£12 to £14 for three courses). Hungerford is a paradise for anyone keen on antiques, with 26 shops and a market for browsing. Seven ground-floor rooms are accessible to wheelchairs, though they have no special disabled facilities, and there is one step up into the reception area.

Many walks; canal trips (including horse-drawn); canal and trout fishing (permits can be arranged from local clubs); site of Special Scientific Interest next door, with rare plants and birds just outside windows; small, beautiful and professional Watermill Theatre

HUNGERFORD

24/41

The Bear Hotel, Charnham Street, Hungerford, Berkshire
RG17 0GL   (Tel. 0488 682512)
On the main A4 in Hungerford
Restaurant opens 7.30pm–9.30pm Sun–Thurs; 7.30pm–10pm Fri–Sat
£75 single, £85 double b&b, £85 single executive, £95 double executive b&b

Established as far back as 1297 and carefully restored over recent years, the Bear Hotel epitomizes all that is expected of a traditional English inn, while offering 20th-century modern conveniences. Timber beams and antique furnishings enhance both the public areas and the well-appointed bedrooms. Bedroom suites, four-poster and half-tester rooms are available as are courtyard rooms complete with a view of the River Dunn. The richly decorated restaurant is highly regarded for

its regional French wines and seasonal, gastronomic à la carte cuisine (three-course meals about £25), while the weekly house menu offers set lunch for £13.95, and a set dinner for £19.95. If you want a more casual meal, try the Kennet room or the cocktail bar (bistro-style food and light snacks). The main bar is elegant and spacious, with large French windows that open on to the courtyard with its charming pergola. The hotel and restaurant may be accessible for the disabled.
Walks on the Kennet and Avon canal; fishing on the canal and the River Dunn

HUNTINGDON

Old Bridge Hotel, Huntingdon, Cambridgeshire PE18 6TQ
(Tel. 0480 52681)
On the main Huntingdon inner ring road, off the A604
£71–£88 single, £96–£110 double b&b
The Old Bridge was built in the 18th century as a private bank, with lawns running down to the River Ouse. Comfortable rooms offer pleasant views over the river. Each is individually decorated with special attention paid to fabrics and pretty touches such as handmade bedspreads. The reception areas have recently been refurbished: one striking new feature is the mural in the terrace lounge. The à la carte restaurant seats 40, has a set menu at £21 for four courses and regular favourites such as a large roast sirloin of beef and a fresh fish dish. For more seclusion but at no extra price the Cromwell room seats 30 for private parties. The terrace lounge is a less formal setting for meals (stir fries and vegetarian dishes are a speciality here). Friendly and professional staff will help to arrange any sporting activity for you. The proximity of the main road makes access very easy, though it does take the edge off the otherwise peaceful setting. No disabled facilities, though the pathway acts as a ramp.
Walking; canoeing at local club; boat hire; fishing nearby

IPSWICH

Butt and Oyster Pub, Pin Mill, Ipswich, Suffolk IP9 1JW
(Tel. 0473 780764)
Off the B1456, follow signs to Pin Mill; pub is at the bottom of
lane
Open 11am–11pm Mon–Sat in summer (11am–3pm, 7pm–
11pm in winter); noon–3pm, 7pm–10.30pm Sun
An unspoilt traditional pub with good facilities and friendly
service. The pub has a long history and is mentioned in travel
writings of 1565. The views over the estuary are magnificent
and the water laps the lower walls of the pub at high tide.
Home-cooked food with daily specials on the board costs
about £1.20 for a starter and £4 for a main course. Ipswich-
brewed cask-conditioned beers are a speciality and the bar
serves Tolly mild, bitter and original. There is seating outside
at the water's edge and plenty of boating activity to
contemplate: the pub is home to many of the old Thames
sailing barges, and trips on the estuary can be arranged. An
annual barge race takes place at the beginning of July, and the
finishing line is just outside the pub. The location is popular
with children as the shallow rivulets allow for hours of messing
around. Beware of oncoming traffic, the lane to Pin Mill is
narrow and parking is difficult. No facilities for the disabled.
Walking; watersports; fishing nearby; muddy foreshore of a beach

IPSWICH

Mortimer's on the Quay, Wherry Quay, Ipswich, Suffolk
IP4 1AS   (Tel. 0473 230225)
Call for directions
Open noon–2pm Mon–Fri; 7pm–8.15pm Mon; 7pm–9pm
Tues–Sat. Closed Sun, bank holidays and the day after;
24 December–5 January and two weeks in August
Although it is not easy to find, it is well worth the effort.
Mortimer's is housed in a glass-roofed, 18th-century ware-
house. It is simply furnished, lacks the ostentation of many

inferior restaurants and offers high-quality service and food. Fish, seafood and shellfish are fresh daily, including a mixture of the local catch and a delivery down the coast from Grimsby. The menu depends on the fishermen's best offerings. A three-course meal with coffee costs about £12–£16. One of the specialities is fillet of lemon sole Dieppoise, which is steamed and served with mussels, prawns and mushrooms in a white wine and cream sauce. There is seating for 60; the 10 waterside tables offer impressive views over the docks, marina and the estuary. Note also that parking on the waterfront is difficult at lunchtimes because of local offices. There is disabled access but no special facilities.

Interesting walks along the dock; fishing (rod licence needed); marina and sailing school next door

KING'S LYNN

IOI 🏠 ⊗ 🖃

Riverside Restaurant, King's Lynn Arts Centre, 27 King Street, King's Lynn, Norfolk PE30 1HA   (Tel. 0553 773134)
Located within the Arts Centre, the Riverside restaurant is attractively set out and pleasantly colour coordinated with a good view of the River Ouse from the window tables and the terrace. The river is very active, dropping and rising 27 foot every day. At high tide the water is busy with shipping from the nearby docks. The restaurant is housed in a 500-year-old warehouse looked after by the National Trust – the natural brick is an integral part of the decoration. The à la carte menu is based on home-cooked English food; roast rack of lamb with accompanying vegetables costs £11.50. The Arts Centre gives visitors to the restaurant plenty to do and see before and after their meal as it has a gallery, artists' workshops and a theatre. No facilities for the disabled (though plans for an access ramp are in progress).

Arts centre

KINTBURY

inn ⁵⁄₅ 🏠 ◁ ▭

The Dundas Arms, Station Road, Kintbury, Berkshire
RG15 0UT (Tel. 0488 58 263/559)
Off the A4, the Hungerford to Newbury road
Bar open 11am–3pm, 6pm–11pm Mon–Sat; noon–2pm, 7pm–
10.30pm Sun
£50 single, £60 double b&b
A pretty whitewashed inn located in a quiet little village,
opposite the station, with civilized accommodation, amicable
staff, and the Kennet and Avon canal on both sides. The one
bar overlooks the canalside garden and serves decent food from
an extensive menu and Morland's bitter, Morland's mild,
Dorset IPA and Adnams bitter. A large collection of blue and
white china covers the wall, and the bar top is made out of
shiny old penny pieces. The wine list received the Egon Ronay
South of England Cellar of the Year 1990 accolade. The
restaurant does not overlook the water but serves seriously
good food at £25 for three courses. The chef uses fish from
Cornwall and local game. Canalside tables in summer allow
visitors to watch the highly painted barges go by and greet the
friendly ducks. The pub gets busy at lunchtime, even out of
season. Pets are accommodated by arrangement only. No
facilities for the disabled, though there are ground-floor rooms
and helpful staff.
Walking; fishing (need a permit from local club); ballooning nearby

LONDON COLNEY

🍺 🏠 ◁ ▭

The Green Dragon, Waterside, London Colney,
Hertfordshire AL2 1RB (Tel. 0727 23214)
Village is off the M25; pub just off main street, by bridge
Open 11am–3pm, 5.30pm–11pm Mon–Sat; noon–3pm, 7pm–
10.30pm Sun
Close to a major road, yet in the midst of beautiful
countryside, this recently refurbished 16th-century pub enjoys
a lovely position at the start of several pleasant country

footpaths. A stream runs quietly by its garden tables, through weeping willows and past the large green. The interior of the pub is traditional and cosy, with open fires and a huge and famous collection of brasses. The landlords have recently added a kitchen and a smart dining area, with good river views, and they offer a range of food, from bar snacks to three-course dinners. The atmosphere is relaxed and friendly. No facilities for the disabled.

Walks through fields, along the stream and up to some lakes; fishing and bird sanctuary nearby

MAIDENHEAD

Boulters Lock Hotel, Boulters Island, Maidenhead,
Berkshire SL6 8PE   (Tel. 0628 21291)
Off Junction 7 of the M4
£75–£125 single, £90–£175 double b&b

Standing on a small island in the middle of the Thames, the hotel was originally built as a mill house and cottages in 1726. The mill race still flows underneath the restaurant. Close to Boulters lock, the longest and deepest lock on the river, it used to be a gathering place for high society during Victorian and Edwardian days, when the area was often known as 'Mayfair on Thames'. Nowadays the hotel provides comfortable accommodation and good food in this pleasant spot. Many of the bedrooms have water views, and are elegantly decorated and well equipped. The restaurant, offering lunch at £18.50 and dinner at £26.50 (£30.50 on Saturday evenings for the hotel's own dinner dance), looks downstream towards Maidenhead, and has even better views from all of the tables (open 12.30pm–2.30pm, 7.30pm–9.30pm (1am on Saturdays) all week). There is a large patio terrace which is very pleasant in summer. The hotel is not suitable for the disabled.

MAIDENHEAD

🏠 30/53 ～ ⚔ ⚗ 💳

Thames Riviera Hotel, at the Bridge, Maidenhead, Berkshire
SL6 8DW   (Tel. 0628 74057)
By Maidenhead bridge
£90 single, £100 double, suite £125; breakfast £5–£7
This hotel is situated by the old bridge which originally helped
to bring prosperity to Maidenhead. The building dates from
the 1870s, and recent refurbishments have preserved the
Edwardian feel. Close to the water, the views from the
restaurant and the terrace are pleasant and picturesque. Neither
the coffee shop nor the bar, however, can lay claim to water
views, and both have slightly gloomy atmospheres. The
rooms are light and airy, and many of them have balconies and
good water views. The bridal suite, complete with four-
poster, has good views of Brunel bridge, which has the longest
brick arch span in the world. The service is friendly and
professional, and there are extensive conference and banqueting facilities. There are no facilities for the disabled.
*Walking; boat hire nearby; Ascot racecourse and Windsor Safari Park
both nearby*

MAIDSTONE

🏠 18/40 ～ ⚔ ⚗ 💳

Chilston Park, Sandway, Lenham, Kent ME17 2BE
(Tel. 0622 859803)
Lenham village off the A20, then follow signs to Boughton
Malherbe
£72–£149 single, £94–£198 double b&b
Boasting 250 acres of parkland and a spring-fed lake, this
beautiful Grade I listed building dates back to the 13th century.
The hotel was remodelled in the 1700s and remains grandly
furnished: even the staff are turned out in traditional costume.
The idea behind the hotel is to recreate an old-fashioned
country house party, and there are open fires, and at dusk
hundreds of candles are lit, to give a very special atmosphere.
The rooms are spacious and ornate, some with four-poster

beds. The hotel is owned by Judith and Martin Miller (authors of *Miller's Antiques Price Guide*), so the house is full of gorgeous antique pieces; depending on your attitude, you'll either find it grand or grotesque. The restaurant seats 80 and has 12 window tables, though seven others enjoy lake views. Set lunch costs £18.50, five-course dinner £32.50. Sunday lunch is £19.50, afternoon tea £8.50. There are no facilities for the disabled.

Walks along Pilgrims' Way; fishing (rods available); golf (three miles away); riding (Oathill, 20 minutes away); gliding (six miles away); windsurfing and waterskiing (Maidstone lakes); champagne, opera, antiques and 'Murder Mystery' weekends; hot-air ballooning by arrangement; archery, clay pigeon shooting

MARLOW

The Compleat Angler, Bisham Road, Marlow Bridge, Marlow, Buckinghamshire SL7 1RG   (Tel. 0628 484444)
On the A404 between Maidenhead and Marlow
£110–£150 single, suites from £250

This famous hotel, occupying the spot on the Thames where Izaak Walton wrote his classic work on fishing in 1653, could not be much closer to the river. Beside the bridge and opposite the church, set in its own beautiful gardens, this hotel offers luxurious accommodation in lovely surroundings. There is plenty of space to enjoy the river from the gardens and from the waterside conservatory. The angling theme is continued throughout the hotel; bedrooms are all named after fishing flies and the best ones, which are slightly more expensive, have gorgeous river views. The large restaurant is also on the river, with the same superb views and extremely good, if unadventurous cuisine. There is a helipad for guests arriving by air. No facilities for the disabled.

On-site fishing (equipment not supplied); boating; tennis; walking

MARSHSIDE

The Gate Inn, Marshside, nr Canterbury, Kent
(Tel. 022786 498)
One mile north of Chislet, on Marshside Road
Open 11am–2.30pm, 6pm–11pm Mon–Fri; 11am–3pm, 6pm–
11pm Sat; noon–3pm, 7pm–10.30pm Sun
This down-to-earth, genuine country pub is bordered by a
stream on two sides, and the garden often has ducks, geese and
pub resident Derek the one-eyed chicken wandering through
it. The atmosphere inside the pub is entirely unpretentious –
there are no carpets on the floor, no jukeboxes or fruit
machines, and the beers are kept in the back room on tap;
Shepherd Neame Old Ale and Bishop's Finger are the local
brews. During Lent, the pub refuses to sell lager. Good bar
food, such as soup and sandwiches, is available at lunchtime,
and is generous, healthy and reasonably priced. There are good
water views from the bar. The pub is popular with those who
prefer simple utilitarianism to frippery and who enjoy the
traditional atmosphere of this friendly pub. Access for the
disabled.
Fishing (rods supplied); fly fishing nearby; walking

MILDENHALL

Riverside Hotel, Mill Street, Mildenhall, Suffolk IP28 7DP
(Tel. 0638 717274)
Off the A11, on the west side of town
£40–£66 per room b&b
This listed red-brick hotel has lovely landscaped gardens
running down to the banks of the River Lark. It has recently
undergone some refurbishments, and the restaurant is now in
an extremely pleasant conservatory. Nearly all the seats have
good river views, as do those on the outside terrace. The food
is of a high standard. During the summer they have barbecues
in the garden. The bedrooms are very pretty, with floral prints
and tasteful furnishings, and one of the rooms has a four-poster

The hotel has a famous Georgian staircase, which is worth inspecting. There are no facilities for the disabled.

Interesting walks; fishing (rod licence needed, the hotel has fishing rights); rowing boats for hire; bridge weekends

MONK SOHAM

2/3 12

Abbey House, Monk Soham, nr Woodbridge, Suffolk
IP13 7EN   (Tel. 072882 225)
Off the A1120, the Stowmarket to Yoxford road
Closed Christmas and New Year
£16–£18 pp b&b

Formerly a Victorian rectory enjoying a quiet Suffolk countryside location, Abbey House's present owners have created a comfortable and quality guest house set in 10 acres of secluded gardens complete with ponds, black swans, oaks and beeches. The genteel atmosphere is informal, warm and welcoming and enhanced by tasteful antique furnishings, soft colour schemes and a magnificently restored cast-iron fireplace in the dining area. Evening meals can be provided for residents and their guests by prior arrangement at £10 a head. Catering is in the traditional English style and features the house's own meat and vegetables. Guests are welcome to look at the Jersey cows, ducks, sheep, peafowl and other livestock in the grounds. The owners are delightful and most welcoming. A magnificent base for exploring many local attractions and places of interest such as the Norfolk Broads, historic Norwich, coastal bird reserves, and most of the 'Constable Country'. No facilities for the disabled.

Open-air swimming pool; countryside and coastal walks; sailing and windsurfing in Aldeburgh; pond fishing; nearby beaches

MOULSFORD
inn ~ 8/13

Beetle and Wedge, Ferry Lane, Moulsford-on-Thames, Oxon
OX10 9JF   (Tel. 0491 651381)
Just off the A329 between Streatley and Wallingford
£60 single, £70 double b&b
This cosy Thames-side inn has lovely views and a pleasant,
relaxed atmosphere. The bar has log fires, and serves
Wadworths 6X, Adnams best bitter and Badger's Tanglefoot.
There is also an informal à la carte restaurant connected to the
bar, which has an open charcoal grill, and serves lunch and
dinner. In the main body of the inn, the more formal
restaurant places strong emphasis on the quality of the food,
which could be described as robust French cuisine with an
English accent, and is said to be extremely good. The three-
course dinner costs £21 per person, and includes coffee and
home-made chocolates at the end. The extensive and tranquil
riverside gardens offer barbecues every day in summer.
There is a college barge which is available for hire. Pets
by arrangement only. There are ground-floor rooms and
lavatories for disabled visitors.
*Fishing by arrangement; rowing boats for hire (10 miles away), walks
along river and through water meadows*

NEEDINGWORTH
inn ~ 5/12

Pike and Eel, Overcote Lane, Needingworth, St Ives,
Cambridgeshire PE17 3TW   (Tel. 0480 63336)
Off the main road through Needingworth
Bar open 10.30am–3pm, 6pm–11pm Mon–Sat; noon–3pm,
7pm–11pm Sun
£35 single, £48 double b&b
This popular pub, situated well off the beaten track, dates back
to the 17th century. On the banks of the River Ouse, it has
large lawns running down to the water, where there is a marina
and a thatched bar where barbecues are held in the summer.
There are two restaurants, both with views of the river,

although the glass-walled Garden Room restaurant has the best of them, and a bar, also with fine views of the gardens and river. There is a good selection of food available, from ploughman's, via steaks, to full-blown à la carte meals. The bedrooms are comfortable and homely, with washbasins, televisions, and pleasant rural views. There are two peaceful lounges off the bar. There are no facilities for the disabled.
Golf; stables nearby; walking; watersports; fishing (with fishing rights)

NEWBRIDGE

The Maybush, Newbridge, nr Witney, Oxon OX8 7QD
(Tel. 0865 300624)
On the A415 exactly halfway between Abingdon and Witney
Open 11am–11pm Mon–Sat in summer (11am–3pm, 6pm–11pm Mon–Sat in winter); noon–3pm, 7pm–10.30pm Sun
This pleasant, quiet pub is right on the Thames, and very close to where it joins that River Windrush – you can see the Windrush gently snaking through the fields in the near distance. There is a small terrace with tables and lovely views over the river and the meadows. During the summer barbecues are held here, and there is some mooring for boats. Inside, the decor of the single bar is simple, and there are several tables with good views. The pub serves Morland ales, and also does a wide range of bar grub, such as steaks, fish and pasta; there is also a selection of vegetarian dishes. All in all, this is a nice, simple, typical country pub in a beautiful position. The pub is accessible to disabled visitors, though there are no special facilities.
Walks along the Thames; fishing

NEWBRIDGE

The Rose Revived Inn and Restaurant, Newbridge, Witney, Oxon OX8 6QD   (Tel. 0865 300221)
On the A415 Abingdon to Witney, or float downstream and moor alongside the garden

£30–£45 per room b&b

Pretty, large old riverside inn, on the upper reaches of the Thames. The à la carte restaurant, complete with impressive 16th-century fireplace, has tables outside on the terrace with good water views. The bar, again with good water views, has flagstone floors and open fires, and serves a range of bar meals, sandwiches and the like. The beers on draught include Stella Artois, and Morland's Revival and Original. The rose theme is stressed, with rose-patterned wallpaper and pictures of roses decorating the walls. The extensive garden by the water seats 250, and is lit at night by old-fashioned street lights. The civilized, pleasant and well-appointed bedrooms all have good views overlooking the river. There is no charge for overnight mooring. It can become very busy during the summer. There are no facilities for the disabled.

Watersports; fishing; walks

NEWBURY

🏠 24/32 🏘12 ◁ 🗌

Millwaters Hotel and Restaurant, London Road,
Newbury, Berkshire RG13 2BY   (Tel. 0635 528 838)
Newbury signposted off the A4
£77–£140 per room

The tumbling rivers Kennet and Lambourn border the grounds of this pretty Georgian country house. Inside is extensively refurbished, with spa baths and mini-bars in some of the bedrooms; many of these overlook the rivers, and all are tastefully decorated, if a little bland. The spacious, not to mention barn-like, restaurant seats 70; some tables inside and on the patio overlook the really lovely award-winning gardens, which are floodlit at night. There is a summer house with waterside terraces for private parties. Despite being close to the industrial wasteland that surrounds Newbury these days, the hotel is an oasis of watery tranquillity, and the gardens are outstanding. There are facilities for the disabled.

Walking; watersports; fishing in grounds on Kennet, Lambourn and lake; gliding by arrangement; special interest weekends include fishing, watercolour painting, music, riding and horse racing

NORWICH

The Ferry Inn, Reedham, Norwich, Norfolk NR13 3HA
(Tel. 0493 700429)
On the B1140, off the A47 Norwich–Great Yarmouth road
Open 11am–3pm, 6.30pm–11pm Mon–Sat; 7pm–10.30pm
Sun Easter–end October; and 11am–2.30pm, 7pm–11pm
Mon–Sat; noon–3pm; 7pm–10.30pm Sun November–Easter
Be warned that approaching this functional inn from the south
entails a short ferry crossing, as the establishment's name
suggests. The Ferry inn enjoys a rural, tranquil location and
owns one of the last working vehicle ferries in East Anglia
which runs from 8am–10pm daily, transporting a maximum
of three cars. Across a quiet lane, the inn's garden-bench
seating overlooks the swans and moored boats of the River
Yale. Inside, the two bar areas (one with a sun lounge) offer a
certain amount of rustic character with their brass and copper
decorations, antique rifles and log fires coupled with modern
entertainments such as games and fruit machines. A fair
selection of generously portioned bar meals are on offer,
ranging from ploughman's at £3.50 to seasonal game at £6, and
beers include Adnams, Woodforde's and Beck's. No facilities
for the disabled.
Fishing rights (rod licence needed); camping nearby

NORWICH

Hotel Nelson, Prince of Wales Road, Norwich, Norfolk
NR1 1DX   (Tel. 0603 760260)
Opposite railway station on east side of town
£73.50–£130 per room b&b
Functional and modern, this purpose-built red-brick hotel has
been sensibly designed to maximize its riverside position.
There are large floor-to-ceiling windows in the lounge, and the
water views are also good from other areas of the hotel. It sits
on the banks of the River Wensum, and has nice waterside
gardens. The bedrooms are comfortable and airy, decorated in

restful colours, with thoughtful extras such as fruit juice, mineral water and chocolates, and many of them have views of the Wensum. There are two restaurants, one on the ground floor, next to the river, and the other on the first floor, with a pleasant balcony looking over the river. The staff are refreshingly professional and most welcoming. There are lavatories, and there is a modified bedroom for the disabled.
Riverside walks; river cruises

OLD HUNSTANTON

Le Strange Arms Hotel, Golf Course Road, Old
Hunstanton, Norfolk PE36 6JJ   (Tel. 0485 534411)
Off the A149 between Wells and Hunstanton
£50 single, £68 double b&b
In an impressive position right on the seafront, this Grade II listed hotel dates from 1600 and has fine lawns leading down to the beaches. The hotel's name comes from the local land-owning family, the Le Stranges, and the hotel occupies the more interesting and historical part of town. There are good facilities for families including a children's play area, children's menus and baby-listening, and there are spacious adjoining bedrooms. There is a snooker room, with a full-sized table. Half of the tables in the 50-cover restaurant look out to sea. There is a bar in the old stables, which also enjoys good sea views. The staff are helpful and friendly. There are no facilities for the disabled.
Walking; beach; watersports and fishing can be arranged by the hotel (rod licence available in Hunstanton, equipment not supplied); golf nearby

OTLEY

Otley House, Otley, Suffolk IP6 9NR   (Tel. 0473 890 253)
Village on the B1079
Open 1 March–1 November
£40–£48 per room b&b

This charming, Grade II listed country manor house nestles in three acres of peaceful grounds complete with two smallish lakes, which used to be part of the moat round the house. French windows open on to smart lawns, wild ducks bob gently on the lake and the atmosphere is extremely tranquil. Inside the house, one tends to feel more like an invited guest than a passing traveller. The light and airy bedrooms are filled with antiques and freshly cut flowers. All guests eat around the same table in the dining room, equipped with crystal glasses and silver cutlery (set dinner £14.50). There is no choice of menu – let the owners know your pet hates when you book. After dinner there is a billiard room where guests gather for coffee, and this is the only room where smoking is permitted. For an elegant and civilized stay in beautiful countryside, Otley House would seem to to offer exceptional value. There are no facilities for the disabled.

Croquet lawn; fishing by arrangement; walking; riding; watersports at Woodbridge, Walderingfield and Orford; Woodbridge golf courses; beach at Aldeburgh (30 minutes' drive)

OXFORD

Cherwell Boat House, Bardwell Road, Oxford OX2 6SR
(Tel. 0865 52746)
Call for directions
Open noon–2pm, 7.30pm–10pm Tues–Sat; noon–2.30pm, 7.30pm–10pm Sun. Closed Mon all year, and Sun evenings in winter

This popular Oxford institution is on the River Cherwell, and the window tables look out over the ranks of moored punts and the meadows leading away towards Marston. The restaurant seats 50, and offers very good, simple food. The menu changes weekly, and there are only two or three choices per course, but the choices are well-balanced and often delicious. The price for the set dinner is £13.50. They also possess an outstanding wine list which is well worth investigating. The decor is plain and unspectacular, but it is compensated by the proximity of the Cherwell, and in the summer you can eat al fresco on the terrace. The boathouse as a whole can become very crowded in the summer with punters arriving and departing. There is access and lavatories for the disabled.

Punting from boat house next door to restaurant (mid-March to mid-October); walks in the university parks

PYRFORD LOCK

The Anchor, Pyrford Lock, Ripley, Woking, Surrey
GU23 6QW   (Tel. 09323 42507)
Off the A3, pass Wisley Gardens, continue along same road to pub
Open 11am–11pm Mon–Sat Easter–September (11am–3pm, 6pm–11pm Mon–Sat October–Easter); noon–3pm, 7pm–10.30pm Sun
This modern, open-plan country pub was built in 1936 and extended five years ago. It has very good views of the canal, the lock and a hump-backed bridge. There is a large canalside terrace with tables, where teas are served in the summertime, and a large waterside garden with seating for 50. Inside, in the large bar, the picture windows look out over the canal, and one can watch the narrow boats passing slowly by. Pleasant parents' and children's room upstairs, which is decorated with narrow boat bric-a-brac. The bar serves Directors, best, and John Smith's beers; and there are bar lunches and dinners. No facilities for the disabled.

Canalside walks; Wisley Garden; boat hire at Guildford and Farncombe; rowing boat hire at Byfleet (one and a half miles)

RAMSHOLT

Ramsholt Arms, Dock Road, Ramsholt, Woodbridge, Suffolk
IP12 3AB   (Tel. 0394 411229)
Village signposted from the B1083 (call for detailed directions)
Bar open 11am–11pm Mon–Sat in summer (11am–2.30pm, 7pm–11pm Mon–Sat in winter); noon–3pm, 7pm–10.30pm Sun
£25 pp b&b

Unless you know the area you may be tempted to give up before you get there: the pub is on a private estate and has no inn sign. Persevere. The setting and the view are stunning and a far cry from city life. The pub is beside an old barge quay; the River Deben flows quietly by to the sea. Local enthusiasts would be more than happy to enlighten you on the wildlife of the water and the vicinity. Two bars overlook the water, and serve Adnam's bitter and a selection of guest beers, and also food. The accommodation is modest, but clean and well maintained, and is able to boast royal visitors (the Duke of Edinburgh and the Prince of Wales), from the days when the pub was a shooting lodge. There is a restaurant, which opens at lunchtime and in the evening. Children are welcome in the dining room but not in the guest accommodation. No facilities for the disabled, but helpful staff.

Interesting walks; sailing; beach nearby

RICKMANSWORTH

IOI 🏠 ⊗ ⊟

Black Jack's Mill, off Park Lane, Harefield, Middlesex
UB9 4HL   (Tel. 0895 823120)
Call for directions
Open 12.30pm–2pm, 7pm–10pm; closed Sun evening and all day Mon

A splendid watery setting, with the Grand Union Canal just behind the restaurant, the river in front of the garden and a lake beyond that. Part of the canal runs under the building and turns a cormetic wheel. Parts of the building are 900 years old, and are recorded in the Domesday Book. The food is Italian and English (set Sunday lunch £11.50) and there is seating for 45, with six tables having a water view. There are some tables outside in summer. Water views from inside can be slightly disappointing (some tables with canal view, others river and lake view), but one can take drinks outside in summer on to the patio. The mill used to be the haunt of film stars when Denham studios were open, and Rosemary Clooney, Bob Hope and Sir John Mills used to eat here often. There are some facilities for the disabled.

Fishing nearby; sailing club opposite; bird watching; walks along canal; boat rental in Uxbridge (four miles away)

ST ALBANS

10/26 12

St Michael's Manor House, Fishpool Street, St Albans, Hertfordshire AL3 4RY   (Tel. 0727 864444)
Follow signposts towards cathedral
£70 single, £85 double b&b (four-poster-bed rooms and special weekend rates also available)
In a very tranquil setting, yet only 10 minutes' walk from the cathedral and the main town, the hotel offers the benefits of both town and country location in one. The front façade faces St Albans's historic cathedral, while the hotel's particularly attractive rear conservatory backs on to five acres of award-winning and charming garden, complete with a picturesque lake. Also facing the green surrounds of the lake are 40 of the 120 seats in the restaurant, which serves a set lunch at £16, dinner at £18 and also offers a comprehensive à la carte menu averaging £22 for three courses. (Restaurant open 12.30pm–2pm Mon–Sun; 7pm–9pm Mon–Sat; 7pm–8pm Sun evening buffet.) The comfortable bedrooms are pleasantly decorated with pastel-coloured soft furnishings. Dogs are accepted by prior arrangement with the hotel management. With its adapted bathroom facilities and ramps, the restaurant is suitable for the disabled, but an overnight stay is not recommended.
Golf; local sports cente with swimming pool; walking; many local historical sites to visit

ST IVES

0/22

The Dolphin Hotel, Bridge Foot, London Road, St Ives, Cambridgeshire PE17 4EP   (Tel. 0480 66966)
In the town centre
£53 single, £63 double, £73 family room (sleeps 4) b&b
This purpose-built hotel with simple accommodation is

conveniently placed at the edge of an attractive and traditional market town, right on the edge of the River Ouse. It is a popular location with both fishermen and boating enthusiasts. If the bedrooms do not boast a water view, the hotel's 'Waterside Restaurant' more than compensates with a good aspect from virtually all of its 120 seats. The modern English/French influenced cuisine includes table d'hôte lunch and dinner at £12.50, or à la carte meals in the region of £17.50 for three courses (restaurant open noon–2pm, 7pm–9.30pm every day). The Dolphin also has a bar, residents' lounge and night porter service and plans are afoot to incorporate a function suite during a large-scale extension programme in spring 1991. Pets are accepted by prior arrangement only. The hotel may be accessible for the disabled.

Walking; boat trips; fishing by arrangement (rod licences available nearby)

ST LEONARDS-ON-SEA

IOI 🏠 🚫 ▭

Röser's, 64 Eversfield Place, Hastings, St Leonards-on-Sea, East Sussex TN37 6DB   (Tel. 0424 712218)
Open noon–2pm, 7pm–10pm; closed Sat lunch and all day Sun and Mon

Directly on the St Leonards seafront and just opposite the pier, this 35-seat restaurant set in a Victorian terraced residence offers reasonable sea views across the road and promenade from the three front tables. The food is inventive but some may consider it slightly pricey although owner/chef, Gerald Röser, clearly puts great thought and energy into it. He uses a wide range of leaves, including many Japanese ones that give a startling boost to the flavour of the salads. Sushi features on the menu when the supply of fresh fish permits; also tartare of scallops and oysters. Set lunch costs £15.95 and the three-course dinner à la carte averages £24 including VAT and service. The 400-strong, award-winning wine list should appeal to all palates and is priced from a reasonable £9 to a frightening £235. Not a restaurant for the casual eater, but a real treat for the food connoisseur. Group catering for up to 40 guests is available in a first-floor function room with panoramic sea view. The restaurant may be accessible to the disabled.

Beach; watersports, including windsurfing; waterskiing in the harbour; fishing from pier; boat trips from harbour (Deep Sea Fishing Club nearby); walking

ST LEONARDS-ON-SEA

🏠 25/52 🏕 ⬦ ▭

Royal Victoria Hotel, Marina, St Leonards-on-Sea, East Sussex TN38 0BD   (Tel. 0424 445544)
£83.50 single, £132 double b&b
Built in 1828, the hotel was refurbished in suitably grand style for a visit by Queen Victoria. The first flight of the impressive staircase ends at an enormous wall mirror, creating such a successful illusion of space beyond that the management found a centrally placed plant necessary to protect guests from embarrassing self-injury! The bedroom suites are luxuriously appointed and the 25 sea-view suites feature old sash windows large enough to gain access to the roof. The first-floor restaurant seats 120 diners and is open to non-residents with excellent sea views from eight of the tables. The set dinner costs £18 and a separate seafood menu is always on offer. Elegant public rooms include an arched and columned lounge with fine sea views, plus an intimate cocktail bar. In the luxuriously appointed bedroom suites, children under 12 may share with parents free of charge. Small pets are only accepted by prior arrangement at a nominal fee. Not specially adapted for the disabled, but the hotel has lifts and may be accessible.

Beach; river fishing nearby; sea fishing from Hastings can be arranged; windsurfing, sailing and waterskiing can be arranged; yacht hire; many walks; riding and golf nearby

SEAFORD

🛏 🏕 ⬦ ▭

The Golden Galleon, Exceat Bridge, Seaford, East Sussex BN25 4AB   (Tel. 0323 892247)

On the A259, the Seaford to Eastbourne road
Open noon–2.30pm (3pm in summer months), 7pm–10.30pm
A traditional, tied pub just opposite the River Cuchmere, featuring low oak beams, red Turkish carpeting and an open log fire in winter. Bar meals range from soups (£2) to steaks (£12), although the specialities are generally Italian. Both the bar and the garden, with bench and patio seating, overlook the river and the point where canoeing enthusiasts set off on an Outward Bound course – a potentially entertaining event for passive onlookers! Easily reached from Eastbourne or Brighton, the pub serves Directors and John Smith's beers. Dogs must be kept on leads. Children are admitted during the summer months. No facilities for the disabled.
Walks in National Trust land; canoeing nearby; fishing; beach

SHABBINGTON

The Old Fisherman Pub, Shabbington, Buckinghamshire
HB18 9HJ   (Tel. 0844 201247)
Off the A329 at Thane, follow signs to Wheatley
Open 11am–3pm, 5.30pm–11pm Mon–Sat; noon–2.30pm, 7pm–10.30pm Sun
Enjoying a lovely, peaceful situation on the River Thane, this simple but charming 17th-century pub is beautifully placed for a quiet summer's drink. There is a garden, with tables, that runs down to the river. The owner/landlord was born and bred in the village of Shabbington, and the pub is equally popular with locals and tourists. Bar snacks are available at prices up to £3.50 and beers served include Morrell's of Oxford. No facilities for the disabled.
Walking

SHILLINGFORD

Shillingford Bridge Hotel, Ferry Road, Shillingford, Wallingford, Oxon OX10 8LZ   (Tel. 086732 8567)
£30–£35 single, £75–£100 double b&b

Restaurant open 12.30pm–2pm, 7pm–10pm (9.30pm Sun) all week

The hotel has a truly beautiful riverside setting, with splendid views of an attractive reach of the River Thames. In the summer, there are seats out in the garden, where verdant lawns descend to the river bank and moored boats line the water's edge. Specializing as a venue for corporate or private events, the hotel is well equipped for banquets for up to 150 guests; ideal for small conferences or wedding receptions. From many tables in the 150-seat dining room guests can enjoy a pleasant view of the river while sampling the three-course meals, table d'hôte (£12.50) or à la carte (£18.50) menus. The bedrooms are adequately furnished and all have private *en suite* facilities and colour television. The hotel will be undergoing decorating work and refurbishment during early 1991 and it is not suitable for the disabled.

Outdoor pool and squash courts on site; golf, coarse fishing, river craft hire and walks nearby

SONNING-ON-THAMES

The Great House at Sonning, Thames Street, Sonning-on-Thames, Berkshire RG4 0UT   (Tel. 0734 692277)
£79 single, £99 double b&b

A sister hotel to Sir Christopher Wren's House (see under Windsor), the Great House at Sonning overlooks a broad meander in the River Thames which is frequented by wildfowl. The hotel has four acres of beautiful grounds, riverside gardens with seating on an extremely large summer terrace and boasts two restaurants, one of which is non-smoking. The bedrooms are well equipped, though lacking the appeal of the gardens. Table d'hôte traditional English meals are set at £12.50 for lunch and £18 for dinner in the 96-seat main restaurant, where all dining tables overlook the river, and a full à la carte menu also offers three-course meals for approximately £19. Alternatively, the more casual 'Hideaway' restaurant in the beamed Elizabethan area of the hotel provides wholesome English meals in the £10–£12 price band. Pets are accepted but are not admitted to public rooms. The hotel is not adapted for the disabled although the restaurants may be accessible.

Walking; watersports; fishing (rods available at hotel); tennis courts on site

SOUTHWOLD

The Harbour Pub, Blackshore Quay, Southwold, Suffolk
IP18 6TA   (Tel. 0502 722381)
From the A1095 to Southwold, turn right at the King's Head and head for the water tower on the other side of the golf course
Open 11am–3pm, 6pm–11pm Mon–Sat in summer (11am–3pm, 7pm–10.30pm Mon–Sat in winter); noon–2.30pm, 7pm–10.30pm Sun
A quaint and refreshingly unpretentious pub on the quay. Its charm lies in simplicity and is enhanced by a sign that says 'Beware – ducks crossing'. The 400-year-old building has two bars: the lower one overlooks the River Blyth; the upper one faces the marsh. Mercifully, there is no chrome plating, no jukebox, and no one-armed bandits to spoil the pub's old-fashioned atmosphere. A small scruffy garden with play area for children runs down to the water where ducks and geese wander freely. With no plates, knives or forks in sight, the food (fish, sausage or – topping the range – scampi and chips for £2.50) is largely fried and includes anything that can be served wrapped in a paper parcel. Food is available Friday and Saturday evenings in winter and all day, all week in summer. Children and pets are allowed in the garden only and dogs must be kept on leads. Not suitable for the disabled.

Landlord Ron Westwood will give directions for interesting walks; children can go crabbing in the river just across from the pub; fishing in the river (no licence needed); beach (10 minutes' walk along the river)

STAINES

4/11

The Swan Hotel, The Hythe, Staines TW18 3JB
(Tel. 0784 454471)
Take first left south of Staines bridge
£35–£65 per room b&b
Bar open 11am–11pm Mon–Sat; noon–2.30pm, 7pm–
10.30pm Sun (snacks noon–2.30pm, 5pm–9.30pm)
This delightfully restored old inn was built in the 17th and 18th
centuries and enjoys a Thames-side setting with a pleasant
sycamore-shaded terrace beside the towpath. There are two
bars serving real ales including ESB and London Pride: both
bars overlook the river and are furnished with upholstered
settles, armchairs and original exposed fireplaces. Scattered
horse brasses, copper tankards and kettles add to their charm.
Bedrooms are comfortable and thoughtfully decked out with
pine furniture and peachy colour schemes. Catering ranges
from a sandwich in the bar to a full meal in the restaurant; all in
all, there is seating for 70 diners. Pets are allowed into the bar
area but not the restaurant. The inn is not adapted for the
disabled but may be accessible. There is one entry step and staff
are more than willing to offer assistance when necessary.
Walking; fishing

STANDLAKE

3/4

The Old Rectory, Church End, Standlake, Witney, Oxon
OX8 7SG   (Tel. 0865 300559)
Near the A415, just before the B4449, right by the church (call
for more specific directions)
Closed December–January
£24.50–£48.50 single, £55.20–£66.50 double b&b
A classy bed and breakfast establishment in a large, characteristic Cotswold stone rectory dating back to the 13th century.
The surrounding lawns lead to the River Windrush and are
sheltered by tall beech hedges, pine trees and a 500–year-old
yew tree. The house has many features of architectural interest,

and a beautifully proportioned 15th-century dining room with several large sash windows and a pleasant view of the river and meadows. The dining room will open for residents' dinner on request. The comfortable drawing room is well furnished with antiques and a log fire and bedrooms range from attractive to the truly magnificent and luxurious. The best they offer is a river-view four-poster suite with pink and gold bathroom. A warm and friendly welcome is assured and value for money guaranteed. The rectory is just 10 miles from Oxford and conveniently situated near plenty of places to eat. Not suitable for the disabled.

Fishing; watersports; interesting walks; close to Oxford

STORRINGTON

Abingworth Hall, Thakeham Road, Storrington, West Sussex RH20 3EF   (Tel. 07983 3636)
Two miles west of the A24, on the B2139 between Storrington and Coolhan
£63 single, £88 double b&b, £145 suite

Set in ample, pretty gardens with its own one-acre lake and islands, this gracious, elegant and historic old hall has a country house atmosphere. The estate dates back to the 14th century, although the current house was built in 1910 after fire destroyed its predecessor. The 50-seat restaurant, spanning three interconnecting rooms of varied layouts, provides French nouvelle and traditional English cuisine (lunch £18.50, dinner £27.50) with French, German, Italian and Spanish wines. The oak-panelled drawing room faces south and is shaded by a canopy of wisteria and its dark-wood decor contrasts severely with the lighter shades of the dining room and cocktail bar. A 20-seat conservatory overlooks the water. Rooms vary widely (the best is the double-lake-aspect suite) although all have a huge German stool bath, comfortable beds and plenty of space. Additional facilities include an on-site helipad. Although not specially adapted, the hotel offers eight ground-floor rooms which may be suitable for the disabled.

Heated outdoor swimming pool (May to September); tennis court;

nine-hole pitch and putt course; walks to South Downs (maps
available); beach and watersports (eight miles away); coarse fishing
on lake (bring equipment)

STREATLEY

🏨 23/46 🛶 🐕 💳

The Swan Diplomat Hotel, Streatley-on-Thames, Berkshire
RG8 9HR   (Tel. 0491 873737)
In Streatley, just off the A329
£81 single, £113 double, £198 suite b&b
A sunny, spic-and-span and extremely professional Scandin-
avian-run hotel on the banks of the Thames, with pleasant
views of the old river bridge, and 23 acres of grounds. Giant
carp swim beneath bridges in the grounds (no fishing here!).
Inside the red-brick building, bedrooms are decorated in
muted pastels with mahogany furniture; over half have a river
view and some have riverside balconies. The cane, pink and
white restaurant seats 80 with many river-view tables and
serves classical French cuisine with set lunch at £18.50, dinner
£21.50 and à la carte meals for around £29.50. Light lunches
and teas are available for non-residents. A Magdalen College
barge moored alongside the hotel provides an excellent
cocktail party venue. Both the barge and the hotel's function
rooms contribute to its increasing success in the mini-
conference trade. There are two ground-floor rooms adapted
for the disabled and all public rooms and facilities are
accessible.
*Leisure club with gym and pool on site; watersports and fishing
nearby; walking; clay pigeon shooting; golf; squash; tennis; rowing
boats and bicycles may be rented*

SUDBURY

🏨 44/53 🛶 🐕 💳

The Mill Hotel, Walnut Tree Lane, Sudbury, Suffolk
CO10 6BD   (Tel. 0787 75544)
Off the A131 to Chelmsford
£45 single, £68 double b&b

Set on the River Stour with its own stretch of river for fishing, the 300-year-old mill features a restaurant and 'Meadow Bar' which are separated by the old mill wheel. Set in the old mill house, the restaurant seats 80 with seven water-view tables from which to enjoy a set lunch (£9.75), a set dinner (£14.50) or à la carte meals for about £19. The accommodation is in simple, individually styled bedrooms with pleasant views over the mill pond and surrounding acres of peaceful water meadows. On arrival at the reception lobby, guests may be fascinated (unnerved, even) by the presence of the mummified remains of a cat, which was supposed, in ancient times, to ward off evil spirits. The atmosphere of the mill is enhanced during the colder months by two roaring log fires in the day rooms. For overnight stays, the mill may be suitable for the disabled and access to the restaurant and bar is ramped.

Many interesting walks; excellent coarse fishing (prior notice required); golf (two miles away); many antique shops

SUTTON

The Anchor, Sutton, Ely, Cambridgeshire CB6 2BD
(Tel. 0353 778537)
Off the B1381
Open noon–3pm, 6.30pm–11pm Mon–Sat; noon–3pm, 7pm–10.30pm Sun

This 350-year-old inn is very much a winter pub, though well worth a visit in summer too. From the banks of the river at the Anchor, the views are exhilarating and it is an understandably popular spot with knowledgeable bird watchers as thousands of swans congregate in the surrounding flooded fens between November and February. The pub is spacious and simple yet traditional and homely, with log fires for cold, winter days. The landlord is most welcoming and enthusiastic about the locality, and very committed. There are no less than four bars, three of which are right on the water. There is an outdoor patio with seating and a very good bar menu offering fresh seafood, daily specialities and vegetarian meals. Three courses cost less than £10. Beers include Tolly bitter. The Anchor has specially adapted disabled toilets and wide doorways to public areas.

Walking; ice skating in winter when shallow meadow waters freeze;
fishing; very good bird watching (bird sanctuary nearby)

TEYNHAM

The Ship Inn and Smugglers Restaurant, Conyer Quay,
Teynham, Sittingbourne, Kent ME9 9HJ   (Tel. 0795 521404)
From Teynham, take signs to Conyer
Open 11am–3pm, 6pm–11pm Mon–Sat; noon–3pm, 7pm–
10.30pm Sun
A white-painted pub by a busy, working harbour with any
amount of history. The pub's interior, although somewhat
cramped, is convincingly decked out as a stone-walled
smugglers' tavern: strange dummies lurk silently in odd
corners; canvas-wrapped parcels are stacked on shelves;
silhouettes of furtive men and sailing ships stand poised against
the windows; and fishing nets hang from the ceiling. The
highly original nature of the pub's decor tends to obscure much
of the water view, but a small garden faces the boats on the
harbour water. The bar and restaurant bar have an extensive
snack menu including fresh oysters and fish daily. A full à la
carte restaurant meal costs in the region of £18 (open noon–
2.30pm, 7pm–10.30pm Mon–Sat; noon–3pm, 7pm–10pm
Sun). The pub's real speciality is the quantity of unusual drinks
on offer: there are nearly 160 wines, 250 whiskies (including
175 malts), 150 liqueurs and 50 brandies and rums. Children
are admitted to the restaurant only; dogs to the bar only. The
pub is not suitable for the disabled.
Saxon Shore Way walks; swale fishing; trout farm nearby;
Sittingbourne Sports complex; on-site Ship's Library for purchase,
exchange and reference

THAMES DITTON

The Albany Inn, Queens Road, Thames Ditton, Surrey
KP7 0QY   (Tel. 081-398 7031)
Open 11am–3pm, 5.30pm–11pm Mon–Sat; noon–3pm, 7pm–
10.30pm Sun

This large 1890s pub, originally built for the Duke of Albany's paramour, enjoys a spicy history and sits directly on the Thames riverbank with spacious car parking and extensive riverside terrace and garden seating. The roomy Victorian interior features a circular bar and predominantly dark-wood furnishings; there are excellent views across the Thames and to distant Hampton Court with its green expanse of grounds, river banks and boating. The pub lunches include a cold buffet and hot meals such as chicken in tarragon and mushroom, hot pots and steak and kidney pie; price range £3.95 to £4.25. Real ales include Bass and Charrington's IPA. No facilities for the disabled.

Walking; boats for hire at Hampton Court; river trips to Kingston and London; skiff and punting club; fishing in Albany Reach

TITCHWELL

Titchwell Manor, Titchwell, King's Lynn, Norfolk PE36 8BB
(Tel. 0485 210221)
On the main A149 coast road
£31 pp b&b
Formerly a manor house, this traditional hotel provides roaring log fires in winter and a warm and friendly family welcome. Set back from the main road and overlooking the Norfolk marshes and the sea beyond, the hotel has recently undergone a commendable facelift and now offers guests a comfortable, homely, Laura Ashley-style environment. Lunchtime bar snacks are available in the smaller dining area and the two restaurants (one of which has an attractive aspect over the salt marshes and sea) serve table d'hôte and à la carte meals with dinner priced at around £14.50. During the summer months, guests are invited to sit out in the pretty, walled rear garden adjoining one of the restaurants. The hotel has four ground-floor rooms and wide-access bathrooms which may be suitable for the disabled.

Walking; windsurfing (at Brancastle Snaithe two miles away); sailing; fishing can be arranged by the hotel; boat trips; nearby beaches; golf courses; cycle hire; bird watching

UPSTREET

The Grove Ferry Inn, Grove Ferry, Upstreet, nr Canterbury, Kent CT3 4BP   (Tel. 022786 302)
Off the A28 east of Upstreet
Open 11am–11pm Mon–Sat; noon–9.30pm Sun May–September (11am–2.30pm, 7pm–11pm Mon–Sat; noon–3pm, 7pm–10.30 pm Sun in winter)
The marvellously traditional and varied Grove Ferry Inn has three bars and gardens and two of each enjoy an appealing situation beside the River Stour. To the rear of the inn, a long stretch of landscaped river frontage has outdoor summer seating for at least 100 people, plus a beer garden shaded by a canopy of trees. Tastefully and warmly illuminated both in and out, the hotel is particularly attractive at night when the dozens of copper bells, pots, kettles and even coal scuttles suspended from the ceiling gleam amid the richly traditional decor. Beers served include Director's and the pub's own label 'Ferryman's', and there is an extensive restaurant menu with many daily specials. Food is substantial and English, with mixed grills, steaks, fish, chicken and various hot and cold snacks ranging from £3.95 to £9.95 per dish. Afternoon teas and children's meals are also available. Additional facilities include a 90-seat family room. At present, the pub is not suitable for the disabled, but the management plan to change this as soon as possible.
Walks through 11-acre picnic site nearby; Saxon way (one-week walk from Dover to Medway); Stodmarsh Nature Reserve (three miles away); hourly river boat trips from pub; rowing; cabin cruising; fishing (day tickets available from bailiff)

WADHURST

Newbarn, Wards Lane, Wadhurst, Tunbridge Wells, Sussex TN5 6HP   (Tel. 089288 2042)
Signposted from the B2099, on the Wadhurst to Ticehurst road)

£18–£20 pp b&b; self-catering cottages per week £142–£258
(sleeps two), £208–£377 (sleeps four–five)
A secluded, 17th-century farmhouse in a tremendous waterside setting. There is a pond to one side of the house, and in
front of it 15 acres of landscaped gardens descend to the edge of
Bewl Water – a vast man-made lake – which is the largest
stretch of water in the south-east and has a good 17-mile walk
round the circumference. The excellent views of the blue lake
below and hills beyond can be enjoyed from both the ground
and first floors of the hotel. The light decor in the bedrooms
complements the old pine floors and low ceiling beams. An
intimate dining room overlooks the water and seats six for
breakfast only. 'Carter's Cottage' and 'The Hopper's Hut',
two very attractive self-catering cottages, offer a good aspect
over Bewl Water, and feature homely log-burning stoves and
comfortable furnishings. Additional amenities include a games
room with table tennis, pool and darts. Not suitable for the
disabled.
Walks around the circumference of Bewl Water; National Trust
properties nearby; bicycles on loan; boat cruises; windsurfing;
canoeing; rowing from Bewl Water Visitors Centre (on the A21, 20
minutes away); trout fishery

WALTON-ON-THAMES

The Swan, 50 Manor Road, Walton-on-Thames, Surrey
KT12 2PF   (Tel. 0932 225964)
Open 11am–3pm, 5.30pm–11pm Mon–Fri; 11am–11pm Sat;
noon–3pm, 7.30pm–10.30pm Sun
This pleasant, Victorian, white-painted pub boasts a spacious
interior and a large attractive garden leading down to the road
by the River Thames. Its peaceful and relaxing location offers
views across the river to the facing houses and boats moored at
the river bank. Summer barbecues take place in the illuminated
garden (private barbecues can be arranged on request). The
pub interior may seem a little bland as the copper ornaments
and horse brasses are somewhat dwarfed by the enormous
rooms, but it is worth a visit for the roast Sunday lunch,

(reasonably priced at £6.95), or the considerable range of bar meals served daily (between noon and 3pm and 6pm and 9pm) at less than £10. The Swan serves Young's traditional beers. A separate cottage is available for private luncheons, meetings or seminars. No facilities for the disabled.

Walks along river; fishing (bring equipment); boat hire next door; two marinas nearby; public moorings for 10 boats

WANSFORD

The Haydock Hotel, Wansford, Peterborough PE8 6JA
(Tel. 0780 782223)
Signposted from the A1 and A47 near Peterborough
£70 single, £89–£110 (four-poster) double b&b
Restaurant open noon–2.30pm, 7pm–10pm
A gracious, golden stone-built coaching inn, dating back to the 17th century, on the edge of the River Nene. Despite its proximity to the A1 and A47, Wansford remains a peaceful village and provides an idyllic setting for a relaxing stay. The flagstoned entry hall, with antique seats and longcase clock, sets the scene for the gracious and plush atmosphere of hotel. The restaurant seats 95 people, is open to non-residents and offers mainly English cuisine, with dinner à la carte costing £18.50. The hotel counts two lounges (one of which is the setting for informal buffets at mealtimes), bar meals from 7.30pm to 10.30pm and a lovely, formal garden among its many other attractions. Bed and breakfast rates include early morning tea or coffee and morning papers. One *en suite* bedroom and a bathroom near the public areas are specially fitted for the disabled.

Walks; watersports at Ferry Meadows (five miles away); fishing (rod licence needed, available from the Anglian Water Authority in Oundle); pétanque courts; cricket field in hotel grounds

WINDSOR

🏨 ⁵⁴/⁹² � 🚫 ▭

Oakley Court Hotel, Windsor Road, Water Oakley, Windsor,
Berkshire SL4 5UR   (Tel. 0628 74141)
Off the A308 between Windsor and Maidenhead
£109–£430 per room/suite
With 35 acres of mature grounds reaching to the bank of the
River Thames, this imposing Victorian Gothic mansion offers
plush, though slightly characterless, rooms in keeping with the
building's historic background. Day rooms include an original
library, yellow and white river-view drawing room with
ornate plasterwork and billiards room complete with 300-
year-old table. Primarily suited to private functions and
corporate entertainment, the hotel boasts conference, banqueting and exhibition facilities for between four and 100
people, plus organized activity events for larger groups by
prior arrangement. The 120-seat Oakleaf restaurant offers four
water-view tables and highly reputed modern French cuisine
(set lunch £18.25, set dinner £27.50). Three-course lunches à la
carte cost about £24 and a full vegetarian menu is available. No
facilities for the disabled.
*Walking; fishing (hotel has own rights on river); archery, clay-
pigeon shooting, rally driving, hot-air ballooning and other group
activities by arrangement; croquet lawn; heliport; pitch and putt
course; riding nearby*

WINDSOR

🏨 ¹⁸/⁴⁰ 🛭 ◇ ▭

Sir Christopher Wren's House, Thames Street, Windsor,
Berkshire SL4 1PX   (Tel. 0753 861354)
On riverside at Windsor–Eton bridge
£89 single, £109 double, £119 premier double b&b
In keeping with its architectural appearance, this pleasant,
medium-sized hotel has tastefully decorated day rooms
furnished with antiques, including a soothing lounge with a
splendid marble fireplace. As its name suggests, the house was
originally designed and inhabited by Sir Christopher Wren in

1676 during his period as Member of Parliament for Windsor and it has a fascinating historical background complete with resident ghost. The river is clearly visible from many bedrooms (three superior rooms have riverside balconies) and 30 window seats in the 75–120-cover restaurant. Guests can select from a reasonable range of meals à la carte or opt for table d'hôte lunch and dinner at £12.50 and £18.50. During the summer months (from June until the weather becomes chilly) the hotel opens its additional river-view terrace restaurant. There is limited private parking and the hotel is not suitable for the disabled.

Walking; watersports; fishing

WOLVERCOTE

The Trout Inn, 195 Godstow Road, Wolvercote, Oxford
OX2 8PN   (Tel. 0865 54485)
Off the A40 north of Oxford (call for precise directions)
Open 11am–11pm April–August (11am–3pm, 6pm–11pm
September–March) Mon–Sat; noon–3pm, 7pm–10.30pm Sun
(all year). Restaurant open noon–2pm Mon–Sun; 7pm–10pm
Mon–Sat all year

This very pretty and highly traditional Bass Charrington 'Vintage Inn' spurns jukeboxes and games machines to preserve its idyllic and tranquil waterside setting beside the River Thames: peacocks wander along the river terrace and boats moor alongstream. There are no less than five bars, four of which overlook the water, including the original 800-year-old 'Stable Bar'. A sixth bar is planned for 1991. The pleasant restaurant offers tantalizing dishes such as jugged venison braised with vegetables, bacon and red wine (£11.95). Three-course meals average £15 and a variety of salads and grills, plus vegetarian meals (on request) are available. In the snack bar, prices range from £2.70–£6 with barbecues and an outdoor Pimms and champagne bar at evenings and weekends during summer. Drinks offered include a good selection of wines, malt whiskies and real live bitters; Bass Charrington's IPA. Additional attractions include function rooms, Christmas meals and an annual fireworks display on the inn's own river island. The inn is accessible to the disabled and an advance telephone call assures personal assistance from the helpful staff. *Walking; fish sanctuary*

WROXHAM

Hotel Wroxham, Broads Centre, Hoveton, Wroxham,
Norfolk NR12 8AJ   (Tel. 0603 782061)
£45 single, £69 double b&b
The town of Wroxham, considered to be at the centre of the Norfolk Broads, is a busy, major crossing point for both road and waterways and this modern hotel, which forms part of a shopping centre, is right on the water's edge. From many bedrooms and the restaurant, the hotel overlooks a local gathering point for boats and boat enthusiasts. Welcoming non-resident bookings, the restaurant offers a wide selection of à la carte meals, a carvery lunch for £4.25 and three-course carvery dinner at £10.50. For £18.50 both residents and non-residents can dance the night away to popular live music at the hotel's Saturday dinner dances. The hotel may be accessible for the disabled as it has ground-floor bathroom facilities and wide doorways.
Walking; boating (self-drive launch, £6.50); fishing from the quay (rod licence available locally, £1.50)

YALDING

The Anchor Inn, Twyford Bridge, Yalding, Kent ME18 6HG
(Tel. 0622 814359)
Off the A26, the Maidstone to Tonbridge Road
Open 10.30am–11pm Mon–Sat; noon–3pm, 7pm–10.30pm Sun
£25–£35 single, £40–£55 double b&b
A coaching inn in distant times, the Anchor became a bargees' inn when the Hampstead canal was cut in 1744, and it was extended to a hotel 200 years later. It is placed at the point

where the canal joins the River Medway, and so benefits from a double water frontage. The long canalside garden borders two sides of the inn. The ancient, thatched part of the pub is highly atmospheric, with ceilings that are disconcertingly low for the taller visitor (hence the doorway sign reading 'Duck or Grouse'), old timbers, crooked walls and exceptionally solid, traditional furniture. Good bar meals are available until 10pm daily and three of the inn's bars overlook either the canal or the river, as do eight of the modern, airy bedrooms. The steakhouse restaurant seats 33 and offers three-course meals for around £15 (open from 8.30am–midnight). Drinks in the bars include real ales, Webster's, Ruddles and John Courage best bitter. Although there are no special adaptations, both the hotel and restaurant may be accessible to the disabled.

Walks in fields and along Medway; canoeing and boating (boatyards nearby); fishing in season on canal and River Medway (rod licence from tackle shops)

The Isle of Wight

BEMBRIDGE

inn ~ 1/5 🏠 ◁ ▭

Crab and Lobster, Forelands, Bembridge, Isle of Wight
PO35 5TR   (Tel. 0983 872244)
Open 10.30am–3pm, 6pm–11pm Mon–Sat in summer (11am–
3pm, 6.30pm–11pm Mon–Sat in winter); noon–3pm, 7pm–
10.30pm Sun. Restaurant closed November–Easter
£13 pp b&b
This old country inn, dating from the early 19th century, is
situated in a unique clifftop position with panoramic views
over the Solent and the Channel. The two bars and restaurant
all sport the same nautical theme with an interesting array of
prints covering the walls. The timber and brick interiors of the
bar are complemented by pretty, cottage-style decor and
comfortable period furnishings. Low lighting creates a warm
atmosphere with a fun and lively ambience, and a wide range

of beers, ciders, wines and spirits is available. There is also an excellent choice of bar snacks on offer. The leaded bay window in the dining room affords some spectacular views and it is here that one can take advantage of the fresh seafood on the evening à la carte menu. The comfortable bed and breakfast accommodation offers perhaps the best value for money on the island. Very friendly staff. No facilities for the disabled.
Walking; watersports; fishing; beach

BONCHURCH

5/10

Peacock Vane, Bonchurch, Ventnor, Isle of Wight PO38 1RJ (Tel. 0983 852019)
£50 single, £80 double b&b
Peacock Vane is a charming house of outstanding character in a lush green setting, set among willow and beech trees and surrounded by beautifully landscaped gardens. While the style may not be to everyone's taste, the elegance found throughout the rooms is undeniable. Recently taken over, the owners have completely refurbished and carefully restored the entire hotel; the decor and furnishings reflect the grandeur of the Victorian era. Entrance is via the conservatory, where tea, coffee and snacks are served. This leads to the intimate Peacock Parlour (good for informal, bistro-type food). The formal Directors' dining room seats 16 people round the large oval table with a low hung chandelier. The larger Ivory Room restaurant (open to non-residents) is elegant and the cuisine already has a good reputation. The individually designed bedrooms all sport period paintings and antique furniture, tasteful decor and fully equipped *en suite* facilities that offer the height of luxury. In the drawing room again antiques and plush furnishings abound but despite the rich elegance, an air of relaxed cosiness reigns. The charming staff work with dedication and pride, courtesy and attention. No facilities for the disabled.
Walks on Ventnor Downs; surfing; fishing; beach

BONCHURCH

¶◯¶ ⚐ ◈ ▭

Teddy Bears Picnic, Village Road, Bonchurch, Isle of Wight
(Tel. 0983 855232)
Open 10.30am–9pm
The Teddy Bears Picnic is a delightful tea room and fully
licensed restaurant of some repute, set by the side of the pond
in the picturesque village of Bonchurch. It is small and simply
furnished and decorated; the low-walled terrace allows for
more guests during the summer. The terrace affords the best
views over the fish-filled pond, the wooded banks and thriving
activity on the pretty lane. Everything on the menu from the
cakes and snacks to full meals is home produced, and there is a
special children's menu. The Sunday lunch menu and table
d'hôte offer good value for money. The home-made cakes
attract the most attention here, and are thoroughly recommended even by the famous showbiz stars that frequent the
establishment. No facilities for the disabled.
Walking; fishing; beach

BONCHURCH

▦▦▦ 12/19 ⚐ ◈ ▭

Winterbourne Hotel, Bonchurch, Ventnor, Isle of Wight
PO38 1RQ   (Tel. 0983 852535)
£41–£48 pp b&b
Closed November–March
Winterbourne was home for Charles Dickens when writing
David Copperfield. In a letter to his wife, he described the house
and grounds as '. . . the prettiest place I ever saw in my life . . .'
It is a country house of considerable charm and character
combining an air of tranquillity with a good standard of
comfort. Set in beautiful grounds with extensive, well-tended
lawns and gardens, waterfalls, streams and a swimming pool,
it overlooks some remarkable coastline and the sea. The
spacious rooms are stylishly furnished and decorated, with all
conveniences provided and many concessions to comfort. The
romantic restaurant has an excellent reputation and uses fresh

local produce. A comprehensive wine list is also available. These splendid surroundings create a serene but informal atmosphere which is serviced by a genial host and friendly staff. No facilities for the disabled.

Walking; watersports; beach

CHALE

Clarendon Hotel and Wight Mouse Inn, Chale, Isle of Wight PO38 2HA   (Tel. 0983 730431)
£30 dinner and b&b

The Clarendon Hotel was once a coaching inn. Dating from the 17th century, it maintains its air of antiquity, character and charm and now provides excellent hospitality, with good standards of comfort, a wide range of food and wine and a selection of 365 whiskies! The friendly, helpful and attentive staff are headed by the proprietor, John Bradshaw, whose dedication and creativity won the establishment the award the Eon Ronay/Coca-Cola Best Family Pub of the Year in 1990. This was well deserved: there are good play areas and facilities for children both inside and out, and an impressive children's menu. The bedrooms are charmingly furnished with antique and period furniture. Home-from-home touches and fine paintings and prints set these rooms apart. The hotel dining room, with wonderful views of the sea, is comfortable and tasteful; a tremendous collection of English watercolours adorns the walls. The hotel and pub also offer a minibus service, available at special rates for ferry collection and island tours. May be accessible for the disabled.

Walking; watersports on nearby beaches; fishing; trout farm nearby; beach

COWES

Fastnet Restaurant, 124 High Street, Cowes, Isle of Wight PO31 7AY   (Tel. 0983 299251)
Open 10am–2.30pm, 7pm–10pm Mon–Sun

The Fastnet Restaurant is ideally situated on Cowes High Street facing the working marina and with views of the Solent. It is a long, narrow space but the simple, bright white decor and furnishings make it airy and light. The large front windows give panoramic views and lead on to the summer terrace where many of the rich and famous have dined while watching the thriving activity and the yacht races. Obviously, it gets very busy in and around Cowes Week, so booking is essential. The restaurant has an enviable reputation for serving fresh, local produce, cooked by the continentally trained chef. A comfortable and informal place with a convivial atmosphere generated by the friendly and good-natured staff. No facilities for the disabled.

Walking; watersports; fishing; beach

COWES

The Globe, The Parade, Cowes, Isle of Wight PO31 7QJ
(Tel 0983 293005)
Open 11am–11pm (10.30pm Sun) in summer; 11am–3pm, 6.30pm–11pm (10.30pm Sun) in winter
This attractive pub is located on the seafront of Cowes next to the working marina. Recently refurbished, the decor and furnishings are simple, stylish and elegant but with a relaxed, leisurely atmosphere throughout. The extensive menu caters for all palates and purses, from bar snacks through to full meals with the emphasis on fresh, local produce, and a good variety of vegetarian options. The two bars are divided into eating and drinking areas and there is a very agreeable conservatory (non-smoking). A wrought-iron spiral staircase leads from the dining area to the upper floor where private functions are held. The extensive views across the Solent to the mainland are really quite spectacular, especially when the boat races are underway. Friendly and helpful staff make for an enjoyable visit. May be accessible for the disabled.

Walking; watersports; fishing; beach

COWES

🏘 ㎡ 5/25 🏌 🕊 ▭

The New Holmwood Hotel, Queens Road, Cowes, Isle of
Wight PO31 8BW   (Tel. 0983 292508)
Restaurant open 12.30pm–2pm, 7.30pm–9pm
£65–£75 double, £100 suite b&b
A unique and lovely location on the quieter side of Cowes,
right by the water's edge and Egypt Point, affords this hotel
some panoramic views of the Solent and a wonderful vantage
point for sunsets. Recently taken over, the new proprietors
have refurbished both the hotel and restaurant in elegant style
using comfortable furniture and some beautiful furnishings
and fabrics. They've managed to keep the hotel's charm and
character, and also the helpful and friendly staff. Bedrooms are
individually decorated, and the luxurious *en suite* bathrooms
are something to write home about. The charming and
relaxing restaurant is tastefully decorated in subdued pastel
tones, and the views are magnificent. Following the com-
pletion of their extensive refurbishment programme, the hotel
now has a sun terrace with heated pool and spa bath, three
elegant lounges, a cocktail bar and conference facilities. Two
rooms adapted for the disabled.
Walking; watersports; fishing; beach; private moorings

FRESHWATER BAY

🏘 ㎡ 15/40 🏌 🕊 ▭

Farringford Hotel, Freshwater Bay, Isle of Wight PO40 9PE
(Tel. 0983 752500)
£22–£35 pp b&b
A gracious country house, once the home of Alfred Lord
Tennyson, the Farringford is steeped in history. It stands in 33
acres of beautiful parklands and gardens with sweeping views
of the bays and peninsulas of the island. With views of the sea
on one side, the hotel adjoins approximately 100 acres of
National Trust downlands on the other. Each of the attractive
and spacious rooms is traditionally furnished and decorated
with private bathroom, radio, television and direct dial

telephone. The large, elegant restaurant offers table d'hôte and à la carte menus making use of locally caught fish, island-grown vegetables and fresh farm produce (open 12.30pm to 2pm, and 7.30pm to 9.30pm). Candlelit dinner dances are very popular on Saturday nights. The views of the downs and golf course from the cocktail bar and the Tennyson drawing room are really quite spectacular. Mementoes of the famous poet are on display in the library. No facilities for the disabled.

Nine-hole golf course; tennis court; croquet lawn; bowling green; games room in hotel; walking; windsurfing; sea fishing at Yarmouth; beach

NITON

Buddle Inn, St Catherine's Road, Niton, Isle of Wight
(Tel. 0983 730243)
Open 11am–11pm Mon–Sat in summer (11am–3pm. 6pm–11pm Mon–Sat in winter); noon–2.30pm, 7pm–10.30pm Sun
Situated on the southernmost point of the island, this old smugglers' pub is a delightful collection of recently refurbished 16th-century buildings surrounding a central garden. It still retains many of its original features including the flagstone flooring and inglenook fireplace. Both the bars sport low-beamed ceilings and rustic furniture; the atmosphere is cosy, and locals and tourists can enjoy darts, pool and occasionally live music. There is a good choice of food on offer including ploughman's, salads and a variety of specials using the fresh seafood. Morning coffee, afternoon tea, snacks and cakes are available throughout the day. There are good parking facilities and coach parties are welcome. The inn may be accessible to the disabled.

Walking; fishing; beach; watersports (four miles away)

RYDE

Royal Esplanade Hotel, Esplanade, Ryde, Isle of Wight
PO33 2ED   (Tel. 0983 62549)

£25 pp b&b

Built in 1837, the Royal Esplanade offers good, old-fashioned sea-front grandeur. The ground floor has just been refurbished, with the slightly dated elegance replaced with new silk screens, plush fabrics and stylish furnishings. However, thanks to the dedicated staff, none of the comfortable and homely atmosphere has been lost. The hotel's amenities include a heated outdoor swimming pool for the summer months situated in a lovely palmed terrace garden. The bedrooms are spacious and comfortable; those at the front of the hotel are particularly attractive. Local beers are on offer at the bar. The lounge and bar areas have plenty of quiet character, and comfortable furniture. Although a listed building of some historical and architectural interest, this hotel still attains the same high standards expected of modern-day establishments. Some rooms may be suitable for disabled visitors.

Outdoor swimming pool; windsurfing (and tuition) nearby; golf; squash; tennis courts; equestrian centre; steam railway

SEAVIEW

The Old Fort, Esplanade, Seaview, Isle of Wight PO34 5HB (Tel. 0983 612363)

Restaurant open 7pm–10pm; closed Sun and Mon in winter.
Pub open 11am–11pm Mon–Sat; noon–3pm, 7pm–10.30pm Sun

Once a terrace of three cottages dating from the late 19th century, the Old Fort occupies a wonderful position right on the end of Seaview's esplanade, by the sea. Like many of the island's pubs, hotels and restaurants, the views are particularly impressive. This is a café, pub and restaurant, the latter on the upper floor. The café and pub boast a large menu that offers a selection of meals including vegetarian, hot and cold dishes, with much of the emphasis being on the locally caught seafood. There is also a good children's menu available. The friendly staff generate a comfortable atmosphere that is enlivened by the occasional theme nights and the pianist on Friday nights. The restaurant upstairs has a more formal environment. The stylish furnishings, complementing the panoramic views of the sea, make a visit here something special. There is disabled access to the pub, but not to the restaurant.

Walking; watersports (just yards way); fishing; beach

SHORWELL

The Crown Inn, Walker's Lane, Shorwell, Isle of Wight
PO30 3JZ　(Tel. 0983 740293)
Open 10.30pm–3pm, 6pm–10pm Mon–Sat; noon–3pm, 7pm–10pm Sun
In the exceptionally pretty village of Shorwell, this pub, dating from the early 15th century, was once a staging post. It is located in the heart of some truly historic sites with good access to all the other facilities on the island. The trout stream running through the charming, well-tended gardens plays host to a variety of wildlife including a flock of ducks. There is also a good play area for children. The intimate interior, with its low-beamed bars and welcoming log fires, is comfortably furnished with good facilities for families. A varied menu, including vegetarian dishes, offers value for money with all food made from fresh, local produce on the premises. The staff pay attention to comfort and detail which helps to make the Crown inn a perfect pitstop. The pub may be accessible for disabled visitors.

Walking; fishing at trout farm down the road; beach 10 minutes away

ST LAWRENCE

Old Park Hotel, St Lawrence, Ventnor, Isle of Wight
PO38 1XS　(Tel. 0983 852583)
Closed November–March, though open over Christmas
£27–£38 pp dinner and b&b
Old Park was once a small farm dwelling but over the years it has been enlarged and is now an imposing, Gothic-style grade II listed house. Away from the main road, it is set in

magnificent woodland with extensive grounds that reach to the sea. The decor and furnishings in the public areas reflect the grandeur and status of the house with chandeliers, heavy oak doors and gilt-edged mirrors in the comfortable lounge. The beamed bar area is well stocked and there is also a coffee shop open throughout the day serving light snacks. The spacious restaurant is simply but comfortably decorated and the managers pride themselves on being able to cater for special diets including strained or junior food for children. The family suites are one of the hotel's strongest points. The rooms in the west wing (more luxurious than those in the annexe) have recently been refurbished and many boast William Morris-design wallpaper and antique brass bedsteads. Some ground-floor rooms are suitable for disabled visitors.

Fully equipped leisure centre at hotel; popular tropical bird park; ornithology and murder mystery speciality weekends; walking; fishing; beach

TOTLAND

Waterfront Restaurant, The Promenade, Totland Bay, Isle of Wight PO39 0BQ   (Tel. 0983 754130)
Restaurant open 11am–2.30pm, 7pm–10pm Mon–Sun. Café open 10am–midnight in summer (11am–10pm in winter)
Not the best-looking building on the island, but talk to anyone and they'll recommend the food. The Anglo-French specials created from the fresh, local produce have an outstanding reputation. The dining area is pretty if simple but it provides an excellent vantage point from which to watch the passing of the famous cruise liners and spectacular sunsets over this action-packed bay. It is a lively venue serviced by friendly and jovial staff and due to its popularity, it really is essential to book in advance. The adjoining café serves coffee, tea, ice cream and a selection of snacks. It also provides a take-away service. The restaurant is accessible to disabled visitors.

Walking; jetskiing, waterskiing and surfing; fishing; safe beach

VENTNOR

The Spyglass Inn, Esplanade, Ventnor, Isle of Wight
PO38 1JX   (Tel. 0983 855338)
Open 11am–11pm Mon–Sat in summer (11am–3pm, 7pm–
11pm Mon–Sat in winter); noon–2.30pm, 7pm–10.30pm Sun
Reputed to be the mildest and most protected resort on the
island, the Spyglass inn sits at the end of this famous fishing
cove with its own seawall and terraces. The building used to be
the saltwater bathhouse and with the aid of sympathetic
refurbishment, the venue still boasts many of its original
features. There is the obligatory nautical and sailing theme to
its decor and furnishings, but take some time here. It is packed
with fascinating pictures and wonderful antiques that set off
the timbered interior perfectly. In summer, the terraces
become a hive of activity as the live entertainment gets into
swing with varied music – usually traditional jazz and blues.
There is a pianist playing every weekend. An extensive menu
ranges from ploughman's and burgers to fresh, locally caught
crab and lobster (which you can watch being brought up the
seawall to the inn). The pub serves its own real ale and offers
morning coffee and afternoon tea making everyone, young or
old, most welcome. There is wheelchair access to the pub.
Walking; Victorian boats for hire; fishing; beach

WHIPPINGHAM

Barton Manor Vineyard and Gardens, Whippingham, Isle of
Wight PO32 6LB   (Tel. 0983 292835)
Open 10.30am–5.30pm daily (1 May to second Sun in
October); weekends in April; Easter holidays
Although the £2.50 entrance fee to this wine bar and café may
seem a little steep – even if Princess Margaret has eaten there! –
the price of admission for Barton Manor is money well spent.
Visitors gain access to the vineyards, the beautiful and
extensive gardens and the award-winning restoration of Prince
Albert's farm buildings that house the winery, a wonderful

collection of V8 vintage cars and, of course, the wine bar. The wine bar offers a basic menu of excellent quality and sells English wine produced on the premises. The proprietor is keen to emphasize that their English wine is very different from 'British' wine. The lawns and gardens are beautiful and lovingly tended, boasting fabulous daffodil displays in spring, an outstanding water garden, a scented garden and the NCCPG's National Collection of 'Red Hot Pokers'. And, lest we forget the manor's justification for being included in these listings, there is a delightful lily-covered lake, home to a variety of wildlife including some stunning black swans. Just a stone's throw from Osborne House, Barton Manor is well worth a visit. No facilities for the disabled.

WHIPPINGHAM

IOI 🏠 🕭 ▭

The Folly Inn, Folly Lane, Whippingham, Isle of Wight
(Tel. 0983 297171)
Open 11am–3pm, 6pm–11pm every day (and longer in summer)
An extensive chalet-style building on the side of the Medina estuary, just south-east of Cowes. Simple, rustic furniture creates an atmosphere that is relaxed, informal and lively. The wood-panelled decor is teamed with cottage-style furnishings making the large areas more intimate and comfortable. Views of the boating and yachting fraternity on the estuary are fascinating: it's always a hive of activity down there. An excellent family room with games caters for children. The menu is kept simple but maintains a high quality and offers good value for money. The large terrace and garden provide ample seating to accommodate the summer crowds. The pub has its own moorings and pontoons with a water taxi service to and from the jetty adjoining the pub. Whippingham is a conservation area with a vast array of wildlife, all of which can be viewed from the pub itself. Good parking facilities are available. No facilities for the disabled.
Walks to Newport marina; sailing nearby; fishing

WHIPPINGHAM

Padmore House Hotel, Whippingham, East Cowes, Isle of
Wight PO32 6LP   (Tel. 0983 293210)
Closed Christmas week
£27–£35 per room
The hamlet of Whippingham is famous for its church,
designed by Prince Albert. Padmore House is situated next to
it, overlooking the river and Medina valley. It is a charming
and elegant ivy-covered building with a Jacobean elevation to
the rear and Queen Anne-style architecture at the front. The
grounds extend to five acres and incorporate formal lawns,
flowerbeds and paddocks. The house is decorated throughout
in traditional, pretty, cottage-style fabrics and furnishings
which create a relaxed and tranquil environment. The wood
panelling, period pieces and lace take you back to the more
genteel ambience of days gone by. The restaurant is equally
pretty and has a good reputation for the standard of its cuisine
served by efficient and courteous staff: Sunday lunches are
especially popular. The evidence on display in the lounge area
of Queen Victoria's visits paints a fascinating picture. No
facilities for the disabled.
Walking; sea fishing (two miles away)

WOOTTON BRIDGE

The Sloop Inn, Wootton Bridge, Ryde, Isle of Wight
PO33 4HS   (Tel. 0983 882544)
Open 11am–11pm Mon–Sat; noon–2.30pm, 7pm–10.30pm
Sun
The Sloop inn is located very close to Fishbourne and the
Portsmouth ferry. It combines eating and drinking areas
served by friendly staff in a relaxed and informal atmosphere.
The pub was converted from an old mill and is now one of
Whitbread's Brewers Fayre chain. The large interior is
attractively decorated and comfortably furnished with stylish
fabrics and furnishings. Being part of a chain, the pub is able to

offer an extensive range of facilities including all those for the disabled, an excellent family room and also a mothers' room. The eating area looks out over the marina where there are public moorings and the development of extra facilities for the sailing set in the pipeline. The menu is comprehensive, offering good value for money on their freshly prepared meals. There is wheelchair access and fully adapted lavatories for disabled visitors.

Walking; fishing nearby; beach

YARMOUTH

The Bugle Hotel, The Square, Yarmouth, Isle of Wight
(Tel. 0983 760272)
£40–£50 per room b&b
Once the distribution point for beer on the island, the Bugle boasts a 300-year history. Character and old-world charm are very much the key components to this simple but friendly hotel: nooks, crannies and winding corridors abound. The spacious bedrooms are simply but adequately furnished and decorated. All are comfortable. The beautiful, wood-panelled restaurant is elegant and intimate, serving food with an excellent reputation. The menu comprises seasonal dishes using fresh, local produce and includes fish brought in daily. The two bar areas, with occasional live music, serve bar snacks and meals and offer good value for money. The wood-panelling and heavy beams create an intimate and cosy ambience with a lively atmosphere provided by the mix of tourists and locals. Much is made of the courtyard garden where barbecues are served daily throughout the summer. Also of note are the special spit roasts. Staff are charming, friendly and dedicated in the pursuit of improving standards and customer comfort. No facilities for the disabled.

Walking; fishing; beach; watersports

YARMOUTH

George Hotel, Quay Street, Yarmouth, Isle of Wight
PO41 0PE   (Tel. 0983 760331)
Closed over Christmas
£22–£70 per room
Situated directly on the seafront, this gracious 350-year-old
house was once home to the governor of the Isle of Wight and
boasts Charles II as one of the more famous guests. There are
two bar areas that are elegant yet lively. The stylish pub is
decorated and furnished with humour on a nautical theme. The
dining areas are gracious and romantic, especially the conservatory. The food has a good reputation: menus are seasonal
and varied. The spacious rooms are full of character and charm
with wood panelling, elegant antique furniture, tasteful decor,
open fireplaces and home-from-home touches throughout.
The pretty and well-tended garden looks out across the water
and has the unusual features of its own lobster tank, from
which one can choose supper, and an extensive barbecue area;
the views are quite special too. A relaxed, informal atmosphere
pervades this establishment, with its genial owner and helpful,
friendly staff. The restaurant is accessible to disabled visitors,
but not the accommodation.
Walking; fishing; watersports; beach

*Wales and
the Heart of England*

Telegraph GUIDE

WALES AND WEST MIDLANDS

Anglesey

Holy Island

Red Wharf Bay

Llan

Llansan

BANGOR

inn

Betws-Y-Coed

SWYNE

Portmeirion

Abersoch

Bardsey

inn

Dolg

Penmaenpool

Aberdovey

CARDIGAN

ABERYSTWYTH

BAY

Aberaeron

CARDIGAN

DYFE

Fishguard

Dinas

Ramsey Is.

St David's

ST. GEORGE'S

Druidston

Haven

Skomer Is.

Little Haven

Ammanford

Skokholm Is.

Cresswell Quay

GLAMO

Tenby Is.

Caldey Is.

SWANSEA

BRISTOL

CHANNEL

CHANNEL

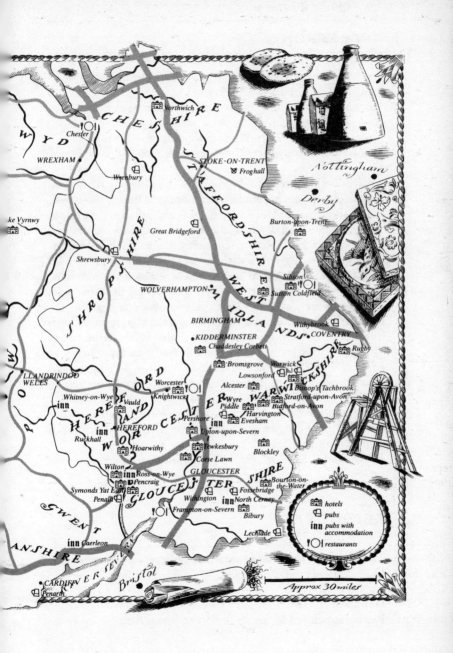

CHESHIRE

Northwich

Chester

WREXHAM

Wrenbury

ke Vyrnwy

STOKE-ON-TRENT

Froghall

Nottingham

Derby

Burton-upon-Trent

STAFFORDSHIRE

Great Bridgeford

Shrewsbury

SHROPSHIRE

WOLVERHAMPTON

WEST

MIDLANDS

Sibson

Sutton Coldfield

BIRMINGHAM

Withybrook

KIDDERMINSTER

COVENTRY

Chaddesley Corbett

Rugby

LLANDRINDOD
WELLS

Bromsgrove

Warwick

WARWICKSHIRE

Lowsonford

Worcester

Alcester

Bishop's Tachbrook

inn

Whitney-on-Wye

Vauld

Knightwick

Stratford-upon-Avon

HEREFORD

Wyre
Piddle

Bidford-on-Avon

Ruckhall

inn

HEREFORD

WORCESTER

Pershore

Harvington

Evesham

Hoarwithy

Upton-upon-Severn

Wilton

Tewkesbury

Blockley

inn

Ross-on-Wye

Corse Lawn

Pencraig

GLOUCESTER

Symonds Yat East

Penallt

GLOUCESTERSHIRE

Bourton-on-
the-Water

Withington

Fossebridge

inn

North Cerney

Frampton-on-Severn

Bibury

GWENT

Lechlade

inn   Caerleon

hotels

pubs

inn   pubs with
accommodation

ANSHIRE

RIVER SEVERN

Bristol

restaurants

CARDIFF

Penarth

Approx 30 miles

ABERAERON

The Harbourmaster Hotel, Quay Parade, Aberaeron, Dyfed
SA46 0BT   (Tel. 0545 570 351)
Junction of the A482 with the A487, the Cardigan to
Aberystwith road
Open noon–3pm, 7pm–11pm (noon–11pm in June, July,
August and September) Mon–Sat; noon–3pm, 7pm–10.30pm
Sun
A harbourside listed building, one of the oldest in Aberaeron
and originally the harbourmaster's house. Despite the name,
the Harbourmaster Hotel is actually a pub. Small and simple in
design with a friendly and unpretentious ambience, the pub
offers highly traditional decor with many old local photographs decorating the walls, and is extremely popular with
local fishermen. Both bar and the restaurant look out across the
boats in the harbour to the colourful houses on the other side;
in the summer, you can take drinks outside and sit on the
harbour wall. In the bar, a varied snack menu has recently been
introduced which offers selected light meals from eight
different countries and includes cold and Sunday lunches at
£3.50. Drinks from the bar include Marston's Pedigree and
Bass ale on draught. The restaurant makes maximum use of
fresh ingredients, including fish purchased from harbourside
boats, and serves cold lunches, Sunday lunches and à la carte
dinners: three-course meals cost from £7.20 to £18.50. No
facilities for the disabled.
*Pebble beach; crabbing; deep sea fishing trips can be arranged from
harbour*

ABERDOVEY

The Maybank Hotel and Restaurant, Aberdovey, Gwynedd
LL35 0PT   (Tel. 065 472 500)
Village on the A493
Hotel and restaurant closed 9 January–10 February.
Restaurant closed Mon–Sat to non-residents from

1 November–15 February
£21.45–£25.85 pp b&b; £33–£40.64 pp dinner and b&b
Set in the centre of a picturesque village perched between the
hillside and the coast, the hotel offers beautiful, restful views
over the village and the Dovey estuary from its large bay
windows. Bright, clean and light inside, both the Victorian-
style sitting room and the restaurant look out to pretty public
gardens directly opposite the hotel, and the sea beyond. A
three-course dinner from the à la carte menu costs about £17.
Bedrooms are attractive and offer many little extras. Children
under 10 stay at half price and under threes stay free if
occupying their parents' room. Dogs are accepted at a charge
of £1 per day and a small surcharge is applied to credit card
payments. Not suitable for the disabled.
Fishing in estuary; river fishing (licences available in village); sea
fishing (trips can be arranged in village); sailing at Dovey Yacht
Club; golf at village course; windsurfing (tuition available);
Outward Bound Centre courses in canoeing, sailing, rock climbing
and camping; RSPB sanctuary nearby; walking; beach

ABERDOVEY

9/11

The Penhelig Arms Hotel, Aberdovey, Gwynedd
LL35 0LT   (Tel. 065472 215)
Village on the A493
£26–£35 pp b&b
An outstanding restaurant and public bar are the focus of this
warm and welcoming harbourside hotel. All tables in the
restaurant overlook the sea and original three-course dinner
menus feature fresh game and local seafood and cost £14.50.
Local fishermen and dogs congregate in the bar, which may
well be the only one in Wales with bidets in the loos. In
summer, lunches from the varied bar menu can be eaten out of
doors at harbourside tables. All bedrooms have private
facilities with colour television, radio and tea-making equipment. There is wheelchair access to the restaurant and the bar.
Walking; pony trekking; windsurfing (tuition available); fishing in
estuary; river fishing (licences available in village); sea fishing (trips

can be arranged in village); beach; golf on 18-hole links course with reduced fees for guests; Outward Bound Centre with courses in canoeing, sailing, rock climbing and camping

ABERDOVEY

Plas Penhelig Country House Hotel and Restaurant,
Aberdovey, Gwynedd LL35 0NA   (Tel. 065 472 676)
Open mid March–December
£37.50–£40.50 pp b&b

A long, winding drive climbs up to this clifftop Edwardian country house with views south over the Dovey estuary and Cardigan Bay. Set in seven acres of beautiful listed gardens, with orchards, original Edwardian greenhouses and a unique walled kitchen garden, the hotel restaurant is almost completely self-supporting in organic fruit and vegetables. A pretty stone terrace with flowers and seating overlooks the water. Most of the tables in the restaurant (which seats 38 people) offer a water view while you dine; a three-course dinner costs from £14.50 and is sure to include locally raised meat and game or fish from nearby rivers. Traditional decor in public areas includes an oak-panelled entrance hall and beamed lounge with chintz-covered armchairs and open fire, stained-glass windows and fresh flowers. Bedrooms are modern and conventional; the most pleasant rooms are to be found in the turret. Local trains stop by request at the Penhelig Halt railway station at the bottom of the hotel drive. Hotel and restaurant may be accessible to the disabled.

Croquet green; putting green; walks in Snowdonia, Cader Idris; watersports; fishing can be arranged (bring equipment); golf; beach; bird watching; windsurfing; Outward Bound Centre nearby

ABERSOCH

The Porth Tocyn Hotel, Abersoch, Pwllheli, Gwynedd
LL53 7BU   (Tel. 075881 3303)
Two and a half miles south of Abersoch; hotel right at the end of the road

Open Easter–mid November
£30–£45 pp b&b
Converted from a row of miners' cottages and set in 25 acres of
its own farm land, this neat little hotel has been run by the
Fletcher-Brewer family for 40 years and both the atmosphere
and the proprietors, who have an exhaustive and highly
entertaining knowledge of local history, are wonderfully
unstuffy. The comfortable, chintzy sitting rooms with period
furniture, reading materials and plenty of fresh flowers, afford
excellent views from the Lleyn Peninsula over Cardigan Bay to
Snowdonia. There is a cosy, unobtrusive bar area. The
restaurant has a straightforward approach to good food and
much of the hotel's excellent reputation is based on the
successful mixture of conventional and adventurous cuisine:
choices range from a two-course meal with coffee at £16.50 to
the full-blown five-course menu with a wide selection of dishes
at a very reasonable £22. The wood-panelled, homely dining
room seats 50 and while most tables have a water view, five are
directly beside the window. There are three ground-floor
bedrooms available which may be suitable for the disabled.
*Tennis court; outdoor pool; a good base from which to explore the
beautiful Heritage Coastline with 26 unspoilt beaches and many
beautiful vantage points; plenty of walks (hotel offers its own book of
walks); watersports in Abersoch; sea fishing; riding can be arranged;
nine-hole golf nearby*

ALCESTER

🏠 9/18 🏇 ⬦ ▭

Arrow Mill, Arrow, Alcester, Warwickshire B49 5NL
(Tel. 0789 762419)
£60 single, £68–£84 double b&b
An attractive 19thcentury mill conversion with a history
dating back 900 years, Arrow Mill offers individually
decorated, spacious, pine-furnished bedrooms retaining
characteristic timber and brickwork. The public areas have
plenty of rustic charm with exposed beams and log fires which
provide a comfortable and intimate atmosphere; the original
water wheel, still driven by the mill stream, is displayed in the

Gun Room bar. The restaurant, which enjoys an excellent reputation and offers three-course meals for around £14.50 is manned by friendly and helpful staff and seats 72 with 11 water-view tables. The restaurant and the Gun Room and Miller's bars are open to non-residents. Development plans for the future include a stable conversion to provide 11 further ground-floor bedrooms, including one which will be specially adapted for the disabled.

Walks; fly fishing for trout on site; clay pigeon shooting; archery; coarse fishing; gliding and hot-air ballooning nearby

AMMANFORD

The Mill at Glynhir, Llandybie, Ammanford, Dyfed
SA18 2TE   (Tel. 0269 850 672)
Off the A483, on the Llandeilo road; (call for full directions)
Closed at Christmas
£29.50 pp b&b, £31.50–£37.50 pp dinner and b&b
A modern conversion of a 17th-century water mill, built on the steep side of a valley overlooking the Black Mountains of the Brecon Beacons National Park and walking distance from the ruins of Carreg Cennen Castle, perched on the edge of a 330foot-high cliff. A pretty stretch of the River Longhar runs through the garden and provides a mile of trout fishing. Bedrooms are modern and individually named after the many local castles and include the luxury Glynhir suite which incorporates the original stone wall of the mill. The noise of rushing water is clearly audible from all bedroom windows. Because of the steepness of the hill, the hotel is built on several levels with access to the front door and reception via a small footbridge. Both the 30-seat dining room and the sitting room are decorated in modern style but retain the 3-foot-thick walls of the old mill. Three-course meals with coffee cost from around £12.50. Additional attractions include a subterranean indoor pool with underwater jet stream, and views out on to the valley and the remains of an ancient steel foundry in the hotel grounds. £1 a day charge for dogs. No facilities for the disabled.

Walking (Brecon Beacons National Park); trout fishing at hotel, sea trout and salmon fishing locally; 18-hole golf (free to residents, equipment hire organized in advance on request); riding nearby

BETWS-Y-COED

🏨 7/13 🏠 ⬦ 💳

Ty Gwyn Hotel, Betws-y-Coed, Gwynedd LL24 0SG
(Tel. 06902 787)
On the A5, 100 yards south of Waterloo bridge before entering village
£17–£35 pp b&b, some four-poster beds
Charming and cheerful 'olde-worlde' 17th-century coaching inn, furnished with lovely antiques and situated in the Vale of Conwy town known locally as the 'Gateway to Snowdonia'. The hotel offers cosy and comfortable accommodation, with traditional public areas including an ancient beamed bar area complete with inglenook, log fires, oak settles and deep window seats overlooking the River Conwy. The chintzy restaurant offers a good selection of reasonably priced dishes using many local ingredients, including a set three-course meal at £12.95. Light meals are also available from the extensive bar menu. Four-poster and half-tester bedrooms are available. All rooms are tastefully furnished and come complete with the sound of rushing water – light sleepers be warned! Topping the range is the Alpine suite, offering a private lounge, balcony and health spa tub. A small patio at the rear of the hotel overlooks the valley. The Bunkhouse behind the inn is well-suited to group bookings and provides accommodation for 24 at £8 pp b&b. One ground-floor room is AA approved as suitable for the disabled.
Golf; climbing; walking; watersports (seven miles away); fishing (salmon, sea trout and trout)

BIBURY

🏨 12/18 🏠 ⬦ 💳

Bibury Court Hotel, Bibury, Cirencester, Gloucestershire
GL7 5NT   (Tel. 028574 337/324)

Bibury on the A433 between Burford and Cirencester; hotel
stands behind the church
£40–£45 single, £60–£66 double b&b

Once a family residence, this beautiful Jacobean mansion of
outstanding dimensions enjoys a glorious setting in six acres of
private grounds bordered by the River Coln. Reputedly visited
by Charles II and the Prince Regent, the hotel's history
includes a celebrated period of litigation which is said to have
inspired Charles Dickens's *Bleak House*. A true reminder of the
age of gracious living, Bibury Court is elegant, tasteful and
spacious throughout with panelled rooms, four-posters and
much fine antique furniture. Additional facilities include a
cocktail bar, television salon, pool room and conference
rooms. A relaxed atmosphere is created by the charming and
informal proprietors who run the establishment as a country
house rather than a hotel. Restaurant prices average £15 for a
three-course meal. Short-break rates are available on request.
No facilities for the disabled.

Interesting walks; tennis; squash; golf; sailing, windsurfing,
waterskiing, jetskiing and more at nearby Cotswold water park;
riding and shooting (by arrangement); racing; croquet, putting and
fishing on site

BIBURY

🏨 ≈ 10/20 🐕 👜 ▭

The Swan Hotel, Bibury, Cirencester, Gloucestershire
GL7 5NW   (Tel. 028574 204)
On the B4425 (A433) between Burford and Cirencester
£45 single, £85 double b&b

A picturesque, 18th-century, creeper-clad, Cotswold-stone
coaching inn enjoying a central location in the village of
Bibury. Set in immensely pretty gardens from which a natural
spring descends to the River Coln, the inn retains much of its
original character with comfortable lounges, traditionally
presented restaurant and individually decorated cottage-style
bedrooms of varying sizes. The Swan will be undergoing
large-scale refurbishment and renovation between January and
March 1991, although the new owners intend to retain and

complement the original character and traditional style of the premises. Plans include fully *en suite* facilities with spa bath for the newly decorated cottagey bedrooms and refitting the elegant 1930s restaurant and bar area. A four-course dinner in the restaurant costs £22.50; Sunday lunch £16.50. Many bar meals and snacks, including afternoon cream teas in the lounge, are available with the upper price band at around £8 for a three-course meal. An outside seating area with river view is planned for the present courtyard. Restaurant and bar may be accessible for the disabled.

Interesting walks; trout fishing (for hotel residents); sailing, waterskiing, jetskiing, windsurfing and more at nearby Cotswold water park; tennis, squash and golf nearby

BIDFORD-ON-AVON

White Lion Hotel, High Street, Bidford-on-Avon,
Warwickshire B50 4BQ   (Tel. 0789 773309)
By the bridge in the centre of the village
Restaurant open noon–2pm three days a week according to demand; 7pm–9pm Sun–Thurs; 7pm–9.30pm Fri–Sat
£50 single, £70–£85 double b&b
Visitors to this half-timbered and whitewashed house situated on the banks of the Avon are sure to appreciate the quiet, waterside location with views across to Bidford's picturesque eight-arched bridge and the rolling Cotswolds. The recently refurbished, intimate bar exudes a comfortable and relaxed atmosphere and the pretty, informal 40-seat restaurant, with a river-view balcony, has started to build a good reputation with visitors. Specializing in fresh fish dishes but also offering vegetarian meals, the restaurant has a good à la carte menu with three-course meals in the region of £18 per person, while the bar menu concentrates on lighter meals for £2.95–£5.75. The neatly maintained bedrooms are decorated in Laura Ashley style. The hotel's welcoming atmosphere is enhanced by friendly and helpful staff but it is not suitable for the disabled.

Gliding club with micro-lighting nearby; boat; children's play area; fishing and mooring rights on River Avon; hot-air ballooning nearby

BISHOP'S TATCHBROOK

🏨 ≈ 4/10 ⌂ 12 ✗ ▭

Mallory Court Hotel, Harbury Lane, Bishop's Tatchbrook,
Leamington Spa, Warwickshire CV33 9QB
(Tel. 0926 330214)
Off the A452 out of Leamington Spa, follow signs to Harbury
£95–£190 double, £325 double suite b&b
This large country house hotel, a member of the prestigious
Relais et Chateaux group, is set in the heart of rural Britain, in
10 acres of private grounds encompassing extensive lawns,
formal rose garden and water and herb gardens. Converted in
1913 from a private residence, Mallory Court has 10
individually decorated and named rooms of the very highest
standard and benefits from lovely views across the beautiful
rolling countryside of the northern edge of the Cotswolds. The
Blenheim suite is particularly splendid with an art deco bath
and trompe-d'oeil painted ceiling. The attractive panelled
restaurant, open to non-residents, seats 50 with six water-view
tables and offers modern French classical cuisine with menus
which are light and innovative, created using fresh herbs and
vegetables from the estate gardens. The set lunch costs £22.50;
set dinner £38.50. The hotel features an elegantly presented
pink lounge and drawing room for reading or relaxation and is
well placed for exploring Warwick, Leamington Spa and
Stratford-on-Avon. Restaurant may be accessible to the
disabled.
Tennis court; croquet; outdoor pool; squash court

BOURTON-ON-THE-WATER

🏨 ≈ 4/12 ⌂ ✗ ▭

The Old Manse Hotel, Victoria Street, Bourton-on-the-
Water, Gloucestershire GL54 2BX   (Tel. 0451 20642)
£37.50 single, £60 double b&b
A lovely country hotel at the centre of what must be one of the
quaintest Cotswold villages. Accommodation is in individually decorated rooms with pretty furnishings, including a
honeymoon suite with *en suite* double spa bath and one room

with a half-tester bed. The spacious bar – with an open fireplace which is lit in winter – serves a variety of basket meals, seafood, meat and pasta dishes at lunchtime as well as offering a cold-buffet counter. Two- and three-course lunches or four-course dinners in the warm and attractive restaurant cost £7.95, £8.75 or £14.75 respectively, and a varied vegetarian menu is on offer. Special two-day breaks are available from £75 per person per two nights including breakfast and dinner. The ground floor is adapted with ramps and specially fitted bathroom facilities for the disabled, making the restaurant easily accessible although an overnight stay is not recommended.

Walking; fishing can be arranged through hotel; motor museum; model railway museum; perfumery; Birdland; model village

BROMSGROVE

Grafton Manor, Grafton Lane, Bromsgrove, Worcestershire B61 7HA   (Tel. 0527 579007)
In Bromsgrove, off the A438 and Worcester Road
£80–£165 per room b&b
Commissioned in 1567 and rebuilt in the early 18th century, this beautiful Grade II listed manor house in stone and pink brick is surrounded by 30 acres of lovely grounds bordering a lake. The hotel has been painstakingly restored and is carefully tended by a charming family who offer gracious dining and accommodation in rooms of individual character equipped with all modern conveniences. The dining room seats 48 and offers a set three-course lunch at between £15.50 and £21.50 and a four-course dinner at £27.50. The lake in the hotel's grounds is preserved as a swan sanctuary and the only tiny blot on the landscape is the sight of the motorway. Discreet estate maintenance and improvement is continually underway, including the planting of a natural screen of 1500 trees to mask the motorway view. Pets are not accepted in the hotel although kennels are available in the grounds. The manor is accessible to wheelchairs and may be suitable for disabled guests.

Walking; golf nearby

BURTON-UPON-TRENT

Riverside Inn Hotel, Riverside Drive, Branston, Burton-upon-Trent, Staffordshire DE14 3EP   (Tel. 0283 511234)
Off the A5121 to Burton-upon-Trent
£26–£55 single, £48–£65 double b&b
The focus of this light, airy and formal hotel set in an original but much-modernized inn is its large and highly reputed riverside Garden Room restaurant, which seats 180 diners and caters for both private and business clients. Seven water-view tables are available from which to enjoy international and traditional English cuisine. River views are extremely pleasant and a neat garden extends from the hotel to the river bank. Decor is straightforward and largely pink and the bedrooms, although sometimes limited in space, are well maintained and equipped and set in a separate wing of the building. The hotel has a largely commercial clientele and it is therefore less expensive to visit at the weekend than midweek. Additional facilities include a bar, lounge, three banqueting rooms (seating a total of 150) and hotel golf course. The restaurant is accessible to wheelchairs although an overnight stay is not recommended for the disabled.
Walking; watersports; coarse fishing on River Trent; fly fishing nearby; three local golf courses; race meetings at Uttoxeter and Nottingham (40 minutes away); nearby Meadowside sports complex offers swimming, squash and saunas

CAERLEON

The Hanbury Arms, Uskside, Caerleon, Gwent
(Tel. 0633 420361)
On the A4236, just before Caerleon bridge
Open noon–3pm, 6pm–11pm Mon–Sat; noon–3pm, 7pm–10.30pm Sun
Rooms open summer 1991, £15–£20 pp b&b
Ancient and basic, the Hanbury Arms is an original 16th-century inn located in an area of great historical interest; not

only does the fortress of Isca (AD 75) mark Caerleon as one of the most important Roman military sites and the third principal Roman garrison in the UK, but it is also considered to be one of the possible locations of Camelot. Tennyson and Arthur Machen have been numbered among its patrons. There is a lounge bar and a public bar overlooking the River Usk, which produces exceptionally high tides. In the bar, beers served include Hancock's HB and draught Bass and snacks are available. In summer, a large beer garden on the water's edge seats 100 for outdoor drinking. The inn is reached via two shallow steps and, although not specially adapted, it may be accessible to the disabled.
Roman amphitheatre; Roman baths and exercise halls; legionary museum (Tel. 0633 423134)

CAMBRIDGE

The George Inn, Bristol Road, Cambridge, Gloucestershire
GL2 7AL   (Tel. 0453 890270)
On the A38, the Bristol to Gloucester road
Open 11am–2.30pm, 6.30pm–11pm Mon–Sat; noon–3pm, 7pm–10.30pm Sun. Closed 25 and 26 December
A pleasant garden on the banks of the River Cam offers pretty riverside seating for patrons of this comfortable, well-aintained pub which runs regular special events and theme evenings providing different bar dishes from around the world. Large, relaxing and set in an idyllic rural area, the George inn offers cosy, cottage-style surroundings, lively staff and an excellent location for family excursions to many places of historic interest. During the summer months the pub operates a garden barbecue and grill beside the river. Overlooking the river, the traditional bar/restaurant seats 146 people in five areas (40 seats have a view of the river) and offers an extensive à la carte menu costing about £8 for a three-course meal. Specialities include a variety of fresh fish dishes and unusual regional recipes such as 'Kromskies' (otherwise known as deep-fried, diced and breadcrumbed

gammon, beef and lamb). Beers served include Boddington's. The pub may be accessible for the disabled.

Many interesting walks including the late Sir Peter Scott's Wildfowl Sanctuary at Slimbridge, one mile's walk away; salmon fishing in the River Cam and the Gloucester Sharpness canal

CHADDESLEY CORBETT

Brockencote Hall, Chaddesley Corbett, nr Kidderminster,
Worcestershire DY10 4PY   (Tel. 0562 777876)
On the A448, the Bromsgrove to Kidderminster road
Closed 26 December–mid January
£63–£106 per room b&b

An impressive Georgian house set in 70–acre grounds encompassing a lake which is home to Canada geese, ducks, herons and occasionally swans. Public areas are light and airy with stripped pine and maple doors and handsome panelling and include a small but bright reception lounge with marble fireplace. The individually decorated bedrooms of varying sizes boast every convenience and are elegantly styled and furnished with quality dark wood. *En suite* bathrooms are mainly modern although a few retain period pre-war fittings. The hotel offers a comfortable relaxed atmosphere with friendly and helpful service. Seating 45, the dining room provides a set lunch for £16.50 and a three-course dinner for £25.80. An excellent location both for conferences and country visits, with on-site secretarial and laundry facilities, but not suitable for disabled visitors.

Walks in grounds and Wyre Forest; Warwick Castle, crystal factories, and safari park nearby

CHESTER

Telfords Warehouse, Tower Wharf, Raymond Street, Chester
(Tel. 0244 390090)
Call for directions

Bar open 11.30am–3pm, 6pm–11pm Mon–Sat; noon–3pm,
7pm–10.30pm Sun
Restaurant open 7pm–10pm Mon–Thurs; 7pm–10.30pm Fri
and Sat; noon–2.15pm and 7pm–10pm Sun
Named after the builder, Thomas Telford, this converted 250-
year-old brick-built warehouse spans the canal and is decorated
with many canal pieces, including the original crane which is
still found in the beamed building. Formerly a storage house
for coal, flour and grain, in 1987 the warehouse was converted
to a friendly and cheerful 92-seat restaurant specializing in
good, cheap Italian cuisine but also offering a traditional
English à la carte menu. Three-course Italian pizza or pasta-
based meals are available for approximately £7; three-course
English à la carte meals for around £10. Four water-view tables
are available in the restaurant and the open and spacious pub,
with full glass frontage affording an excellent canal view,
serves real ales including Theakston's bitter. Quite difficult to
find if you are approaching by road but a good stopping-off
point if you are on the canal. Live jazz during Sunday lunch.
No facilities for the disabled.

CORSE LAWN

Corse Lawn House Hotel, Corse Lawn, Gloucestershire
GL19 4LZ   (Tel. 045 278 479)
Off the A417, the Gloucestershire to Ledbury road, on the
A4211
£65 single, £85 double b&b
An elegant two-storey Grade II listed red-brick Queen Anne
house decorated and furnished with exquisite taste and style
throughout. The hotel is situated on a long and graceful
common complete with fringed trees, hedges and scattered
houses. A new bedroom wing has been erected and tones
sympathetically with the original building. The hotel's calm
and attractive front lawn sports a large duck pond and pretty
garden seating. The bar area offers light meals and snacks and
the restaurant provides provincial French cuisine and an
extensive wine list, with weekday lunches at £15.50; Sunday

lunch at £17.50 and dinner at £22.50 every day. Lunch is served from noon to 2pm, dinner from 7pm–10pm, and non-residents are welcome. Two private dining rooms, seating a total of 55 diners, are available for private functions. The hotel enjoys a good reputation for quality food and service in a relaxed and comfortable atmosphere and has five ground-floor rooms with specially fitted *en suite* facilities for the disabled.

Walking; fishing; croquet; tennis; swimming pool (open air); riding

CRESSWELL QUAY

The Cresselly Arms, Cresswell Quay, Dyfed SA68 0TH
(Tel. 0646 651210)
Village signposted off the A4075
Open 11am–3pm, 5pm–11pm Mon–Sat; noon–3pm and 7pm–10.30pm Sun

The delightful old stone creeper-clad pub in the Pembroke-shire Coast National Park is frequented by both car and boat traffic, though the boaters have to leave with the tide. The interior is traditional, with a high beam and plank ceiling, wall benches, red and black flooring tiles and simple furnishings. The pub has two bars with open fireplace or working Aga, one of which overlooks Cresswell Quay Creek. Beers served include Hancock's HB, tapped from barrels behind the bar, and a local brew nicknamed 'Firewater'. Light meals on offer are fairly limited but keenly priced and include sandwiches for 50p and ploughman's lunch at £1.50; the sides of Welsh bacon hanging above the Aga have been known to yield slices to peckish locals. Picnic tables are situated on the quay with a view over the creek. The pub may be accessible for the disabled but does not offer adapted facilities.

Fishing from quay; private fishing (a quarter-mile stretch, permits available from Cresselly Estate, equipment not supplied); walking

DINAS

The Sailors Safety Inn, Pwll Gwaelod, Dinas Cross, Dyfed
SA42 0SE   (Tel. 03486 207)
Bar and restaurant open 11am–11pm seven days a week
Situated right at the end of the isolated cove of Pwll Gwaelod,
below windswept Dinas Head on the famous Pembrokeshire
coastal path, this wonderful 16th-century pub, once a
smugglers' haunt, has all the right ingredients: a bottomless
pool, the ghost of Black Bart, and the original wrecker's light
illuminating the entrance to the bar. Decor is refreshingly
simple, with a warm, relaxed atmosphere enhanced by a fine
old stone fireplace, whisky-keg seats and fishing nets that lend
a nautical air. The magnificent oak bar was originally a ship's
dresser, brought back from Calcutta in 1922. The pub is
renowned for its food, both in the Galley (bar snacks and
lunch) and Aux Parots (French cuisine; set dinner £15)
restaurants, and for its range of real ales. In the summer, there
are seats outside overlooking the bottomless pool. Fairly easily
accessible for the disabled.
Small private beach below pub; rod and line fishing from cove

DOLGELLAU

Borthwnog Hall Country House Hotel and Restaurant,
Bontddu, Dolgellau, Gwynedd LL40 2TT   (Tel. 0341 49271)
On the A496, the Dolgellau to Barmouth road, by the toll
bridge across the Mawddach estuary
£34 pp b&b, £45 pp dinner and b&b
A perfect example of a Regency country house, which looks
out over the estuary to the Aran mountains to the east, and
Cader Idris to the south. The hotel stands in beautiful grounds
adjoining the RSPB nature reserve of Garth Gell and is
centrally placed for walking or touring the Snowdonia
National Park. Bedrooms are decorated with individual
character and public areas are homely and welcoming with
open fires during the winter months. Drinks may be taken in

the hotel's garden or on the 600-foot promenade-style waterside terrace. The dining room, seating 28, offers set dinner for £12.25 and a three-course à la carte meal set at around £16.50 per person. The hotel may well be unique in that it has its own art gallery, set up by owner Vicki Hawes, which shows original paintings, sculptures and pottery by Welsh artists. The gallery is open daily from 10am to 5pm and prices start at £20. Borthwnog Hall is unfortunately not suitable for the disabled although the restaurant is accessible.

Canoeing and windsurfing on estuary; golf at Dolgellau and Harlech; Snowdonia National Park

DRUIDSTON HAVEN

The Druidston, Druidston Haven, nr Haverfordwest, Dyfed SA62 3NE   (Tel. 0437 781 221)
Two miles north of Broad Haven, on the cliff above Druidston Haven
£24 pp b&b; four cottages, two with water view, each sleeps five–eight people £170–£380 per week; party bookings only 4 November–14 December, and 6 January–14 February
Perched directly above the quiet and unspoilt Druidston beach, this is a delightfully unconventional hotel with few rules or formalities. There is homespun decor and simple accommodation and it is a haven for those who love the outdoors or informal artistic, music, craft and theatre evenings. The restaurant and flagstoned cellar bar open out on to a terrace with spectacular views of St Bride's Bay. The inventive home cooking, presented with flair, uses many fresh local ingredients and ranges from Mexican, through Indonesian and Indian, to Italian and Welsh. Dinner costs between £13 and £16, including wine, and can be prepared for almost any special dietary needs if advance notification is given. Accommodation is in simple, spacious bedrooms which are comfortable but do not feature the usual hotel gadgetry. There is not only accommodation for the disabled but also activities with instruction for disabled group bookings.

Beach; climbing, sea-canoeing and field archery instruction on the premises; riding on beach; walks on Pembrokeshire Coast National Park footpath; windsurfing courses locally; scuba diving; beach fishing below house (river and reservoir fishing seven to 10 miles away, trout pool one mile away)

EVESHAM

Riverside Hotel and Restaurant, The Parks, Offenham Road, Evesham, Worcestershire WR11 5JP   (Tel. 0386 446200)
Off the B4510, the Offenham road
£50–£75 per room b&b
Set in three acres of grounds by the River Avon, this comfortable country house hotel enjoys a scenic location in a former 15th-century deer park once belonging to Evesham Abbey. The hotel is prettily decorated with attractive furnishing in the thematically designed bedrooms, all of which have *en suite* bathrooms and a view of the garden sloping to the river and vale beyond. A garden terrace, seating 50, with river view, is used for light meals or drinks when the weather permits. The elegant dining room, with large bay windows looking out to the river, specializes in English and French cuisine, and makes maximum use of local ingredients; the set lunch costs £12.95, the set dinner £15.95. Lunchtime snacks are also available in the downstairs bar from Monday to Saturday. Reduced-price short breaks are available. No facilities for the disabled.
Fishing (equipment provided); private moorings; hire boats available at the hotel

FISHGUARD

Hotel Plas Glyn-y-Mel, Lower Town, Fishguard, Pembrokeshire SA65 9LY   (Tel. 0348 872296)
Hotel signposted from Lower Town
Open March–October
£35 single, £30 pp twin b&b
Situated two minutes from Fishguard harbour, this sheltered Georgian country house overlooks the River Gwaun, which

runs through the hotel's 20 acres of secluded grounds complete with a hermit's cave and well. The atmosphere of the hotel is very much that of a private house, with antique furniture and open fires in public rooms. All bedrooms have tea and coffee-making facilities and the two double-bed suites afford excellent family accommodation. The restaurant offers interesting modern cuisine (set dinner £16) with the emphasis on seafood and local produce, plus a balanced selection of wines. Dogs are accommodated by prior arrangement at a cost of £2 per day. Additional attractions include a cosy, river-view lounge, a bar with an unusual period fireplace and a conservatory, with productive vines and a fig tree, overlooking the gardens. No facilities for the disabled.

Hotel has quarter-mile of salmon and trout fishing on the River Gwaun (bring own equipment); beach nearby, and Newport Sands (nine miles away)

FOSSEBRIDGE

The Fossebridge, Fossebridge, nr Cheltenham,
Gloucestershire GL54 3JS   (Tel. 0285 720721)
Bar open noon–2pm, 6pm–9.30pm Mon–Thurs; noon–2pm, 6pm–10pm Fri and Sat; noon–2pm, 7pm–9.30pm Sun
£75 double b&b

A delightful Georgian house that is tastefully decorated throughout and sports some really exquisite fabrics. A Tudor coaching inn attached to the house contains the Bridge bar and the Bridge bar restaurant, for informal meals, with main courses costing from £5.50 to £12.50: there are exposed beams and an inglenook fireplace that creates a warm cosy atmosphere. The main hotel restaurant is situated on the first floor, seats 60 people and overlooks the River Coln (open noon to 2pm and 6pm–9.30pm; the table d'hôte menu costs about £22 for three courses). The hotel is surrounded by four acres of grounds, which include a trout lake. No facilities for the disabled, though there are no stairs into the bar.

Fishing (for residents, on trout lake); golf at Cirencester (six miles away); walking; riding nearby

FRAMPTON-ON-SEVERN

🍴 🏠₁₂ ✂ ▭

Savery's Restaurant, The Green, Frampton-on-Severn,
Gloucestershire GL2 7EA   (Tel. 0452 740077)
Off the A38 at the end of Frampton Green
7pm–9.15pm (last orders); closed Sun and Mon
Set in one of the most beautiful villages in the area, and on the
longest village green in the country, the restaurant can seat 24
people. On warm evenings, customers often wander, glass in
hand, to look at the swans on the nearby pond. The small,
intimate cottage-style restaurant is attractively furnished in
pink with prints, plants and ruched curtains and offers a
blackboard menu that for the main is straightforward and
British, including salmon from the Wye or Severn rivers. The
set dinner, with a choice of five dishes per course, is priced at
£19.95. Run by friendly proprietors who have a wide
reputation for quality and excellent service, the restaurant is
situated in an area offering many river views and walks,
although there is no direct view of water from the tables. May
be accessible for the disabled.
*Interesting walks; watersports; riding; fishing (information provided
at the hotel); rivers in all directions within a quarter of a mile*

FROGNALL

🍴 🏠 ✂ ▭

The Wharf Restaurant, Foxt Road, Frognall,
nr Stoke-on-Trent, Staffordshire ST10 2HJ
(Tel. 0538 266486)
Off the A52, the Stoke to Ashbourne road
Open 7.30pm–9.15pm (last orders) Tues–Sat; noon–1.30pm
Sun. Closed Mon
A beautifully restored family-run restaurant in an old canalside
warehouse, set in a designated picnic area at the end of the
Caldon canal. Modernization has not diminished the charm of
the Wharf which is very tastefully decorated, with many wood
furnishings. A small but colourful garden surrounds the
entrance and provides the perfect spot for whiling away a long,
warm summer's evening. The friendly owners, who live on a

canal boat behind the restaurant, set great store by substantial home-produced cooking; even the bread is baked on the premises. The adventurous and experimental menus (which always include vegetarian options) change three times a year and offer a set five-course Sunday lunch for a very reasonable £11.50 or an extensive à la carte menu averaging £17 for a three-course meal. Seating is available for up to 32 guests. No facilities for the disabled.

Interesting walks; canoeing is possible; fishing (licence required); canal walk

GREAT BRIDGEFORD

The Mill at Worston, Great Bridgeford, Staffordshire
ST18 9QA   (Tel. 0785 282710)
Off the A5013 from Eccleshall
Open noon–3pm, 6.30pm–11pm Mon–Sat; noon–2pm,
7pm–10.30pm Sun

This well-converted water mill is now a pub, though it is still in working order, and you can drink among the old machinery. There is a museum next door; a comprehensive information booklet gives details of the hoists and gears and the wheel (the museum is open all the time). There has been a mill on this site since 1279; this particular building, of red brick and tile, with symmetrically placed iron-framed windows, came into being in 1814. Inside, the building is spacious, and attractive. Beers on offer at the bar include Marston's Pedigree, and there is an extensive bar menu; meals are available all day, and the top price is £6. A good place to take children: there is a family area in the pub, and a play area with swings outside in the garden. The new owners are planning many changes and improvements. There is also a pretty stream in the garden; it is worth putting up with the London–Birmingham trains which rush past on the opposite bank every five minutes. The pub has access and a lavatory for disabled visitors.

Nature trail for children; museum; a bird watch; walk to Izaak Walton's Cottage; coarse fishing

HARVINGTON

The Mill at Harvington, Anchor Lane, Harvington, Evesham,
Worcestershire WR11 5NR   (Tel. 0386 870688)
Signposted from Evesham–Stratford road
£51 single, £73 double b&b
Set back from the main road in a peaceful spot of the historic
village of Harvington, which is recorded in the Domesday
Book, this recently opened hotel and restaurant has been
tastefully decorated throughout. A Georgian house and former
maltings and baking mill retaining many original features,
such as beams and open fires, it is set in eight acres of wooded
parkland with excellent views of the River Avon across a
beautifully laid lawn that is abundant with wildlife. A relaxed
and comfortable atmosphere prevails and very friendly staff
assure efficient service. The restaurant has 50 seats between
two rooms (all tables view the 200-yard stretch of willow-
shaded water frontage) and is closed for Monday and Saturday
lunch. The set lunch costs £14, the set dinner £19. Special
weekend breaks cost from £85 per person for two nights,
including breakfast and dinner. There are three ground-floor
bedrooms with disabled access.
*The river is popular with leisure boats doing 'The Avon Ring'; river
fishing; moorings; secluded heated outdoor swimming pool; tennis
court; in-season windsurfing nearby (book through hotel); rowing
club (four miles away); gliding (five miles away); walking*

HOARWITHY

Upper Orchard, Hoarwithy, Ross-on-Wye,
Herefordshire HR2 6QR   (Tel. 0432 840649)
Open February–December
Wine-tasting weekends only: beginner's £120 pp, fine £150 pp,
classic £220 pp
The Hurleys are a charming, friendly couple whose know-
ledge and love of wines and walking is infectious. They open
their comfortable farmhouse to the public and serve home and

locally produced food for the duration of a relaxed but informative wine-tasting weekend. Forty of these are held each year
between February and December, and all stages are catered for:
beginners, fine and classic. Guests are welcome to browse
around the well-stocked wine cellar or set off on any of the many
recommended country walks varying from a distance of three to
14 miles. The owners, authors of five book on local pedestrian
routes, are happy to lend their expertise or even wellies and
walking sticks from the hotel's central supply. A homely and
comfortable residence with traditional, cosy sitting room with
armchairs grouped around a log fire. Bedrooms are decorated in
soft pinks and greens with pine or mahogany furniture. Beamed
dining room offers home cooking with emphasis on organic
produce. No facilities for the disabled.
Walking; cycling

KNIGHTWICK

6/10

The Talbot Hotel, Knightsford Bridge, Knightwick,
Worcestershire WR6 5PH   (Tel. 0886 21235)
On the B4197, off the main A44 Worcester–Leominster road
£22 single, £52 double b&b
Nestling in the Worcestershire countryside just yards from the
River Teme, the Talbot Hotel first became prominent as an inn
during the late 14th century. It is now a fully licensed free
house and residential inn providing home cooking and
adequately furnished and decorated rooms with good facilities.
The heavily beamed, attractive lounge bar with its carved or
leatherette armchairs is dominated by a huge open fireplace and
the informal 20-seat Edwardian dining area serves a varied
menu based on local produce with a bias towards meat and
poultry dishes. Vegetarian meals are always available on the
frequently changing menu, which provides à la carte three-
course meals for around £12. This is a family-run hotel with a
friendly ambience which also offers a function room for
weddings and parties plus seating on the garden lawn for
drinks during the summer season. The hotel is not suitable for
the disabled.

Fishing (hotel has rights), squash courts and sauna on site; walking and hunting nearby; pheasant and clay pigeon shooting for groups organized by prior arrangement

LAKE VYRNWY

🏨 16/30 🛶 〰️ 🔄 ▭

The Lake Vyrnwy Hotel, Lake Vyrnwy, Llanwddyn,
Montgomeryshire SY10 0LY   (Tel. 069 173 692)
Off the B4393 from Llanfyllin; well signposted
£53–£103 per room b&b (lake-view rooms from £67)
Cradled in the Berwyn mountains, on the edge of Dyfnant
Forest and the Snowdonian National Park, Lake Vyrnwy is a
spectacularly beautiful place – complete with a romantic,
turreted 'Wagnerian' tower and hidden, drowned village. This
country house hotel and sporting estate enjoys breathtaking
views over the water, sole sporting rights over 24,000 acres of
woodland plus sole fishing rights on the 1100-acre lake. A
display of fishing flies, deep armchairs and roaring fires creates
a warm atmosphere that appeals to both sport enthusiasts and
those simply seeking a peaceful and relaxing country break.
The simple, pretty bedrooms have been tastefully refurbished;
a newspaper and pot of tea magically appear on the bedside
table each morning. The lake is visible to all diners in the 80-
seat restaurant, but the seven tables in the new conservatory
offer a truly spectacular aspect. Lunch costs £9.25, dinner
£18.75 and Sunday lunch £11.75. The restaurant is accessible to
the disabled, but the bedrooms have no special facilities.
*Bicycles and two sailboats for guests; fly fishing (day ticket £8, boat
hire £9); walking trails; clay and game shooting; tennis; bird
watching in RSPB wildlife reserve; ballooning; four-wheel driving
and white-water rafting can be arranged; beaches (no swimming)*

LECHLADE

🍺 🛶 〰️ ▭

The Trout Inn, St John's Bridge, nr Lechlade,
Gloucestershire GL7 3HA   (Tel. 0367 52313)
On the A417 (call for directions)

Pub open 11am–3pm, 6pm–11pm Mon–Sat; noon–3pm, 7pm–10.30pm Sun. Restaurant open 7pm–10pm Thurs–Sat

A Grade II listed old English pub, with flagstone floors and low-beamed bar partly panelled and decorated with stuffed trout and pike, in a rural setting by an old weir pool and the first lock on the River Thames. The Trout inn boasts two water-view bar areas, one of which opens on to the large public beer garden where visitors are welcome to participate in the summertime outdoor games of *pétanque* and 'Aunt Sally' (a famous Oxfordshire game). The spacious bar offers an impressive range of bar snacks and light meals for approximately £3 (available every day until 10pm) and the restuarant, which lists local trout as a speciality, provides three-course meals for about £15. The pub has excellent family facilities both indoors and in the garden, where there is a marquee throughout the summer for private functions. There is no jukebox, but with the aid of live jazz every Tuesday evening a fun atmosphere prevails. Although not specially adapted for the disabled, the pub is easily accessible.

Riverside walks; boating from the nearby marina; coarse fishing; nearby trout farm (fly fishing); pub sells day tickets for fishing on the weir pool; private moorings

LITTLE HAVEN

The Swan Inn, Little Haven, Pembrokeshire SA62 3UL (Tel. 0437 781256)

Village on the A4341, near Broad Haven; pub on sea wall

Pub opens 11am–3pm, 6.30pm–11pm Mon–Sat; noon–3pm, 7pm–10.30pm Sun. Restaurant opens 7pm–10pm Wed–Sat

Perched on one side of the broad, sandy cove, so close to the beach that water comes right up to the windows, the Swan enjoys a sublime position in one of the prettiest villages on the Pembrokeshire coast. In the comfortable bar, large bay windows look out to sea, and the decor is comfortable and unpretentious with traditional high-backed settles, exposed stonework, and old prints. Llanelli-brewed beers, real ales and imaginative snacks (which costs from £1.25 to £5) are served from the solid wood bar while the menu in the 20-seat restaurant focuses on seafood and offers main courses for about £10–£14. The low sea wall provides waterside seating in summer in lieu of chairs outside. Access to the pub is via several steps, although the staff are more than willing to give assistance to disabled visitors.

Pembrokeshire coastal walks; watersports (bring own equipment) at Broad Haven; sandy beach

LLANDUDNO

🏠 9/17 〰 ⌂ ◁ ▭

The Bellevue Hotel, 26 North Parade, Llandudno LL30 2LP (Tel. 0492 879547)
£30–£34 pp dinner and b & b; self-catering holiday flats sleeping 4–6 people, £110–£250 per week
Facing south-east from the foot of the limestone headland of Great Orme, just opposite the old Victorian pier house and opera house, the simple, friendly and sparkling-clean Bellevue is excellent value. Both the sitting room, with its large bay window, and fishing-net-strewn Fisherman's bar have a marvellous view of the beach and the bay beyond. Light lunchtime meals are available in the bar for approximately £3. A pretty 35-seat evening restaurant, offering set dinner for £8, opens out on to a paved sun terrace and beach views. The bedrooms are comfortable and well equipped and all are *en suite* with colour television together with in-house video channel. Next door, Bellevue House offers four fully equipped self-catering holiday flats with access to all hotel facilities including the snooker and games room. No facilities for the disabled.

Walking; watersports with own equipment; fishing; beach; ski slope; toboggan run

LLANDUDNO

🏠 8/21 〰 ⌂ ◁ ▭

St Tudno Hotel, North Parade, Llandudno, Gwynedd LL30 2LP   (Tel. 0492 74411)

On the promenade near the Great Orme, opposite the
Victorian pier
Closed early December–mid January, and three weeks in
spring
£27–£52 pp b&b
Situated in the centre of the town of Llandudno, a pretty, tree-
lined Victorian seaside resort, this attractively decorated and
very well maintained hotel overlooks the pier and north-shore
beach. Facilities at the St Tudno include two lounges, one of
which is reserved for non-smokers, an attractive reception
coffee lounge for morning coffee and afternoon tea and a
Garden Room restaurant seating 60 people. Decorated with
hand-painted floral scenes, hanging baskets and an abundance
of flowers, the restaurant offers many 'Taste of Wales'
specialities with set lunch at £8.50 or £10.50, and set dinners
costing up to £22.50 for the full six-courses. The hotel's
numerous awards include one for the 'Best Hotel Loos in
Britain' and the 21 lavishly ruched, draped and colour
coordinated bedrooms are well equipped, though some are
rather small. No facilities for the disabled.
Heated covered swimming pool; nearby golf; ski slope; walking;
nearby waterskiing and windsurfing in bay; boat trips from pier;
fishing; sandy beach

LLANSANTFFRAID

The Old Rectory, Llanrwst Road, Llansantffraid, Glan
Conwy, Clwyd LL28 5LF   (Tel. 0492 580611)
Signposted on the A470
Closed 7 December–1 February
£52–£62 pp dinner and b&b
A delightful Georgian rectory set in two and a half acres of
pretty gardens with superb views over the Conwy estuary,
Snowdonia mountains and the soaring towers of Conwy
Castle. The country house decor is unfussy and relaxed: guests
dine together around a large antique table, and bedrooms
are comfortably furnished with hardwood half-tester beds.
Wendy Vaughan's cooking reflects a French influence, has

received many awards and is based on the freshest local produce, including salmon, turbot, Welsh lamb and Welsh black
beef. Three-course dinner costs £22 for non-residents. Pre-
dinner harpist evenings are a frequent summer occurrence and
the Vaughans are only too willing to provide assistance and
recommendations for walking tours from their extensive local
knowledge. A non-smoking hotel. No facilities for the disabled.
Walks in Snowdonia National Park; sailing (three miles away); sea
and river fishing (within five miles); beach (three miles away);
Bodnant Gardens (two miles away)

LLANRWST
📷 🏠 ◇ 💳

Tu Hwnt I'r Bont, Llanrwst, Gwynedd, North Wales
(Tel. 0492 640138)
Attached to the west end of Llanrwst bridge, close to town
centre
Open 10.30am–5.30pm Tues–Sun, Easter to first Sunday in
October, and all bank holidays
This National Trust cottage was built in 1480 as Llanrwst's
original courthouse. Now a tea room, the aptly named 'Beyond
the Bridge' sits so close to the River Conwy that it floods several
times each year; a fact illustrated by the marks on one wall
recording the highest flood levels since 1978. The low oak-
beamed ceilings which allow only shorter customers to walk
fully upright justify the presence of 'Mind your head' warnings
in no less than 26 langugages. The rooms are decorated with
original antique furniture and bric-a-brac and are recommended
for the hot scones with jam and fresh cream (£1.60) and bara-
brith (Welsh speckled bread). The light lunch menu includes
meat salads for £3.55 or ploughman's with hot granary rolls and
Welsh cheese for £2.65. Home-made mustard, scones and
specially blended tea are sold on the premises and the upstairs
gift shop sells Welsh craftwork. The tea rooms may be
accessible for the disabled but there are no lavatories at all on site.
Waterskiing, jetskiing and canoeing on nearby lakes; many lakes
within walking distance; salmon fishing on river, trout fishing on
Lake Crafnant nearby; children's swings in park; miniature golf;

*bowls; cricket; football; walks by River Conwy and signposted walks
in Gwydir Forest (half a mile away)*

LOWSONFORD

Fleur de Lys, Lowsonford, nr Henley-in-Arden,
Warwickshire B95 5HJ   (Tel. 0564 782431)
Open 11.30am–11pm Mon–Sat; noon–3pm, 7pm–10.30pm
Sun
A heavily beamed and attractively furnished 17th-century pub
with extensive bar areas including an excellent family room.
The varied and changing bar menu boasts a reputation for
quality, offers up to 16 choices of dish per course and is
reasonably priced at between £1.50 and £3.95 for starters; £4.50
to £7.50 for main dishes and £1.85 for dessert. A children's
menu at £1.95 and vegetarian meals are always available.
Outside the pub, the extensive and pleasant beer garden offers
plenty of seating, ample parking for clients and a good rustic
play area for young children. The Birmingham–Stratford
canal runs along the foot of the garden and provides six boat
moorings, making the pub an ideal stop-off point for those
exploring the waterways. The pub's old-fashioned layout
means that it is not suitable for disabled access.
Boating; walking; fishing

NORTH CERNEY

The Bathurst Arms, North Cerney, nr Gloucester,
Gloucestershire   (Tel. 028 583281)
On the A435
Open 11am–3pm, 6pm–11pm Mon–Sat; noon–3pm, 7pm–
10.30pm Sun
£26–£42 pp b&b
The six individually decorated rooms in this rosewashed 17th-
century pub are each named after a flower, attractively furnished
and have a light, pretty decor. Set in very rural surroundings
(though just off the main road) with a comfortable rustic

atmosphere, this freehouse is an ideal pitstop, especially during the summer months when the barbecue meals are available. Run by an enthusiastic and hospitable couple who are passionately dedicated to providing quality food and drink, the inn has a separate room with an open fire which seats parties of up to 50: an interesting venue for a private function or conference. In summer, barbecues take place in the large riverside beer garden which is bordered by flowers and floodlit during the evening. A small family room is available for young children. The pub may be accessible to the disabled although it has not been specially adapted.

Cotswold water park (waterskiing, windsurfing, horse riding and jetskiing); golf; Roman villa; fishing; walking

NORTHWICH

Friendly Floatel, Northwich, Cheshire CW9 5HD
(Tel. 0606 44443)
Off the A556 north-east of Chester
£49–£58.50 b&b

This hotel is literally on the water: you will find it floating at the confluence of the River Weaver and the River Dane, right in the centre of Northwich. Although the situation is not picturesque, the place has fascinating novelty value. One of the UK's few floating hotels, it is smartly decked out in black and white, to blend with the other buildings in the town centre. Two swing bridges either side of the floatel are the only examples of their kind in the country, and still open up occasionally to admit passing craft. All of the cabins (bedrooms, to landlubbers) have balconies; those that do not look out on to the water have views of the landscaped gardens. The Waterside restaurant, aboard the floatel, seats 65 people and overlooks the floating garden, a fountain and the floodlit water court. The table d'hôte menu costs £11.75; the à la carte menu from £15 (non-residents are welcome). There is a ramp up to the floatel, and three of the cabins on the lower deck are specially designed for disabled visitors, with large bathrooms (and rails), low-level light switches and so on.

Walks, watersports and fishing nearby; sauna and sunbed for residents only

PENALLT

🏠 🏚 🔷 💳

The Boat Inn, Lone Lane, Penallt, Monmouth, Gwent
NP5 4AJ   (Tel. 0600 2615)
Approach via railway footbridge across Wye, from Redbrook, Gloucestershire (on the Monmouth–Chepstow road). Parking in Redbrook Rovers car park
Open 11am–3pm, 6pm–11pm Mon–Sat; noon–3pm, 7pm–10.30pm Sun
As if its idyllic riverside location weren't enough, this pretty Welsh sandstone pub also offers a wide range of immaculately kept real ales. A list of 'Today's Real Ales', 12 to 14 beers long, and the 'original gravity number' for each are chalked up on a blackboard menu. Tapped from a gleaming row of barrels behind the bar, beer is kept cool by a bare stone wall cut into the hillside. The simple interior decor features quarry tile and flagstone floors, and warm wood panelling. Pan Haggerty, Rogan Josh and smoked Wye salmon (during summer months) are among the local bar menu specialities: prices range from £1.20 to £3.95. Streams and a small waterfall trickle down grassy hillside terraces, where the natural, green, terraced garden provides plenty of seating in summer from which to spot the occasional passing badger, deer or rabbit. Canoes can tie up below the pub. Not suitable for the disabled with access via four steep steps.
Wye Valley walks and Offa's Dyke path; canoeing; salmon and coarse fishing

PENARTH

🏠 🏚 🔷 💳

The Captain's Wife, Beach Road, Swanbridge, nr Penarth, South Glamorgan CF6 2UG   (Tel. 0222 530066)
Off the A4267, three miles from Penarth
Pub open 11.30am–3.30pm, 5.30pm–11pm Mon–Fri; all day

Saturday (in summer 11am–11pm); noon–3pm, 7pm–
10.30pm Sun. Restaurants open noon–2.30pm, 7pm–10.30pm
(Smuggler's Haunt restaurant is closed Sun evening, Mon and
Tues morning)
A delightful old pub, with two restaurants and a resident
ghost, looking over a pebbly beach, Sully Island and beyond to
the Bristol Channel. Low tide allows walkers to cross to the
island, though some have been stranded by the incoming tide.
The large traditional bar, with exposed stone walls and wood
floor boards with scattered rugs and Liberty prints, is split into
several areas, one of which is enhanced by a rustic high-backed
settle surround. In the Smuggler's Haunt grill above the bar,
diners can enjoy charcoal-grilled steaks and chicken, served
with a make-your-own salad and potatoes, while gazing upon
the bar's vast stone fireplace from the balcony. Mariner's à la
carte restaurant, serving fish and steak grills, opens on to the
pub's pretty flagstoned courtyard with a rose trellis, dovecote
and white doves. Prices in the two restaurants range from
£3.75 to £10.50 per main dish. No facilities for the disabled.
Walking; beach; watersports and deep sea fishing trips from Penarth

PENCRAIG

Pencraig Court Hotel, Pencraig, Ross-on-Wye, Herefordshire
HR9 6HR   (Tel. 098 984306)
On the A40 just out of Ross-on-Wye
Open April–October
£25–£40 pp b&b
Situated on the top of a hill, this elegant, Grade II listed
Georgian house has spectacular views across the beautiful Wye
Valley and River Wye and affords easy access to the Forest of
Dean and Raglan, Goodrich and Chepstow castles. Well
decorated and furnished and refreshingly spacious inside, the
hotel is light and airy with comfortable public rooms including
a television salon and sitting room. The range of bedrooms are
located on first and second floors and include a four-poster
honeymoon suite. Despite the hotel's close proximity to the
A40, there is a relaxed, tranquil atmosphere, enhanced by the

three and a half acres of extensive lawns, gardens and woodland, around which guests can stroll. The calm, elegant restaurant seats 25 to 30 people and opens for dinner only (£13 for a four-course meal). The hotel has a large private car park set well away from the road. No facilities for the disabled.
Salmon and trout fishing can be arranged; walking

PENMAENPOOL
inn ᵗ⁰/¹²

The George III Hotel, Penmaenpool, Dolgellau, Gwynedd LL40 1YD   (Tel. 0341 422525)
Off the A493, two miles west of Dolgellau
Closed Christmas and New Year
£33–£44 pp b&b
At high tide, boats moor alongside this delightful 17th-century inn, situated on a magnificent headland in the Mawddach estuary amid the inspiring scenery of Snowdonia National Park. The hotel has two bars, both of which overlook the estuary; the Cellar, only open in summer, is a flagstoned, black-beamed bar with nautical decor which opens out to tables by the water and offers toasted sandwiches and a self-serve cold buffet from £3.60, while the Dresser bar, with its excellent estuary views, produces an imaginative selection of food such as smoked trout, Dublin Bay prawns and roast spare rib of pork. In the hotel's restaurant (which seats 45 people, with three water-view tables) the menu features game and fresh seafood with a three-course dinner costing from £15. Six bedrooms are in the creatively restored shoreside railway building and although each room has a slightly different charm, all 12 have wonderful views over the estuary. No facilities for the disabled.
Precipice Walk; New Precipice, Cader Idris and Torrent walks nearby; sea and river fishing; beach; golf; riding (one mile away); pony trekking; gold and slate mines

PERSHORE

The Angel Inn and Posting House, 9 High Street, Pershore, Worcestershire WR10 1AF   (Tel. 0386 552046)

Bar open 10am–11pm Mon–Sat; noon–3pm, 7pm–11pm Sun
£40–£60 double room b&b (two four-poster rooms available)
Set in the heart of Pershore, a thriving market town which dates
back to AD 972 and displays many buildings of great character
and historic interest, this tempting coach inn enjoys period
decor in all the public areas and an especially attractive and
relaxing oak-panelled restaurant with room for 50. Set lunch
is priced at £13.95 and dinner à la carte ranges from £7.50 to
£12 per main dish. Alternatively, light meals and bar snacks
(from £1.75 to £4.50) may be taken throughout the day in the
lounge area, where guests and passers-by are also invited to
take coffee or Pershore cream teas. The inn assures helpful
and efficient service with accommodation in pleasant, individually decorated rooms kitted out with all modern conveniences. A spacious garden behind the hotel leads down to
private moorings along the river bank. The hotel may be
accessible to the disabled but does not have special facilities.
Walks and fishing nearby

PORTMEIRION

The Portmeirion Hotel, Portmeirion, Gwynedd LL48 6ET
(Tel. 0766 770228)
£65–£145 per room/suite b&b
At the water's edge on the little, wooded peninsula of
Portmeirion, with sweeping views across the Traeth Bach
estuary to the mountains beyond, the Portmeirion Hotel's
position alone is sublime. It stands near an 18th-century
colonnade, a medieval town hall, a glorious jumble of colour-
washed cottages, a pantheon and a campanile which together
make up the Mediterranean-flavoured fantasy village built by
Sir Clough Williams-Ellis between 1925 and 1973. The hotel
interior is luxurious with a typically 'Portmeirion' theatrical
flavour. From the 'Italian', 'Indian', 'Peacock' or indeed any
of the individually decorated and named bedrooms, guests
enjoy superbly clear views of the estuary and with the
columns in the curved restaurant coming from a wrecked
ketch, at high tide it's like dining in an 1930s ocean-going

liner. Lunch costs £13.50, dinner £22.50. Seasonally priced self-catering cottages nearby are available from £195 to £575 per week for two to eight people, but be sure to book well in advance. The hotel facilities include disabled toilets, but the rocky, sloping terrain of Portmeirion may be discouraging for the disabled.

Heated outdoor pool open from May to September; tennis court; walking; pony trekking; watersports; fishing; several sandy beaches

RED WHARF BAY

The Ship Inn, Red Wharf Bay, Anglesey   (Tel. 0248 85 2568)
Off the A5025
11am–11pm Mon–Sat; noon–3pm, 7pm–10.30pm Sun
Open from Easter to the end of October
An extremely pretty, crooked, whitewashed 16th-century inn directly on the waterside in Red Wharf Bay. The welcomingly traditional interior and the three bars in this inn are decorated with old clocks, fishing paraphernalia, ships' wheels and ropes, Toby jugs and have old fox-hunting cartoons adorning the walls. All bars and the 34-seat upstairs restaurant (generally available for private functions only) overlook the bay and the 10 square miles of Cockle Sands where scores of boats are moored in summer. The large lawn of the beer garden stretches to the beach and provides outdoor picnic table seating for up to 120 customers during the warmer season. The Ship inn is well known and highly popular for its delicious and unusual bar food, such as parsnip cobbler and venison sausages, averaging £3.80–£4.40 in price though specialities such as home-cured gammon steaks cost £7.75. The menu is revamped daily and all dishes come with garnish, potatoes and accompanying vegetables. Beers served include the landlord's eponymous Kenneally's bitter. The inn has a specially widened door and may be suitable for the disabled.

Walking; windsurfing and canoeing in bay; fishing; beach

ROSS-ON-WYE

Hope and Anchor, Riverside, Ross-on-Wye, Herefordshire
(Tel. 0989 630030)
From the A40/A49 roundabout, follow signs to Ross
Open 11am–11pm Mon–Sat (mid June to end of August);
11am–2.30pm, 5pm–11pm Mon–Sat (Sept to mid June);
noon–3pm, 7pm–10.30pm Sun
The pleasant and lively bar area overlooking the River Wye is
divided by arches, and has a strong boating theme, amplified
by all the boating bric-a-brac. The upstairs parlour bar is cosy,
with Victorian prints on the walls, and armchairs, and opens
into the Victorian-style dining room. Pretty and well-tended
gardens lead directly to the river banks and the extensive river
frontage from which an Edwardian pleasure boat belonging to
the pub is launched in the summer months. Local cider,
Marston's Pedigree and Springfield are on draught at the bar.
Bar snacks are available at lunch and dinner, priced from £1.50
to £3.50. The pub no longer offers bed and breakfast
accommodation, but does have a four-bedroom house for rent
in the holidays (£150–£250 per week, two rooms have river
views). This is 40 yards behind the pub, and is called River
View. There is wheelchair access to the pub.
*Walking; canoeing (PGL); fishing by the pub; Silver Band concerts
on summer Sundays (May–August, 7.30pm–9.30pm on lawn)*

ROSS-ON-WYE

Wye Lodge, 24 Wye Street, Ross-on-Wye, Herefordshire
HR9 7BT   (Tel. 0989 66599)
Off the main Hereford–Monmouth road (call for directions)
£14.50–£19.50 pp b&b
A comfortable 'home from home' atmosphere is offered at
this attractive and fully restored Victorian house, which has a
garden descending to the bank of the River Wye. Although
generally a bed and breakfast guesthouse, providing the full
four-course English breakfast, there is a residents-only river-

view restaurant seating six for dinner on request (from £8.50). The sympathetic conversion of the basement and cellar provides good amenities and accommodation for families. Just yards from the lodge, a garden gateway leads to the river bank and the hotel has the added bonus of being next door to the excellent 'Hope and Anchor' pub (see above). Pets are generally accepted, subject to prior notification and the owners' agreement. There are two ground-floor rooms for disabled visitors.

Many interesting walks; fishing; canoeing nearby

ROSS-ON-WYE

Pengethley Manor Hotel, Harewood End, Ross-on-Wye, Herefordshire HR9 6LL (Tel. 0989 87211)
Call for directions
£50–£110 pp b&b
Set in 15 acres of beautiful countryside, overlooking a trout lake in the heart of Herefordshire, Pengethley Manor is surrounded by attractive lawns, gardens and wooded walks. The hotel's history dates back to the reign of Henry VIII; the fine oak-panelled library has an open log fire in winter. Individually decorated rooms are tasteful and boast very elegant furnishings; some have beamed ceilings. The Georgian restaurant seats 50, with three water-view tables, serves much home produce and has an excellent reputation: cuisine includes Wye salmon, Welsh lamb, and local beef, cooked with fresh herbs from the garden. Vegetarians do not have to make do with 'alternatives': they have their own complete menu. Lunch costs £15, the table d'hôte dinner £18.50. The staff are friendly and obliging. One of the ground-floor rooms has facilities for disabled visitors. There is a helipad.

Nine-hole pitch and putt; outdoor heated swimming pool; trout lake; snooker room; croquet lawn; interesting walks in Forest of Dean and Symonds Yat; sailing; on-site or river fishing can be arranged

RUCKHALL

inn 2/5 &8 ⚔ ▭

The Ancient Camp Inn, Ruckhall, nr Eaton Bishop,
Herefordshire HR2 9QX   (Tel. 0981 250449)
Off the A465 just outside Hereford (call for directions)
Bar open noon–2.30pm, 6pm–11pm Mon–Sat; noon–2.30pm,
7pm–10.30pm Sun
£52 double room b&b (without view £30 single, £42 double)
Perched 80 feet above the River Wye on the site of an important
Iron Age settlement, the inn has beautiful views over the river.
It is a very secluded spot – you are not likely to find it by
accident. Airy, modern rooms offer the convenience of *en suite*
facilities but blend sympathetically with the intimate and
informal surroundings of the 19th-century restaurant and bar
areas, where hand-made wooden furniture and the stone-
walled bars make for a rustic atmosphere. The bar overlooks
the river and serves Woods Parish bitter. Bar meals can be
served on the terrace. The restaurant seats 30 and opens in the
evenings only; bar meals are available at both lunch and supper
(Note that there is no food available on Sunday or Monday
nights). There is disabled access to the pub, restaurant and
lavatories, but not to the accommodation.
*Walks in beautiful countryside; 400 yards of river frontage available
for fishing; golf nearby*

RUGBY

🏨 7/31 & ◁ ▭

Brownsover Hall Hotel, Brownsover Lane, Old Brownsover,
Rugby, Warwickshire CV21 1HU   (Tel. 0788 546100)
Off the A426 between Rugby and Junction 1 of the M6
£40–£100 per room b&b
An imposing mock-Gothic hall, rebuilt by Sir Gilbert Scott in
the 18th century for the Broughton-Leigh family and set in
seven acres of woodland with attractive lawns that lead to the
banks of the river. The interior boasts some impressive
architecture with stone archways and a timbered gallery. The
restaurant seats 60 people: the set lunch costs £9.95, the set

dinner £15.95. The whole hotel has been recently refurbished with elegant yet comfortable furnishings and decor. More developments will be made during 1991 and will add 60 more bedrooms, a banqueting hall and leisure centre. There are already impressive conference facilities. No facilities for the disabled.

Walking; sailing; waterskiing; fishing organized through hotel

ST DAVID'S

14/25

The Warpool Court Hotel, St David's, Pembrokeshire
SA62 6BN   (Tel. 0437 720300)
West of St David's (call for directions)
Bar open noon–2pm Mon–Sun; restaurant open noon–2pm,
7pm–9.15pm Mon–Sun
£35–£48 pp b&b

The Warpool Court Hotel, built in the 1860s as St David's Cathedral Choir School, adjoins National Trust land in the Pembrokeshire Coast National Park and is worth visiting for its superb coastal location overlooking St Bride's Bay, Skokholm and Skomer islands. The building itself houses a unique collection of antique ceramic wall tiles and has a 70-seat restaurant and a bar, both of which enjoy stunning views of the bay and welcome non-residents. Traditional lunch and dinner, at around £12 and £20, are served in the restaurant, although at midday guests and visitors may prefer to sample the bar meals (from £3 to £10). The hotel assures a choice of at least two vegetarian meals at each serving. Extra facilities include two sitting rooms (one with clear water view), cot loan, baby-listening service, plus a large garden with summer seating facing the bay. Pets are only admitted to certain bedrooms and a charge of £4 per day is applied. The ground floor and restaurant are all on one level but there are no special facilities for the disabled.

Covered heated swimming pool (Easter to end of October); all-weather tennis court; sauna; gym; children's play area including table tennis and pool at hotel; free coastal trips in hotel's boat about three times a week, weather permitting; Pembrokeshire coastal path walks;

watersports at nearby Whitesands Bay and Newgale beach; sea fishing; beaches within short drive

SHREWSBURY

The Boathouse Inn, Port Hill Road, Shrewsbury, Shropshire (Tel. 0743 62965)
On the B488 just south west of Shrewsbury
Open 11am–11pm Mon–Sat; noon–3pm, 7pm–10.30pm Sun
Comfortable, quiet and quite cosy with two bars, the inn caters for teachers at lunch and early evening and yuppies at night, according to the staff. It is in a lovely spot, particularly nice on a summer evening, though a little tricky to find if you are coming through the town. The long lounge bar looks across the river to the 'quarry', an extensive park, which can be reached by an attractive iron bridge that crosses the river just beyond the pub. There is a patio area outside the pub, and also a good beer garden. Bar food – for example, ploughman's, or lasagne – is available beween noon and 2pm, and 5pm and 7.30pm; beers on offer include Pedigree bitter, and Whitbread and Flowers. Pets can be accommodated by request. No facilities for the disabled.
Walking; quarry park; watersports; fishing

SIBSON

Miller's Hotel and Restaurant, Main Road, Sibson, Nuneaton, Warwickshire CV13 6LB   (Tel. 0827 880223)
On the A444, the Nuneaton–Burton-on-Trent road
Bar open for meals noon–2.15pm, 7pm–10.15pm Mon–Sun; restaurant open 12.15pm–2.15pm, 7pm–9.45pm all week except Mon and Sat lunch
£49.50–£69.50 per room b&b
Miller's Hotel and Restaurant is set in a stylish mill and bakery conversion that is adequately furnished and decorated with reasonably sized rooms. Decorative fountains are to be found both in and outside the hotel and a small stream, turning a large

waterwheel, runs through the bar area. For residents and non-residents alike there is a stone-walled, beamed dining area which serves a traditional roast lunch on Sundays for £7.45 (£3.75 for children) and à la carte midday and evening meals at approximately £15. A large selection of hot and cold meals are also served in the bar lounge and are priced in the region of £1.75 to £4.65. The range of accommodation in double, twin and single rooms includes colour television, tea- and coffee-making facilities and *en suite* bathrooms. A simple four-poster bridal suite is available, as are conference facilities for a maximum of 80 people. The hotel is well placed for access to Bosworth battlefield, Twycross zoo and Kingsbury water gardens and is suitable for the disabled with ramps and ground-floor rooms.

Walking; Bosworth Field; Twycross zoo; coarse fishing locally

STRATFORD-UPON-AVON

🏨 4/65 🏤 ⬦ ▭

Arden Hotel, 44 Waterside, Stratford-upon-Avon, Warwickshire CV37 6BA   (Tel. 0789 294949)
Opposite entrance to Swan Theatre (call for directions)
Bar open 12.30pm–2pm all week; restaurant open 12.30pm–2pm, 6pm–9pm all week
£54–£68 single, £79–£100 double b&b
The Arden Hotel occupies a very central position overlooking the Swan Theatre, the River Avon and the surrounding green, where a summer marquee is erected providing a good venue for weddings and private receptions. The hotel is actually two very attractive annexed houses, dating from the 17th century and Regency period, but until the intended interior refurbishment is completed, furnishings may seem slightly disappointing. In recognition of its key location in such a theatrically important town, the hotel's 70-seat restaurant offers not only carved buffet lunch for £10.50 and dinner à la carte from 7pm–9pm, but also a special pre-theatre set dinner for around £11 from 6pm to 9pm. The bar, which is regularly patronized by theatre and television actors, is open for snacks and light lunches from £1.40 to £4.50. The dining areas accommodate

non-residents for all meals, morning coffee and afternoon tea. A very pretty, terraced garden with seating looks out over the theatres, green and river. Ten de luxe bedrooms and meeting facilities are available. The hotel is not suitable for the disabled, but the ground-floor restaurant is accessible via two shallow steps.

Walking; windsurfing and fishing can be arranged

STRATFORD-UPON-AVON

Moat House International, Bridgefoot, Stratford-upon-Avon, Warwickshire CV37 6YR (Tel. 0789 414411)
Central Stratford
£82.50–£165 per room b&b
Restaurant open noon–2.30pm, 6pm–11pm Mon–Sat;
12.30pm–2.30pm, 6pm–11pm Sun. Warwick grill open
7pm–11pm Mon–Sun, 12.30pm–2.30pm Sun
A large, modern, low-rise building with extensive facilities for conferences and business functions. The huge flagstoned lobby with open fireplace is a concession to character; otherwise the decor and furnishings, although stylish, are rather uniform. The bedrooms with contemporary furnishings are well equipped with all modern conveniences, including 20 with up-to-date child-minding systems. Attractive lawns and terraces overlook the river and the Royal Shakespeare Theatre as do the new riverside carvery restaurant and the on-site leisure centre. Lunch in the 230-seat riverside carvery costs £11.75, dinner £13.95, and a three-course dinner in the à la carte Warwick grill costs about £20. There are two lively bars, one of which adjoins the in-house Monday-to-Saturday nightclub. Non-smoking bedrooms are available to guests. The hotel's dining facilities are open to non-residents and it is well adapted for the disabled, with two purpose-built bedrooms, lifts, ramps and converted bathroom facilities.

The hotel has its own leisure centre with swimming pool, spa bath, steam room and solarium, gymnasium, sauna, beautician, chiropodist and masseur (open 7am–10pm Mon–Fri, 9am–8pm Sat–Sun); nearby, guests can find an all-weather football pitch and tennis courts, fitness centre, squash, walking and rowing; fishing, watersports and boating can be arranged

SUTTON COLDFIELD

🏨 50/60 ⛳8 🏹 ▭

New Hall Hotel, Walmley Road, Sutton Coldfield, West
Midlands B76 8QX   (Tel. 021 378 2442)
£85 pp b&b, £250 per suite
Run by a charming and friendly couple, this rather exclusive
hotel and restaurant is an oasis set in 26 acres of beautiful
grounds and surrounded by a lily-fringed moat just six miles
from Birmingham. It is a 12th-century, Grade I listed building,
reputedly the oldest inhabited moated manor house in
England. The Elizabethan oak-panelled dining room and
parlour are wonderful; a new drawing room has just been
built. Stained-glass and leaded windows add to the unique
character of the individually decorated rooms. Most of the
bedrooms are in the new wing. There is a very peaceful and
relaxed atmosphere to the whole place. The restaurant
(decreed Restaurant of the Year by the *Good Food Guide* in
1990) is open to non-residents (set lunch £13.50; set dinner
£23), and the cuisine is described as modern English and
creative. There is one specially adapted bedroom for disabled
visitors.
*Croquet lawn; putting green; golf driving net; archery; two floodlit,
all-weather tennis courts; clay pigeon shooting can be arranged for
parties of guests; walks in the 3500-acre Sutton Park nearby; eight
miles to Kingsbury water park; riding nearby; golf course (five miles
away)*

SYMONDS YAT EAST

🏨 18/20 ⛳12 ◁ ▭

Royal Hotel, Symonds Yat East, Ross-on-Wye, Herefordshire
HR9 6JL   (Tel. 0600 890238)
Village signposted off the A40 (call for directions)
Closed in January
£29.50–£34.50 pp b&b

Being at the end of the lane, this hotel – a converted 19th-century hunting lodge – boasts the nicest situation on the Symonds Yat East river front. There is a charming, if slightly dated feel about the opulent decor and furnishings, but the atmosphere is comfortable and relaxed. The hall boasts columns and arches, a galleried stairwell, and hand-carved wooden friezes. The huge lounge, with a log fire, overlooks the River Wye. Extensive and very attractive rose gardens slope gently to the banks of the river. The staff are notably friendly and helpful. There are two restaurants which seat 80 people between them. There is a Finnish garden sauna cabin and a solarium, which guests can use for a small charge. No facilities for the disabled.
Billiards room in hotel; walking; fishing, golf and riding can be arranged

SYMONDS YAT EAST

🏰 7/10 🏠 🚫 🖃

Saracens Head Hotel, Symonds Yat East, Ross-on-Wye, Herefordshire HR9 6JL   (Tel. 0600 890435)
Off the A40 near Monmouth, south of Ross-on-Wye, follow signs to Symonds Yat East
Bar open noon–2pm, 7pm–10pm Mon–Sun
£18.50–£22.50 pp b&b
The Saracens Head Hotel, once a cider mill and stopping place for barges using the river, stands near an ancient river ferry crossing in the idyllic and picturesque Wye Valley and offers wonderful river views from all public areas. A lively atmosphere pervades the establishment from the bar, with its central open fireplace and cocktail area, to the large and extremely popular Riverside restaurant. Both bar and restaurant are open to non-residents at all sittings. The midday and evening bar menu (in the £1.50 to £5 price range) includes soups, salads, ploughman's, and plenty of fresh river fish; table d'hôte lunch is also provided for £11.95. For those preferring to dine à la carte, three-course meals in the Riverside restaurant cost about £15 (restaurant open 7pm–10pm). Beers available at the bar include Bass real ale, Grolsch and Newcastle Brown.

Between the hotel and the river bank, an attractive terraced garden offers extensive open-air seating. The compact but nicely decorated rooms are equipped with all modern conveniences and guests are invited to enjoy 30-channel satellite television in the lounge. The bar and restaurant are accessible to disabled visitors, but not the accommodation.

River trips on hotel's 'Kingfisher' boat with bar and buffet; good walking; swimming and fishing with hotel permission

TENBY

Goscar Rock Hotel, The Norton, Tenby, Pembrokeshire SA70 5AA   (Tel. 0834 2177)
Facing North Beach in Tenby. Note that in summer, no cars are allowed through town between 11am and 4pm, 2 July–September. Use free buses instead
£28 pp b&b, £45 pp dinner and b&b
The pretty Georgian house that is Goscar Rock Hotel has an excellent view along the North Beach to the dramatic Goscar Rock and the curve of the sea front. The dining room and lounge share this view, and there is also a light and modern conservatory. Decor and furnishings throughout are in keeping with the style of the house. The food is described by owner and chef Bill Campbell as 'New English and definitely not nouvelle' (dinner only, not on Sunday evenings; a four-course table d'hôte meal costs £17.20). Fourteen seats in the dining room have a sea view, and there is a family bedroom with connecting children's room. No facilities for the disabled.

Blue Flag beach opposite hotel; fishing trips from harbour; lots of castles in the area; golfing (18-hole course in Tenby); tall ships race in Milford Haven (20 minutes by car) in July

TEWKESBURY

The Royal Hop Pole Hotel, Church Street, Tewkesbury, Gloucestershire GL20 5RT   (Tel. 0684 293236)
£38 pp b&b

A fine, half-timbered hotel in the town centre, attractively decorated and furnished. The hotel has a warm cosy feel and is full of character; the drawing room is better described as elegant. There are log fires in the timbered restaurant, which work to create a wonderfully intimate atmosphere. Regional and seasonal dishes can be found on the menu alongside classical French recipes; beef and Guinness pie is a house speciality. The set lunch costs £7.50, the set dinner £15.75. There are some four-poster beds, and several executive rooms. At the back of the hotel, well-laid lawns and pretty gardens stretch down to the banks of the River Avon; in summer, guests can bring their drinks out here from the bar. The hotel has private moorings on the river, which visitors can use. There are some ground-floor rooms, but none of these are specially adapted for disabled visitors.
Walking

UPTON-UPON-SEVERN

Pool House, Hanley Road, Upton-upon-Severn,
Worcestershire WR8 0PA   (Tel. 06846 2151)
On the A449 (off the A4104 from Pershore)
Closed at Christmas
£17–£25 pp b&b

A charming Queen Anne period house with direct river frontage and lovely views across the meadow. The spacious rooms are tastefully decorated – the flower arrangements are splendid – and offer excellent facilities for families (cots and high chairs can be provided, for example). There is a television room as well as a sitting room. The beautifully laid lawn is screened from the road by a wall and is plenty large enough to accommodate a marquee. Private dinner parties and functions can be catered for. Most of the tables in the dining room look out to the river (the set dinner, for residents only, costs £10). Meals for children and those on special diets can be provided. No facilities for the disabled.
Interesting walks; fishing; marina for watersports in Upton (book through hotel)

UPTON-UPON-SEVERN

The Swan Hotel, Riverside, Upton-upon-Severn,
Worcestershire   (Tel. 0684 62601)
Bar open 11.30am–2.30pm Tues–Sat; 7pm–11pm Mon–Sat;
noon–3pm, 7pm–10.30pm Sun
£37.50 single, £50 double b&b
The hotel dates from 1540, and the bedrooms are decorated in
keeping with the character of the hotel, with traditional
furnishings. The attractive beamed lounge overlooks the river,
and serves bar lunches from a menu that changes daily. The
restaurant, cosy and beamed, is decorated in cottage style and
offers a more extensive menu; there is seating for 50 people.
The proprietors, Peter and Sue Davies, have established a
widespread reputation for excellent food and draught beer
during their 30 years in residence. There is a small garden
overlooking the river. The restaurant, bar and lavatories have
wheelchair access, but not the hotel.
Fishing and walks nearby; marina opposite the inn for watersports

VAULD

Vauld Farmhouse, Vauld, Marden, Herefordshire HR1 3HA
(Tel. 056884 898)
Off the A49, the Hereford–Leominster road (call for
directions)
£25–£50 per room b&b
A beautiful, Grade II listed, 16th-century farmhouse that is
well and truly 'off the beaten track'. This fine half-timbered
building lies in a quiet country lane in the hamlet of Vauld,
known locally as 'sleepy hollow'. The accommodation is
excellent, decorated with comfort, charm and period style in
mind: there are many heavy beams and whitewashed walls. It
would be hard to find a more relaxed, away-from-it-all
atmosphere. There are three duck ponds next to the house, and
conversion is underway on a 17th-century building next door
which will add a restaurant, terrace and four rooms. A four-

course dinner can be provided, by arrangement, for residents only, and costs £12.50 (no lunch); the dining room has a large open fireplace, and a flagstone floor. Pets can be accommodated, by prior arrangement. No facilities for the disabled.
Good walking; canoeing; fishing on Wye, Lugg and Arrow rivers can be arranged; riding and golf nearby

WARWICK
🍺 ⌂ 🍴 ▭

Saxon Mill, The Coventry Road, Guys Cliffe, Warwickshire
CV34 5YN   (Tel. 0926 492255)
On the A429 Warwick–Coventry road
Open 11am–11pm Mon–Sat (11am–2.30pm, 5.30pm–11pm October–April); noon–2.30pm, 7pm–10.30pm Sun
This Grade I listed, fully functional watermill that dates from as far back as 1061, is set in a beautiful location, overlooking the ancient weir pool and the historic ruins of Guys Cliffe House. A public pathway passes the restaurant entrance beside the river, which is visible to bar drinkers via a glass panel in the pub's flooring. The timbered and whitewashed interior of the bars and 98-seat 'Harvester' dining area create a warm and inviting atmosphere. Both the dining room and restaurant bar have excellent river views, as does the summer garden area with bench seating and children's play area. Prices in the à la carte restaurant average £14 for a three-course meal while the bar menu offers a fairly wide range of lighter meals and snacks. Saxon Mill is an ideal setting for family visits but it is not suitable for disabled visitors.
Walking; fishing.

WHITNEY-ON-WYE
inn 1/5 ⌂ 🍴 ▭

Rhydspence Inn, Whitney-on-Wye, Herefordshire
HR3 6EU   (Tel. 04973 262)
At junction of the A438 and A470 between Hereford and Brecon

Open 11am–2.30pm, 7pm–11pm Mon–Sat; noon–2.30pm,
7pm–10.30pm Sun
£23–£25 pp b&b
A lovely 16th-century timbered drover's inn, with a warm and
cosy atmosphere, 'complete with genuine creaks, groans and
draughts', add the charming and informative proprietors. The
inn is a short distance from a tributary stream of the River Wye
(which marks the England–Wales border), and is surrounded
by attractive gardens and beautiful countryside. The individually decorated bedrooms are tastefully in keeping with the
character of the inn, as are the three dining rooms (these
provide seating for 72 people in all. The food has a good
reputation, and a three-course meal from the à la carte menu
costs between £12 and £15). The bar serves Robinson and
Marston real ales, local Dunkerton cider, and bar snacks such
as steak and kidney pie (£5.95). The dining rooms are
accessible to wheelchairs, but not the accommodation.
Walking; canoeing; coarse and trout fishing; golf; riding and gliding
can be arranged

WILTON

Bridge House Hotel, Wilton, Ross-on-Wye, Herefordshire
HR9 6AA   (Tel. 0989 62655)
£48.50 double b&b
A lovely situation that boasts the best river views in Ross, with
no sign of the A40. The 250-year-old hotel stands in one and a
half acres of land running down to the river, and is efficiently
run by a very friendly staff. The spacious rooms are adequately
decorated, and the dining room has just been renovated, to
give a more intimate atmosphere. There is much emphasis on
quality and value for money, especially in the restaurant where
much on the menu is home grown. The dining room seats 20
people (set dinner £8.50), and non-residents are strongly
advised to book in advance. No facilities for the disabled.
Walks in forests and mountains around Wye Valley; watersports;
fishing can be organized through hotel; canoeing

WITHINGTON

The Mill Inn, Withington, Cheltenham, Gloucestershire
(Tel. 024289 204)
Signposted from the A436 and A40
Open 11am–2.30pm (3pm on Sat), 6.30pm–11pm Mon–Sat;
noon–3pm, 7pm–10.30pm Sun
A heavily beamed, attractive Cotswold house with cottage-style furnishings and the obligatory inglenook fireplace. The original 16th-century flooring adds to the authentic atmosphere of the pub, which has a good reputation for food such as trout and chicken Kiev. The staff are lively and friendly, and the clientele is a blend of locals and tourists. A pretty garden beside the stream is excellent for families and for anyone who wants to appreciate this secluded spot fully: there are no buildings in sight across the valley. Several rooms of varying size are available for private functions for 25 to 40 people. There are four rooms for bed and breakfast accommodation (£24.50 to £38 per room; none of them have a view of the river). The inn is accessible for wheelchairs, but there are no special facilities for disabled visitors.
Walking; riding nearby; Roman villa (ask at pub)

WITHYBROOK

The Pheasant, Main Street, Withybrook, nr Coventry,
Warwickshire CV7 9LT   (Tel. 0455 220 480)
On the B4112 between Nuneaton and Rugby
Open 11am–3pm, 6pm–11pm Mon–Sat; noon–2.30pm,
7pm–10.30pm Sun
This 17th-century pub enjoys a delightfully rural situation beside the brook from which the village of Withybrook takes it name and has a lively atmosphere and friendly staff. The two beamed bar areas, filled with artefacts, seat up to 75 people and offer an extensive bar menu including many vegetarian selections with prices ranging from £1.50 to £11.50 per dish. Beers served include draught Guinness and cider, Courage,

Directors and John Smith's. Sunday lunch in the slightly more formal 28-seat à la carte restaurant costs around £10 per person with a wide choice of dishes per course (meals available from noon to 2pm, and 6.30pm to 9.45pm). A large outdoor terrace overlooking the brook provides summer seating for 150 for drinks, light snacks or lunches in the pretty, rustic gardens. The pub is not specially adapted for the disabled but it is fairly easily accessible.

Walking; fishing

WORCESTER

|O| 🏠10 🎣 ▭

Brown's Restaurant, 24 Quay Street, Worcester WR1 2JN
(Tel. 0905 26263)
Open 12.30pm–2pm, 7.30pm–9.45pm; closed Sat lunchtime and Sun evening
Architecturally interesting, this corn mill has been elegantly converted and furnished in modern style. The very comfortable lounge/café seating both in the gallery and ground floor overlook the river and bridge. The restaurant seats about 100 in all; 10 tables have a direct view of the water. The food (described as New English and French, and organic where possible) maintains an excellent reputation; the menu changes every two or three weeks. Char-grilled meat and fish dishes are a speciality. The set lunch costs £15, Sunday lunch £20, and set dinner £30. The restaurant is accessible to wheelchairs, and so are the lavatories.

River sailing; rowing; salmon and trout fishing; walks in Malvern hills, Wyre Forest and Bringsty Common (ask at pub)

WORCESTER

🏨 12/15 🏠 🍷 ▭

The Diglis Hotel, Severn Street, Riverside, Worcester
WR1 2NF   (Tel. 0905 353518)
On a side street leading to the river, adjacent to Worcester Cathedral
£32.50–£43.50 single, £65.50–£76.50 double b&b

In an attractive, listed brick house next to the River Severn, this is a comfortable and relaxed hotel serviced by a friendly and informal staff. It is close to Worcester Cathedral and has a terrace overlooking the river and county cricket ground which is perfect for wedding receptions and private functions. The decor is slightly old fashioned. The restaurant, which is now run separately, seats 46 people, and has five tables which look out on to the river. Bar snacks are available at lunchtime (more substantial meals can be provided, if you have booked in advance, and non-residents are welcome at dinner). The bar is accessible to wheelchairs, but not the accommodation.

Walks along river; Cathedral; Royal Worcester Porcelain factory; river trips available at Worcester Steamer Co.

WRENBURY

Dusty Miller, Wrenbury, Cheshire CW5 8HG
(Tel. 0270 780537)
Open 11am–11pm Mon–Sat (March–September); noon–3pm, 6pm–11pm Mon–Sat (October–February); noon–3pm, 7pm–10pm Sun
A popular spot, especially if you are on a boat; the Llangollen canal passes the pub, and the lock right outside is one of its best features. The pub was originally a working mill that dates back to the 16th century. The present pub is a conversion of the 19th-century mill building, whose wheel was worked by the adjacent River Weaver. The bars have the original heavy beams, and are adorned with old milling and farm equipment. There is seating for 60 people outside in the canalside rose garden. The first-floor restaurant seats 38 people and looks out on to the canal; à la carte dinners cost between £13 and £15. One of the two bars also has a view of the canal, and there is an extensive bar menu, providing food between noon and 3pm, and 7pm and 9.30pm every day. The resident proprietor Robert Lloyd-Jones, who carried out the conversions, is extremely knowledgeable about the area, and has twice won the Innkeeper of the Year award. No facilities for the disabled.

Walking; watersports; fishing; yacht club at Bridgemoor Winsford Flashes; English country cruises next door

WYRE PIDDLE

The Anchor Inn, Main Road, Wyre Piddle, Pershore, Evesham, Worcestershire   (Tel. 0386 552799)
On the B4084, the Pinvin–Evesham road
Open 11am–2.30pm, 6pm–11pm Mon–Sat; noon–3pm, 7pm–10.30pm Sun
A quaint but lively 17th-century pub with traditional beams and inglenooks. There are beautiful views from the dining area and the very pretty garden sloping down towards the River Avon. The staff are delightfully friendly and serve food with an excellent reputation (there is a restaurant, where main courses cost about £8; bar snacks are also available) in a wonderfully homely atmosphere. The bar has Flowers Original and Marston's Pedigree on hand pump. The pub has private moorings on the river, which can be used by customers. No facilities for the disabled.
Walks nearby (Bredon Hill, Malvern hills, Cotswolds); boating and canoeing on river; golf nearby

Central England
and the North

NORTH AND CENTRAL ENGLAND

Telegraph GUIDE

SCOTLAND

NORTH SEA

NORTHUMBERLAND

Cornhill-on-Tweed

Seahouses

Alnmouth

Bellingham

Greenhead inn Brampton

CARLISLE

Caldbeck

Ullswater

CUMBRIA

Watermillock-on-Ullswater

Grasmere
Skelwith Bridge
Hawkshead
Spark Bridge
Ulverston

Ambleside
Windermere
Bowness
KENDAL
Newby Bridge inn Milnthorpe
Arnside
Morecambe inn Heaton with

Chollerford
Haydon Bridge
Bardon Mill

Cullercoats
Tynemouth
Newcastle

TYNE

WEAR

DURHAM

Richmond

MIDDLESBOROUGH

Piercebridge inn

CLEVELAND

Lealholm

Northallerton

Hubberholme inn
Burnsall

NORTH YORKSHIRE

Newton-on-Ouse

Linton

Scarborough

Whitby inn

Bridlington

Stamford Bridge

inn North Dalton

York
Acaster?

HUMBERSIDE

Lancaster

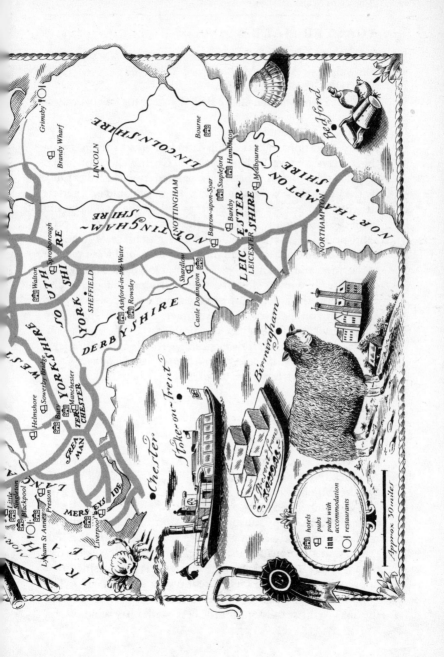

ACASTER MALBIS

inn ⚖ 6/8 🛖 ✗ ▭

The Ship Inn, Acaster Malbis, York YO2 1XE
(Tel. 0904 705 609/703 888)
South of Bishopthorpe on the B1222, just to the east of Acaster
Malbis
£35 single, £45 double b&b

A cosy, traditional inn, the Ship dates from the 17th century; in those days, it was frequented by Cromwell's army and assorted river pirates. The inn is separated from the River Ouse by the pub car park. This slightly mars what could be a perfect site, but you can see the river from one of the two bars, and from the three window tables in the restaurant. The bars offer hand-pulled beers and bar meals; the restaurant seats 40 people and has more elaborate food on offer; steaks and fresh fish are specialities, and a set meal costs £10.95. Downstairs, there is an open fire in winter; upstairs, the bedrooms are pretty and simply furnished. There are private moorings for visitors who are passing on the river. In the summer, a marquee springs up on the lawn. No facilities for the disabled.

Walking; boating (inn has private moorings); coarse fishing (£2 a day), tickets available from the pub; York racecourse five minutes away; mini cruiser (£35 a day), barges and yachts can be hired nearby

ALNMOUTH

🏘 10/10 🛖 ◁ ▱

The Marine House Private Hotel, 1 Marine Road, Alnmouth,
Alnwick, Northumberland NE66 2RW   (Tel. 0665 830 349)
Off the A1068
£29–£33 dinner and b&b

Alnmouth is a sleepy, unspoilt and beautiful seaside village. In medieval times it was an important sea port, and in the 18th century was famous for its smugglers. Originally a granary, then a vicarage, this charming, unsophisticated seaside guest house was converted by its present owners 15 years ago. The golf links is just across from the hotel and the beach runs from the links to the sea. Room 1 is the best, with a bay window and window seat looking out to sea, but all of the rooms have sea views. A terraced garden rises behind the house to the churchyard and also has fine, sheltered sea views. There are two self-catering cottages, and one newly built studio for two (£135–£282 and £122–£196 per week). The dining room seats 30, and all tables look out to sea. Dinner is at 7pm, for residents only. No facilities for the disabled.

Games room; football; cricket; horse riding; golf; walking; windsurfing; sailing; canoeing; fishing; beach

AMBLESIDE

Wateredge Hotel, Waterhead Bay, Ambleside, Cumbria
LA22 0EP   (Tel. 05394 32332)
Closed December to February
£42–£70 pp dinner and b&b
Converted from two 17th-century fishermen's cottages, the hotel is set at the heart of Lake Windermere's bustling tourist centre. There are low-beamed ceilings and farmhouse dressers in the lounge and bars, where nooks and crannies offer private, cosy seating. The windows offer good views of the length of the lake and the swans on the jetty. Bedrooms are bright and decorated with floral prints and cottage-style decor. The dining room seats 48, serving a sumptuous six-course dinner (£19.90), including dishes such as paupiettes of plaice with spinach farcie served on a shellfish sauce followed by fresh mango and raspberry crème brûlée. In summer, morning coffees, lunches and teas are served on the patio and lawns leading down to the lake's edge. No facilities for the disabled.

Watersports; walking; trout fishing (equipment not supplied); private jetty (launch fee from £3.50); lake cruises from £3.75

ARNSIDE

Stonegate Guest House, The Promenade, Arnside, Cumbria
LA5 0AA   (Tel. 0524 761171)
£15 pp b&b

The guest house, built in 1884, is right on the water and pretty promenade in a quiet, unspoilt village, which boasts spectacular views of the Kent Estuary and Lakeland hills. It is situated at the start of one of the week-long Lakeland walks and would be an ideal base for people who want to be close to the famous beauty spot but want to escape the commerciality. The bedrooms are pretty and still have original fireplaces. The dining room seats 20, with six tables overlooking the sea. Lunch is £2.50, and set dinner is £8, serving home-made food such as soups, pâtés, chicken, fish and vegetarian dishes. There is room for 12 on the sea-facing patio, where teas and dinner are served in summer. It is a non-smoking hotel. No facilities for the disabled.

On Cumbrian Cycle Way; walking; watersports; windsurfing; fishing; grass and pebble beach; sailing club on estuary; bird watching

ASHFORD-IN-THE-WATER

Riverside Country House, Ashford-in-the-Water, Bakewell, Derbyshire DE4 1QF   (Tel. 062981 4275)
Off the A6, between Bakewell and Matlock
£80–£90 per room
A Georgian country house hotel with a warm atmosphere and a walled garden that leads down to the River Wye. There is an oak-panelled bar with an open fire for drinks before and after dinner. Rooms are individually decorated, with many floral prints, and with four-poster and half-tester beds. The restaurant is open to non-residents for dinner and Sunday lunch. A four-course dinner is £27.50 and offers a mouth-watering range of nouvelle cuisine such as pigeon and quails eggs salad followed by freshly caught brown trout served with a champagne and dill sauce. However, if you have a particular favourite dish the chef will prepare it for you, given 24-hours' notice. There is an impressive list of 89 wines. No facilities for the disabled.

Local stately homes worth visiting include Chatsworth, Haddon Hall and Hardwick Hall; walks along River Wye in the Peak District

National Park; golf can be arranged; hang gliding and rock climbing nearby; mine visits

BARDON MILL

Eldochan Hall, Willimoteswyke, Bardon Mill, Hexham, Northumberland NE47 7DB (Tel. 04984 465)
Off the A69, through Bellingham
£14.50–£16 b&b

A small stone-built family house, at last 200 years old, converted from two derelict one-up-one-down cottages. It is in a rural position close to the ancient Reiver castle of Willimoteswyke. There are two double rooms for guests and a very attractive residents' lounge with open fire, television and games. Dinner is for residents only and is a good value three-course meal at £8. Vegetarians and special diets can be catered for. Down one side of the garden runs the babbling Blackclough Burn, and there is a small terrace by the stream. Hadrian's Wall, the Roman Fort at Housesteads and the Roman settlement at Vindolanda are all close by. Guests without transport can be collected from Bardon Mill station half a mile away. Added extras include babysitting and laundry services. In many ways the ideal country retreat, very tranquil, very pretty. No facilities for the disabled.

Walking; fishing (by arrangement only); swimming; windsurfing; canoeing; tennis; riding; golf all nearby

BARKBY

The Brookside, Barkby, Leicestershire (Tel. 0533 692757)
Off the A47, east of Leicester; call for detailed directions
Open 11am–3pm; 7pm–11pm Mon–Sat; noon–3pm, 7pm–10.30pm Sun

A 300-year-old pub, in an attractive, popular setting five miles away from Leicester. A small, quietly burbling brook runs outside the front door. The interior is decorated with paintings, brasses and naval memorabilia. The publican's

Toby jug collection, started over 30 years ago, now numbers upwards of 200. The pub is tied to Allied Breweries and serves Tetley's bitter, draught Burton Ale and Ansells Traditional Mild on hand pump. Both bars overlook the water and serve bolstering lunches to businessmen and tourists alike. Main courses cost from £3.50 and the favourite speciality is the beef ruff – a hearty sandwich made with a long French stick. Worth the effort of finding it. No facilities for the disabled.
Walking; fishing

BARROW-UPON-SOAR

The Navigation Inn, 87 Mill Lane, Barrow-upon-Soar, Leicestershire (Tel. 0509 412842)
Take the A6 to Loughborough, then the A675
Open 11am–2.30pm, 6pm–11pm Mon–Fri; noon–3pm, 7pm–10.30pm Sun
The pub is well situated in a secluded area by a picturesque arched bridge and lovely stretch of river where the River Soar joins the Grand Union Canal. There has been a building on this site since the days of the Domesday Book; the pub was formerly a resting place for buyers visiting the gravel mine, and then for the navvies who dug the canal. The lounge overlooks the water, and the decor is tasteful and relaxed. There are four real ales on offer at the bar, and good home cooking; the atmosphere is friendly. Outside, there is open-air seating in garden for when the weather is good, moorings and a good, long, well-worn skittles alley. There is wheelchair access to the ground floor and the garden.
Fishing; walks across fields to Quorndon and Mountsorrel villages

BELLINGHAM

The Riverdale Hall Hotel, Bellingham, Hexham, Northumberland NE48 2JT (Tel. 0434 220 254)
Take the B6320 to Bellingham, turn west towards Charlton
£28–£34.50 single, £24–£29 double/twin b&b

A mid-19th-century villa and stables with a modern extension. The surrounding area was fought over for centuries as it lies 10 miles from Hadrian's Wall and the Scottish border. The hotel sits above its own cricket ground on a terrace above the North Tyne. The bar, games room, indoor swimming pool and extremely fine restaurant all have river views and there is not a single house or farm in sight across the valley. The bedrooms are light and airy and some have four-poster beds. Plans are underway to build 15 garden bedrooms with river views by 1992. The restaurant seats 70 and serves award-winning meals for lunch and dinner. Residents can fish for salmon from the hotel's grounds and the management plays host to about 20 touring cricket teams each year. An annual golf tournament is held on the Bellingham course opposite the hotel. A peaceful, relaxed and comfortable place to stay. There are bedrooms on the ground floor, but the bathrooms are not wide enough to admit wheelchairs.

Indoor heated swimming pool; sauna; cricket; golf; walking; fishing; watersports (motor boats, windsurfers and sailing boats can be hired on Kielder Water)

BLACKPOOL

The Clifton Hotel, Talbot Square, Blackpool FY1 1ND
(Tel. 0253 21481)
On the promenade, opposite north pier
£55 single, £85 double b&b
One of the more classical old promenade hotels. Thoughtful decoration blends in well with the magnificent staircase and stained-glass windows. The hotel has recently been renovated, giving the main bar, cocktail bar and residents' lounge good sea views. Newly refurbished bedrooms have high ceilings and mouldings. The restaurant seats 150 people, and serves lunch, high tea and dinner. The table d'hôte menu for £12.50 is a mixture of English, French and Italian cuisine of basic fish and steak choices. The hotel has very good value weekend breaks especially in the low season: £35 per person for dinner, bed and

breakfast. Other packages include the theatre, dinner dances, racing, bowling and the Blackpool illuminations. Babysitting facilities available. Two rooms have disabled facilities and hotel has disabled access.
Walking; watersports; fishing; theatre; fun fairs

BLACKPOOL

The Pembroke Hotel, North Promenade, Blackpool
FY1 2JQ   (Tel. 0253 23434)
On the promenade
£85 single, £105 double
A hideous new building, but cunningly built so that 80% of its rooms have a sea view. Recent refurbishments have added more rooms and a new marble reception area. Inside, the hotel is extremely comfortable as its four-star status suggests, with good service. There are very impressive conference facilities, and a big swimming pool and disco area. There is one à la carte restaurant, the Crystal Room, where 10 tables have a view of the sea, and also a carvery, the Promenade Restaurant, offering good-looking food (£13.25 for a main course). Pets can be accommodated by request (they're not allowed into the public rooms). There are three rooms that may suit disabled visitors (the bathrooms have doors that open outwards, but there are no handrails), and the hotel has disabled access.
Fishing; beach

BLACKPOOL

Revill's Hotel, 190–4 North Promenade, Blackpool FY1 1RJ
(Tel. 0253 25768)
£20.25–£23.50 single, £17.25–£22.50 double b&b
£23.50–£28.50 pp dinner and b&b
A simple, family-run hotel on the promenade with old-fashioned decor. The sun room runs the length of the hotel and its large windows overlook the sea. The bedrooms facing out to sea are also light and sunny, though the decoration is fairly

basic. The basement bar offers cabaret and other entertainment in the high season and on special occasions in the winter (such as Christmas). The dining room (dinner only) seats 90 people, with six water-view tables: food is straightforward and good value (fruit cocktail, roast, and sweet costs £6.50 to non-residents). A newly opened café/bar serves food all day. The hotel would suit those on a family holiday or anyone wanting a break in Blackpool for very reasonable prices. No facilities for the disabled.
Golf; walking; fishing; beach; theatre

BLACKPOOL

The Warwick Hotel, 603–9 New South Promenade,
Blackpool FY1 1NG   (Tel. 0253 42192)
£27.75–£63.50 pp b&b
A 1930s hotel, composed from four adjacent hotels along the promenade. The large swimming pool, with seven surrounding tables overlooking the sea, is particularly pleasant. The decor in the bedrooms is modern, and there are family rooms with bunk beds and large bay windows. The hotel has a large bar with a friendly atmosphere: bar lunches available. The restaurant seats 120, with 12 sea-view tables. Disabled access to ground floor only; no lifts to rooms.
Blackpool pleasure beach; indoor swimming pool; sun bed; The Sandcastle – an indoor water fun centre

BLACKPOOL

The White Tower Restaurant, Blackpool Pleasure Beach,
Balmoral Road, Blackpool FY4 1EZ   (Tel. 0253 46710)
Open 7pm–10.45pm Tues–Sat; noon–4pm Sun
The restaurant is situated on the second floor of the Wonderful World building; a fine example of 1930s sea-front architecture. Due to its elevation and curving façade the restaurant boasts panoramic views of the sea, the South Pier and the Promenade. It is next to all the lights and sights, rides and excitement of the

pleasure beach. Acclaimed as one of the Fylde's top eating establishments, it offers main courses for between £10 and £15, and Sunday lunch from £7.95. There is seating for 70, and all tables look out over the beach. Coasters Wine Bar on the Promenade is run by the same management and would be a pleasant place to have a drink before eating at the restaurant. It is a new establishment but the design is based on the 1914 casino building which was on the same site. There are facilities for disabled visitors.

Walking; watersports; fishing; pleasure beach

BOURNE

Bourne Eau House, Bourne, Stamford, Lincolnshire
PE10 9LY   (Tel. 0778 423621)
On the A15 north of Stamford
£25–£30 pp b&b
This listed country house looks over the little Bourne Eau river to the 12th-century abbey on the opposite bank, which can be reached by a small wrought-iron footbridge. The architecture is a mixture of Jacobean and Georgian, which contrives to give the house the air of a gentleman's town residence. The lovely Jacobean- and Elizabethan-style rooms are well furnished with matching period antiques. Exposed beams, woodwork and fireplaces are offset by white walls and tiles. One of the sitting rooms has a finely carved 17th-century mantelpiece and a concert piano. The flagstone-floored dining room seats eight; dinner is for residents only. The set menu is £16.50, offering generous portions of home-cooked food using local Lincolnshire produce. Well-tended gardens run down to the pretty stretch of water. No facilities for the disabled.

Walks in Bourne Woods (two miles away); Lincoln and Ely cathedrals; golf (two miles away); sailing, fishing, waterskiing and sailing on Rutland Water nearby; Abbey Lawns across road with tennis courts (hard and grass); cricket, football, swimming, bowls, outdoor and indoor heated swimming pools in local leisure centre

BOWNESS-ON-WINDERMERE

🏨 52/82 🏠 ⬤ ▭

The Old England Hotel, Bowness-on-Windermere, Cumbria
LA23 3DF   (Tel. 09662 2444)
£115 per room (breakfast £7.25)
This Georgian mansion, now a Trust House Forte hotel, is in
an excellent spot on Lake Windermere. The hotel is next to the
Royal Windermere Yacht Club and has views across to Belle
Isle and the Cumbrian hills. The decoration is fairly typical of a
chain hotel; comfortable, with reproduction furniture, bright
chintzes and added touches such as the local author Wain-
wright's books in the bedrooms. Rooms with the best views
cost £10 extra. The bar leads out to a terrace with sweeping lake
and garden views. The dining room seats 120, serves 'classic
English dishes' including fish, duck and rabbit. Most tables
look on to the water, and a three-course dinner with coffee and
sweetmeats costs about £16. Special diets catered for. Popular
with business clientele. Other services include baby-listening,
laundry, hairdressing salon and children's play area and high
teas. Some ground-floor rooms, though no specific facilities
for the disabled.
*Walking; snooker; fishing; heated outdoor pool (May to October);
watersports; private jetty; lake cruises*

BRAMPTON

inn 4/7 🏠 ⬤ ▭

Abbey Bridge Inn, Lanercost, Brampton, Cumbria CA8 2HG
(Tel. 06977 2224)
Off the A69
Open 11.30am–3pm, 6pm–11pm Mon–Sat; noon–3pm, 7pm–
10.30pm Sun
£19.50 single b&b, £37.50 double, £44 double with private
bathroom
The Abbey Bridge inn sits on the banks of the River Irving
next to a red sandstone humped-backed bridge built in the
reign of James II. Within walking distance is the part-ruined
Lanercost Priory (dating back to 1166). A very friendly and

comfortable establishment with simple bedrooms, four with
private bathrooms and three without. 'The Blacksmith's' bar/
restaurant was converted from the 17th-century forge, and the
dining tables are on a gallery up a wrought-iron staircase. The
home-made food (such as deep-fried Brie, chicken satay, and
crispy duck) looks very tasty and a main course costs around
£6. Summer days can be spent sitting in the garden next to the
river. The hotel would be a suitable base from which to explore
Hadrian's Wall, the Lake District and the Solway Firth area.
The downstairs rooms could be used by disabled visitors,
though these are not specially adapted. Meals can be taken at
the bar, and there is trained nursing staff on site.
*Trout fishing (£5 a day); watersports and golf nearby; walking;
Naworth Castle (one mile away)*

BRAMPTON

Tarn End Hotel, Talkin, Brampton, nr Carlisle, Cumbria
CA8 1LS   (Tel. 06977 2340)
Closed February
£38.50 single, £56 double b&b
A 19th-century farmhouse, with old barns, in a beautiful spot
on the banks of Talkin Tarn, in the Talkin Tarn Country Park.
The friendly, family hotel is right on the edge of the lake, with
picturesque jetty and rowing boat. A leisurely walk around the
circumference of the lake takes about 20 minutes. The rooms
have good views and are prettily decorated, in a cottage style
with Laura Ashley furnishings, antiques and patchwork quilts.
The dining room seats 30 people, with six lake-view tables and
serves French haute cuisine with main courses costing between
£10.50 and £12.50. There are vegetarian choices on the à la
carte menu and an extensive wine list accompanies your meal.
Non-residents are welcome. Bar lunches are available from
noon to 2pm, and afternoon tea is served from 3pm to 4.30pm.
There is one ground-floor room, but no specific disabled
facilities.
*Walking; Hadrian's Wall; watersports; coarse fishing; shooting; row
boat rentals; golf course 200 yards away, £10 a day*

BRANDY WHARF

Cider Centre, Brandy Wharf, Waddingham, Gainsborough,
Lincolnshire DN21 4RU   (Tel. 06527 364)
Halfway between Waddinghan and South Kelsey on the B1205
(the Grimsby to Gainsborough road)
Open noon–3pm, 7pm–11pm Mon–Sat; noon–3pm, 7pm–
10.30pm Sun
Right beside the New River Ancholme, the Cider Centre pub
has two bars, one of which overlooks the river. Up to 60
varieties of cider are on offer, 18 of them on draught. Some of
these have an alcoholic content of over 7%, and so are sold only
in half-pints; visitors are advised to drink them slowly, and
with respect. Good cheap bar food is available to punctuate the
drinks. There is an orchard and 'Sydre Shoppe' museum next
door. The Cider Centre offers visitors' berths for river
cruisers, and they also have a caravan site that can accommodate five vans. No facilities for the disabled.
Walking; watersports; fishing

BRIDLINGTON

The Monarch Hotel, South Marine Drive, Bridlington,
Humberside YO15 3JJ   (Tel. 0262 674 447)
On the seafront next to lifeboat station
Closed three weeks over Christmas
£30–£38 single, £25 double pp b&b (£30 pp with bathroom)
Bridlington is a charming seaside resort, especially tranquil out
of high season. There is a good balance between the modern
bright lights and the original Regency architecture. The
Monarch Hotel is typical of a sea-front establishment that is
comfortable but not luxurious; the public rooms are smartly
attractive and the bedrooms well fitted. Good for families
and those who want an accommodating, reasonably priced
seaside break. (For a two- to four-night break, dinner, bed and
breakfast costs £38 per person per night.) The dining room

seats 90, with six sea-view tables. The set menu of three courses is very good value at around £10 and includes fresh fish off the local trawlers such as Bridlington Bay fillet of ling; there are also exciting-sounding vegetarian dishes. There is a lift that can be used by disabled guests, but no special facilities.

Walking; watersports; hire boats; fishing (from pier, licence needed); beach; pleasure boats from harbour along coast; fun fair

BURNSALL

The Red Lion Hotel, Burnsall, Skipton, Yorks BD23 6BU
(Tel. 075672 204)
On the B6160, two miles from Grassington
£17.50–£22.50 b&b
Deep in the dales, the Red Lion is beautifully situated on the right bank of the River Wharfe just across from the village green. The only place from which it is easy to see the water is from the hotel garden where guests can take drinks and food from the bar. The hotel has a separate restaurant, which seats 50. They offer home-cooked food and the set three-course dinner (including coffee) costs £12. There is also a table d'hôte menu and one of the specialities of the house is roast duckling at £11.70. Decor is plain and traditional and the bedrooms are well furnished and comfortable. No facilities for the disabled.

Walking; swimming (half a mile away); fishing nearby (trout £11 a day, grayling £5.50 a day); river beach

BURY

The Boholt Hotel, Walshaw Road, Bury BL8 1PU
(Tel. 061 764 5239)
£43 single, £59 double b&b
This modern hotel has been built on the site of the birthplace of Henry Dunster (1609–59), the first president of Harvard University. It is in its own peaceful, 50-acre grounds on the outskirts of busy town, overlooking a small, man-made lake

with ducks, and next to two larger lakes. The hotel has been commendably involved in the 'greening' of the area, turning factory ruins into meadows and protecting wildlife. A 19-bedroom extension is underway as well as the addition of a squash court and indoor swimming pool with a sliding glass roof. The decor is an odd mixture of pine and red leather in the reception areas. There are two bridal rooms with four-posters. The restaurant is open from 7pm to 9pm and seats 60 people. There is disabled access and ground-floor rooms, but bathrooms are not specially adapted.
Walking; watersports; fishing; picturesque gardens; leisure facilities (including spa bath, sauna and gym)

CALDBECK
🍽 🏠 ⊗ ⊟

Watermill Coffee Shop, Priests Mill, Caldbeck, Wigton, Cumbria CA7 8DR   (Tel. 06998 369)
Open 10am–5pm March–October, and weekends in November and December
The café is part of a restored 17th-century watermill, in an extremely pretty complex with shops and a museum. It was originally built by the rector of the neighbouring 800-year-old church. The idea when restoring the building and grounds was to keep it all looking natural: 'Nothing garden-y'. In this successfully natural environment you can eat your picnic or the café food, listen to the bubbling river and watch cricket in the field beyond. The water wheel works by putting 10p in a slot. Dippers and wagtails live on the river banks among the daffodils and cherry trees. There is a tempting gift shop, with wares ranging from scented candles to framed locally taken photographs. The wholesome food from the coffee shop includes nutty cheese bake and lemon surprise pudding, all for reasonable prices. Other attractions within the complex include craft workshops, a bookshop and a mining museum. Bed and breakfast accommodation is available locally. There is wheelchair access to the café.
Walking

CASTLE DONINGTON

The Priest House Hotel, Kings Mills, Castle Donington, Derby DE7 2RR   (Tel. 033281 0649)
Off the A6, south east of Derby
£50–£54 single, £60–£64 double b&b
A low-beamed, attractive inn with a medieval tower and large grounds in a pretty spot by the River Trent. In the bar, you can find the wheels which used to drive the Chain Ferry across the river; there is also a games room and fruit machines. A good stretch of running water and woodland can be seen from the pub and garden. A new extension has recently added 14 more large bedrooms, some with four-poster beds. The restaurant seats 60 people, and serves a table d'hôte menu from £12.95 and à la carte from £10 to £15. One of the chef's specialities is half sugar roast duck with orange sauce. Hearty bar snacks are also available. The hotel is convenient for the East Midlands airport. One of the bedrooms is suitable for disabled visitors.
Walking; fishing (trout-permit £3 per day); riding; canoeing outside the hotel (bring own equipment); Donington Racing Museum; Alton Towers nearby

CHOLLERFORD

The George Hotel, Chollerford, Hexham, Northumberland NE46 4EW   (Tel. 0434 681 611)
From the A69, take the B6318 at Chollerford
£70 single, £90 double b&b
Once a small 17th-century coaching inn and farm, on the main military road between Carlisle and Newcastle, the George has been extended since the war to form a 50-bedroom hotel, and another 25 bedrooms are under construction. The hotel is set right on the banks of the North Tyne next to the five graceful arches of the 18th-century Chollerford Bridge. A very well-kept and peaceful formal garden leads down to the river; a larger informal garden stretches away upstream. In late August and September the salmon can be seen leaping the weir 100

yards from the hotel. A new restaurant has just been completed on the river side of the hotel (set four-course dinner £15.95). Rooms in the modern extensions have the best river views; furnishings throughout are in traditional country house style. Pets can be accommodated by arrangement only. Two of the bedrooms are easily accessible for wheelchairs.

Hotel has fishing rights for salmon; swimming pool; sauna; spa bath; sunbed; putting; walking

CORNHILL-ON-TWEED

🏨 ≈ 4/13 🏠 ✎ ▭

Tillmouth Park Hotel, Cornhill-on-Tweed, Northumberland TD12 4UU   (Tel. 0890 2255)
On the A698, one mile north of Cornhill-on-Tweed
£52 single, £78 double.

The perfect country house hotel, built in 1882, using stones from nearby Twizle Castle, by the architect Charles Barry (son of the designer of the Houses of Parliament). It is lovingly maintained, and furnished in the Jacobean style, with an impressive gallery, stained-glass windows, and period four-posters in the bedrooms. There are several acres of garden, and five miles of high-quality salmon fishing on the Tweed. A ghillie will guide and advise if necessary. In winter, the River Till, which runs into the Tweed, can be seen from the dining room (which seats 70), drawing room and many of the splendid, enormous bedrooms. Trees block the views in summer. The restaurant serves traditional English food in season and a five-course meal costs £15.50. The guests can enjoy several miles of walking along Twill and Tweed within the 1000-acre estate. No facilities for the disabled.

Walking; fishing; beach (15 miles away); National Trust properties

CULLERCOATS

🏨 ≈ 17/22 🏠 ✎ ▭

The Bay Hotel, Front Street, Cullercoats, Tyne and Wear NE30 4QB   (Tel. 091 252 3150)
Off the A193, opposite Cullercoats harbour
£18–£23 single, £33–£44 double b&b

Previously the local manor house, this is a modest, family-run hotel. It stands above the small harbour of Cullercoats, with a stunning view across the cliffs to the ruins of Tynemouth Priory. The American artist Winslow Homer painted his seascapes from here in 1882–84. The lifeboat is launched from the harbour, and small fishing boats operate from here too. The cocktail bar (very 1970s chrome), dining room (seats 60) and residents' lounge are on the first floor to make the most of the views. Three local bars are downstairs. Some bedrooms have been renovated, but some are still rather basic. For those who want to explore the city, one great advantage is that Newcastle is only 20 minutes away by Metro. No facilities for the disabled.

Walking; watersports; sea fishing can be arranged; beach

FLEETWOOD

39/57

The North Euston Hotel, The Esplanade, Fleetwood
FY7 6BN   (Tel. 03917 6525)
£37 single, £53 double

A semicircular hotel on the promenade, dating from 1841, with an unspoilt façade. In 1991 the hotel will be celebrating its 150th birthday with special events and souvenirs. The friendly staff will be giving guests gifts such as North Euston Hotel rock and note pads. Inside, there is a huge sea-view bar, and photographs of local history on the walls. There are very light bedrooms and suites, with large windows and balconies; some have views of the River Wyre, and some look out over the bay. The restaurant seats 85 and has good watery views from all tables. Lunch is £7.25, and a three-course dinner is £11.20. However, the famed speciality of the house is fish and chips. One hundred large portions of fresh haddock from the dock are served every day in the high season. The Chatterbox café and a family area in the pub make it a suitable hotel for children. There are disabled lavatories and ramps on the ground floor for lounge, bar and restaurant. The lift is not wide enough for wheelchairs but would help infirm visitors.

Walking; watersports; fishing; beach; golf; games room

GRASMERE

Lake View Guest House, Lake View Drive, Grasmere,
Cumbria LA22 9TD   (Tel. 09665 384)
Open April–November
£18 pp b&b, £26.50 dinner and b&b (£3 extra for private
facilities)
In a good location and off the beaten tourist track through
Grasmere, this friendly bed and breakfast would make a good
base for touring the Lakes. It is about 500 yards away from a
pretty lake and a private footpath winds its way down the
garden to the water's edge where guests can sit and enjoy the
tranquillity of Wordsworth country. The house has a sunny
television lounge. Pictures by local artists decorate the walls,
and are for sale. The dining room seats 12 and dinner is served
at 6.30pm for residents only. Bring your own wine.
Vegetarians and those with special diets can be catered for.
Three self-catering flats are available which sleep two to five
people and cost between £149 and £230 per week depending on
the season. Two of these have water views. No facilities for the
disabled.
*Walks; row boats and windsurfers can be hired nearby; small pebble
beach*

GREENHEAD

Holmhead Farm Licensed Guest House and Holiday Cottage,
Greenhead, Haltwhistle, Northumberland CA6 7HY
(Tel. 069774 7402)
Off the B6318 (call for directions)
£18 b&b; holiday cottage for four £150–£250 a week
This 150-year-old farmhouse lies directly in the line of
Hadrian's Wall beside the upper reaches of the River Tibalt and
just below the mound of the ruined 13th-century Thirlwall
Castle. It was built with stones from the Wall, with Roman-
style arches and a candle-lit, beamed dining room, and modern
furnishings. Guests dine together round a large, oak table. The

friendly owners offer good, clean, farmhouse accommodation. A large residents' lounge is equipped with television, radio, records, tapes and board games for the use of the guests. A solarium, sunbed and foot machine are available to soothe tired limbs and sore feet after walking Hadrian's Wall or the Pennine Way. Mrs Staff is a very knowledgeable guide to the area. The river runs down one side of the small garden. In November, exhausted salmon, nearing their spawning ground, can be seen struggling upstream. The ground floor of the cottage is specially adapted for the disabled.

Golf; riding; swimming; tennis; bowls; cycling; walking; windsurfing; canoeing; sailboarding; fishing; Roman army museum

GRIMSBY

Leon's Fish Restaurant, Riverside, 1 Alexandra Road, Grimsby, South Humberside DM31 1RD   (Tel. 0472 356282)
Not the most picturesque location, beside the canalized River Freshney, on a busy corner opposite the shopping precinct, but Grimsby is a working port, and this is a tremendously popular town-centre eatery. Pizzeria-style, the fish is fried in full view, in the central corner of the L-shaped restaurant, and customers seated at oak tables and chairs are served by waitresses in traditional black and white. The fish is purchased from the owner's brother each morning, so it could not be fresher: there is no cod on the menu as Grimsby folk consider it inferior to their favourite haddock. Main dishes cost from £4.50–£6.75. If you are in Grimsby and hungry, Leon's is the place for you. If you want a romantic meal by the water, go elsewhere. No facilities for the disabled, but helpful staff.

Watersports; fishing

HAMBLETON

The Shard Bridge Inn, Shard Lane, Hambleton, Lancashire
(Tel. 0253 700208)
11am–3.30pm, 6pm–11pm Mon–Sat; noon–3pm, 7pm–
10.30pm Sun

The Shard Bridge is set in a very peaceful part of Lancashire, worth discovering along the little country roads, and is reached by a tiny toll bridge which costs the princely sum of 8p per crossing. It is a roomy pub with two bars overlooking the River Wyre. In summer you can sit out on the river bank and admire the pretty view. Bar food is available (including soup, filled rolls, lasagne and steak). Bed and breakfast accommodation is available locally. There is disabled access and the pub is all on one level but there are no special facilities.
Walking; bird watching; waterskiing; jetskiing; boat racing and windsurfing nearby

HAMBLETON

Hambleton Hall, Hambleton, Oakham, Rutland,
Leicestershire LE15 8TH   (Tel. 0572 756991)
£105–£225 b&b
A first-class country house hotel in a picturesque village, on a peninsula by the vast, quiet expanse of Rutland Water. Built as a hunting lodge in 1881, Hambleton Hall is an example of English luxury at its best. Guests are welcomed on arrival by delightful staff, into a formidable reception room with large comfortable armchairs, old paintings and an open fire. The decoration is very impressive throughout, with airy rooms that afford tremendous views of the lake. There are large amounts of fresh flowers and linen in evidence. The dining room, judged Country Restaurant of the Year for 1990 by the *Good Food Guide*, seats 40 to 50 (set dinner £25–£33); all tables have a view of the water. The chef's specialities include char grilled loin of lamb with a tumblet (layers of potato, aubergine, courgette and tomato baked in olive oil and lamb juice) in a sauce of basil and tomato (£18.50). To follow, try the hot sabayon soufflé of wild strawberries with its own ice and coconut tuile. Services offered by the hotel include secretarial, laundry and babysitting. There is disabled access to the hotel, a lift, and six rooms that would be suitable for the infirm but not for the severely disabled.
Walking; trout and pike fishing can be arranged; sailing club Whitwell (two miles); windsurfing; beach; helipad; golf (six miles

away); riding; cycling; local market towns to visit; National Trust properties nearby

HAWKSHEAD

Walker Ground Manor, Hawkshead, Cumbria LA22 0PD
(Tel. 09666 219)
On B5286
£25–£35 pp b&b

A 16th-century house of Lakeland stone, where one feels more a private guest than a paying customer. Wendy and Dennis Chandler are very chatty and friendly, and dine with their guests in the candle-lit dining room or conservatory, which is full of the heady smell of flowers. The house has its original panelling and a priest hole. Upstairs are beautiful old bedrooms, with four-poster beds and individual, personalized decoration. Two of these have private bathrooms and the other has use of two other bathrooms in the house. At the bottom of the wild, cottage-style garden is a small, pretty, tumbling stream which rises and falls depending on the weather. Dinner costs £10–£15 and may include fresh trout from Esthwaite Water or salmon from Scotland served with fresh vegetables from the garden, lightly baked in the Aga, followed by a good selection of cheese, fresh fruit salad or rich mousse. Lunch and teas can be made by arrangement. The Manor is a non-smoking hotel. No facilities for the disabled.

Walking and climbing nearby; fishing and rowing on Esthwaite Water; sailing and steamers on Windermere and Coniston; lake beaches nearby

HAYDON BRIDGE

The General Havelock Inn, Radcliffe Road, Haydon Bridge, Northumberland NE47 6ER   (Tel. 043 484 376)
Open 11am–2.30pm, 7pm–11pm Wed–Sat; noon–2pm, 7pm–10.30pm Sun. Closed all day Mon and Tues
Opened as a private house in 1840, the inn obtained an ale

licence in 1890 to quench the thirst of the local lead miners. The stable and hayloft have been converted into an airy restaurant with river views. The self-taught chef provides well-flavoured home-made food using North Sea fish and local game. A three-course lunch costs £9.50 and a four-course dinner costs £15.50. A mouth-watering example of a main course could be chicken tarragon, cooked with pan-fried onions, lemon, garlic and cracked black pepper in a ginger and tarragon cream sauce. Bar snacks are also available. There is a tidy garden, with fine views of early 19th-century Haydon Bridge, now closed to traffic, and a terrace where diners can eat on fine days. No facilities for the disabled.

Fishing; walking; golf; Hadrian's Wall (four miles away); Roman museums

HEATON WITH OXCLIFFE

The Golden Ball (Snatchems), Lancaster Road, Heaton with Oxcliffe, Morecambe, Lancashire LA3 3ER
(Tel. 0524 63317)
Open 11am–11pm Mon–Sat; noon–3pm, 7pm–10.30pm Sun
Originally called Snatchems, this charming old pub is set in an area where reeds were cut to thatch the roofs of Lancashire. It is steeped in history: the name Snatchems evolved in the days when press gangs from ships on the River Lune would come to the inn and snatch their next crew from among the clientele. Tankards on the wall tell the story of the 'Queen's Shilling'; if this was dropped in your drink you would automatically be hauled off to work at sea. This practice led to the introduction of glass-bottomed tankards so that locals could have some forewarning of any impending curtailment of their liberty. The decor includes the original beams and low doors, and high-backed leather chairs. Real coal fires in the bar and restaurant and a hospitable landlord make the pub warm and friendly. The small restaurant seats 20; and the menu changes weekly. Choices include 16-inch pizzas served in the top of barrels. Bar food is also available. The tide cuts off the road every day (the pub prints a booklet of tide times for

customers). Outside seats on a raised terrace look over the river. Disabled access but no special facilities.

Walking; bird watching; yachting (moorings available); salmon fishing (need permit from Duchy of Lancaster); waterskiing arranged by pub

HELMSHORE

The Robin Hood Inn, 280 Holcombe Road, Helmshore, Lancashire BB4 4NP   (Tel. 0706 213180)
By the textile museum, one mile off the M66
Open noon–11pm Mon–Sat; noon–3pm, 7pm–10.30pm Sun. Closed lunchtime Mon–Wed
A charming old pub, looking out over the River Ogden, with views of the viaduct and two mill ponds from back windows. A beer garden and patio enable customers to enjoy the scenery in the summer months. The interior is small, cosy and totally unspoilt. There have been no attempts to make it look genuine olde-worlde – it just is. The pub boasts hand-pulled beer, open fires and a ghost called Wilf. Toast your own crumpets over two open fires, or treat yourself to a Bury black pudding. One of the rooms has pinball and old football machines. The main theme of the pub, related to being on the water, is the landlord's love of ducks, which adorn the walls and corners in many shapes and forms. An added attraction is live jazz and blues on Wednesdays and Saturdays. Bed and breakfast accommodation is available locally. No facilities for the disabled.

Walking; trout fishing (£8 for three hours, £15 for the day); textile museum next door

HUBBERHOLME

inn ¹ᐟ³ 🏠 8 🐟 ▱

The George Inn, Hubberholme, Kirk Gill, nr Skipton, North Yorkshire   (Tel. 075 676 223)
Off the B6160 at Buckden

Open 11.30am–3pm, 7pm–11pm Mon–Sat; noon–3pm, 7pm–
10.30pm Sun
£35 double b&b
Separated from the River Wharfe by a country road, the
George satisfies one's image of a truly rural pub, picturesque in
its site and its buildings. The mighty fells rise either side of the
tiny hamlet, culminating in Buckden Pike 2302 feet up. The
16th-century, Grade II listed, white-washed stone inn sits in
this valley to the side of a stone bridge, opposite the 700-year-
old churchyard. Inside are original oak beams, stone-flagged
floors and open fires. Apparently the pub was a favourite of
J. B. Priestley. Bar food and hand-pulled beers are on offer.
The bedrooms are plain and simple; the breakfast room has
pews (the building used to belong to the church) and shares the
same view of the river as the bar. The inn is popular with artists
who are inspired by the scenery. Winter-breaks weekends are
very good value. No facilities for the disabled.
Walking; fishing (permit needed)

HULL

IOI 🏠 ✕ ▭

Cerutti's, 10 Nelson Street, Hull, Humberside HU1 1XE
(Tel. 0482 28501)
Near the marina
Open noon–2pm, 7pm–9.30pm; closed Sat lunch, all day Sun,
bank holidays
Housed in Hull's 17th-century stationmaster's house next to
the old ticket office for the Humber Ferry, Cerutti's has the
atmosphere of a provincial gentleman's club. There is a
comfortable bar downstairs and two dining rooms upstairs,
the nicer of which is bright and well proportioned, overlooking the estuary. From here you look down on what was
once the bustling pier of the Ferry, but is now a quiet, traffic-
free piazza. The service is formal but friendly with clientele
being served little eats with their apéritifs before being guided
to their tables. There is seating for 36 people, with six water-
view tables. The menu mainly has a French influence and
focuses on fresh fish and seafood in different sauces: for

example, Halibut Guiseppe (poached halibut with smoked
salmon and avocado on a hollandaise sauce). Main course
prices start at around £11. No facilities for the disabled.
Walks; watersports nearby; museums; art gallery; marina

HULL

49/99

The Marina Post House Hotel, Castle Street, Hull,
Humberside HU1 2BX   (Tel. 0482 225 221)
Signposted 'New Hotel' from the A63; overlooks marina
£69–£110 per room (breakfast £7.50)
A modern hotel on Hull's new marina, designed and furnished
in a traditional style, with a nautical theme in the reception
areas. A good weekend base by the waterfront in a buzzing
town. The restaurant, bar and lounge overlook the marina, the
old dock warehouses and the new docklands residential
developments. The food is described as English, cooked with
plenty of fresh herbs in a light, modern way. A three-course
meal with coffee costs £15.50. The docklands are well worth
exploring, as there is a surprising amount of activity – not least
the building of the new Princes Quay shopping centre on stilts
above one of the old docks. The hotel runs special activity
weekends with themes such as murder and mystery, golf,
watercolours and heritage. The fitness club is equipped with an
indoor swimming pool, sauna and solarium. There are
disabled facilities on ground floor, and one specially equipped
bedroom.
*Golf; ice-skating; sailing and sea fishing can be arranged; mega-
bowling; railway, maritime and William Wilberforce museums*

LANCASTER

The Water Witch Inn, Canal Side, Lancaster
(Tel. 0524 63828)
Open 11am–11pm Mon–Sat in summer (11am–3pm,
5.30pm–11pm Mon–Sat in winter); noon–3pm, 7pm–10.30pm
Sun

A simply-furnished canalside pub, decorated in a Victorian Romany style in the heart of the old city of Lancaster. The stone walls have narrowboat pictures and canal memorabilia. The pub has a roomy feel, and overlooks a clean canal with barges, swans and ducks. A wrought-iron staircase leads up to a secluded eating area with pine benches and dresser. The hot platters include lasagne, scampi, pizzas and vegetable stroganoff at reasonable prices. A pool table, television and jukebox provide the entertainment downstairs. In summer, food is served at bench tables beside the canal. Cars can be parked on the other side of the water and the pub is reached by a small footbridge. No disabled facilities, but there are no steps into the pub.

Walking; watersports at Morecambe; freshwater and sea fishing; beach; canal cruises

LEALHOLM

The Board Hotel, Village Green, Lealholm, Whitby
YO21 2AJ   (Tel. 0947 87279)
Off the A171, the Guisborough to Whitby road
£10 pp b&b
This plain stone house is in the picturesque village of Lealholm, deep in the Yorkshire Dales. Set on a bend in the River Esk, the hotel overlooks the village green and its grazing sheep. A modest, traditional establishment, with two bars downstairs, and pretty, plainly furnished bedrooms upstairs. The residents' lounge has views of the river. Food is available in one bar where the locals play dominoes: fresh Whitby cod, chips and peas will cost you £4. In summer drinkers can sit in the hotel gardens overlooking the river. The hotel has fishing rights on the Esk so guests bringing their own tackle can fish for salmon there free. New owners have recently taken over the establishment but do not plan to make any radical changes and will keep the good-value prices of the accommodation. No facilities for the disabled.

Walking; watersports; fishing

LINTON

🏰 ⁸/²² 🏠 ◁ ▭

Wood Hall, Linton, Wetherby LS22 4JA   (Tel. 0937 67271)
Off the A661, three miles south of Wetherby
£95–£245 per room
A beautiful Georgian mansion with a Jacobean addition and a
new six-bedroom courtyard wing set on a hill overlooking the
River Wharfe. There are good river views from the bedrooms
but not from the ground floor. The interior decoration befits
the exterior: the original plasterwork has been preserved,
while high-quality restoration furniture fills the rooms and
recreates a country house atmosphere. Drinks in the bar are
served on a grand piano and the lounge is rich with books,
paintings and comfy armchairs. Bedrooms are individually
furnished with decoratively painted furniture and modern
conveniences. In the restaurant the chef Simon Wood uses
fresh produce, and presents it with care and simplicity. The à la
carte menu offers dishes such as mousse scallopes and red
mullet served with a hot watercress, salmon, caviar and butter
sauce. There is one specially equipped room for disabled
visitors on the ground floor (on the same level as the restaurant,
bar, lavatories and access from car park).
*Salmon, trout and barbel fishing (bring equipment); snooker; archery,
clay pigeon shooting and hot-air ballooning by arrangement; walking;
National Trust properties; bird sanctuary; Leeds, Harrogate and
York nearby*

LITTLE SINGLETON

🏰 ⁵/¹⁰ 🏠 ◁ ▭

Mains Hall Country House Hotel, Mains Lane, Little
Singleton, Lancashire   (Tel. 0253 885130)
Off the A585
£35–£90 per room
Built in 1537 by an order of monks, Mains Hall is the oldest
building in West Lancashire, originally used by travellers
journeying to Cockersand Abbey. It is found at the top of a
long private drive, in a fine, woodland setting overlooking

the River Wyre. The interior reflects its impressive history with secret hiding-places used by Cardinal Allen of Rossall during the Papist persecutions. An extravagant wood carving decorates the panelled hall and the staircase. Some of the modernization is slightly at odds with the house (electric fires in lovely old fireplaces). One of the rooms has an impressive four-poster bed. The dining room seats 35; all tables overlook the river (dinner £17.50 to £27.50), and visitors to the restaurant are reputed to travel from as far away as London to sample the excellent beef, veal, pheasant and grouse. Two ground-floor rooms (with bathrooms) are suitable for disabled visitors.

Walking; fishing; beach (Blackpool); sailing; golf; bird watching; fishing lessons; cookery courses

LIVERPOOL

The Pump House, Albert Dock, Liverpool L3 4AA
(Tel. 051 709 2367)
Open 11.30am–11pm Mon–Sat; noon–3pm, 7pm–10.30pm Sun

An early-19th-century pump house renovated to a high standard, in a wonderful situation overlooking the water, the square ship Zebu, and the Port of Liverpool building. The conversion of the Albert Dock has been extremely successful, housing shops and exhibitions, and has now become the third most popular tourist attraction in Great Britain. The pub is very roomy, with lots of dark wood, a marble counter, and architectural prints on the wall. Tall ships visit the dock in summer (a very popular attraction). The pub is frequented by Granada celebrities, business people and tourists, who are all welcomed by the friendly staff and invited to enjoy a drink on the dockside and sample the bar food which is available from noon to 2.30pm. This involves generous helpings of a choice of 15 cheeses and four patés served on granary bread and garnished with pickles. There is a ramp into the pub, and a lavatory for the disabled.

Shopping galleries; Tate gallery; Maritime museum; the 'Beatles Story' in the Albert Dock

LIVERPOOL
74/226

The Atlantic Tower Hotel, Chapel Street, Liverpool L3 9RE
Tel. 051 227 4444
At the head of the pier
£73 single, £80 double b&b
A modern hotel, somewhat startling in appearance, situated at
the head of the pier, with good views of Liverpool's old
buildings, Princes Dock and the Mersey. Bedrooms are light
and airy, and there is one entire floor that is kept specifically for
female guests, and another for non-smokers. One bar is in the
style of a Pullman carriage; another is styled like a ship. The
dining room seats 150 people, and 10 of the tables have a view
of the water. There is a baby-minding service. The staff are
friendly despite the vast size of the hotel. There are
comprehensive conference and banqueting facilities. Limited
disabled facilities (such as lavatories in some areas, and lifts for
access between floors).
*Albert Dock and its many attractions (see above); walks at Sefton
Park (one and a half miles away); fishing can be arranged; beach
(three miles away)*

LYTHAM ST ANNE'S
18/70

The Chadwick Hotel, South Promenade, Lytham St Anne's
FY8 1NP   (Tel. 0253 720 061)
£32.50 single, £42.50 double
This modernized hotel has light and airy bedrooms, with
white walls and brass beds; all the rooms have bathrooms, and
some even have spa baths. The lounge has a large expanse of
windows, which gives the impression that the seats have been
set out for an airport over the sea. The dining room, behind the
lounge seats 150 people, and 10 tables have a view of the sea.
There is a cosmopolitan range of dishes on the menu, with the
emphasis on seafood; the set lunch costs £6.40; the set dinner,
£11.20. The Bugatti bar has a classic car theme, but no sea
view. There are two ground-floor bedrooms with facilities for

disabled visitors, and the hotel has wheelchair access.
Walking; watersports; fishing; beach; health club with indoor pool; spa bath; sauna; solarium; games room

LYTHAM ST ANNE'S

15/41

The Clifton Arms Hotel, West Beach, Lytham St Anne's FY8 5QJ   (Tel. 0253 739898)
£75–£130 per room
Originally a small inn on the Clifton estate, this attractive 150-year-old building is in the quiet part of St Anne's, overlooking the sea front. The bedrooms are massive with large windows and light-coloured furnishings. The lounge, cocktail bar, and most of the tables in the restaurant look over the Ribble estuary (lunch £9.75; dinner £15.50). The menus offer fancy dishes such as 'Duet by Moonlight' which is slices of beef and veal, grilled and served with a pink peppercorn sauce. A good place to stay for peace and quiet, though only 15 minutes away from the bright lights of Blackpool. Pets can be accommodated by request. No facilities for the disabled.
Walking; watersports; fishing; beach; golf; tennis; whirlpool bath; free in-house films; spa baths, sauna and solarium

LYTHAM ST ANNE'S

25/100

The Dalmeny Hotel, 19–33 South Promenade, Lytham St Anne's FY8 1LX   (Tel. 0253 712 236)
£25–£91 per room b&b
The Dalmeny Hotel is situated on the promenade overlooking the sea and promenade gardens. The outside suffers from ugly modern architecture but inside it is very comfortable. The rooms are good value, especially the apartments (£50 for four people; from £68 for six people, with kitchenette and some with balcony). A good place for a family holiday as the hotel offers an organized crèche, outside play area, special children's tea menu and half portions, family entertainments and a games room. All children can stay free in the month of June.

There are four different eating establishments to choose from: The C'est La Vie (lunch £10.50, dinner £17.50), The Carvery, (recommended for excellent value and good food), The Barbecue, and The Buttery bar (salads and teas). Other facilities include a non-smoking lounge, ballroom, beauty salon, large indoor swimming pool, squash court, saunas and solariums. Six of the bedrooms have disabled facilities.

Beach; Blackpool illuminations; tennis and four championship golf courses nearby

MANCHESTER

 81/166

The Copthorne Hotel, Clippers Quay, Salford Quays, Greater Manchester M5 3DL   (Tel. 061 873 7321)
Three minutes from the Salford turning of the M62/M63
£75–£85 single, £85–£95 double
A smart, modern hotel on Salford Quay, focusing on business and function trade. There is a sunny and spacious reception area, and comfortable, well-equipped bedrooms. There are two restaurants, which have nine tables with views of the quay and the marina between them: guests are required to wear formal dress in Chandlers, the à la carte restaurant. The Quayside Restaurant has a more informal atmosphere. There is a health and leisure centre within the hotel, comprising multigym, sauna, solarium and swimming pool. Moorings for visitors can be found at Salford Quay. The hotel has disabled access, and one bedroom which may be suitable for disabled guests.

Granada Television studios, Castlefield Urban Heritage Park and Manchester's Chinatown are all within range for visits

MANCHESTER

The Mark Addy, Stanley Street, Salford, Manchester 3 (Tel. 061 832 4080)
Open 11.30am–11pm Mon–Sat; noon–3pm, 7pm–10.30pm Sun

Overlooking a now cleaner River Irwell, the pub is named after the 19th-century hero who rescued 50 people from drowning in the filthy water. Mark Addy was the only civilian to receive the Royal Albert Medal (otherwise known as the Victoria Cross) from Queen Victoria. The river (which looks more like a canal) marks the border between Manchester and Salford, and the pub was originally the waiting room for boat passengers. Mark Addy's story and the history of the quay, the prison, and the landing stage are well documented on the pub walls. All seats in the roomy bar overlook the water. Boddingtons Bitter and Marston's Pedigree serve to quench the thirst. The food on offer is somewhat of a novelty in that the range is so huge. Customers can choose from 70 cheeses from around Europe (and be advised on the best wines to accompany them), 14 meat and vegetarian pâtés, dill cucumbers, all served with freshly baked granary bread, and a doggy bag for those whose eyes are bigger than their stomachs. On the riverside is a pretty, terraced garden with a magnolia tree and private moorings. No disabled facilities but helpful staff.

Granada Studio tours; Castlefield Roman fort; shopping centre; walking

MEDBOURNE

inn

The Nevill Arms, 12 Waterfall Way, Medbourne,
Leicestershire   (Tel. 085883 288)
Village on the B664, pub in centre of the village green
Open noon–2.30pm, 6pm–11pm Mon–Sat; noon–3pm, 7pm–
10.30pm Sun
£40 single, £50 double b&b
This picturesque inn enjoys an extremely quiet setting by the River Welland. An open fire and lots of brass fittings make for a relaxed atmosphere. Fifty ducks have made their home on the water, and have become the main theme of the pub; to be found on the beer mats and flying – in effigy – up the wall. Three newly converted bedrooms in an adjoining cottage are decorated in pretty furnishings. Full English breakfasts are

served in the conservatory overlooking the terraced garden. Two bars offer food such as beef stroganoff, steak and kidney pie, treacle tart and bread and butter pudding. Indoor pursuits include skittles, carpet bowls, darts, Connect 4, shove ha'penny, dominoes and cards. There are riverside tables in the garden and a dovecote over the water. Barbecues are held in the summer months. No facilities for the disabled.

Walking; watersports (three miles away); fishing; game fishing (Eye Brook Reservoir); Rutland Water; cycle track

MILNTHORPE

inn ≈ 6/6 ⌂ 14 ⌀ ▭

The Ship Inn, Sandside, Milnthorpe, Cumbria LA7 7HW
(Tel. 05395 63113)
Open 11am–3pm, 6pm–11pm Mon–Sat (11am–11pm Mon–Sat Easter to October); noon–3pm, 7pm–10.30pm Sun.
Accommodation closed Christmas and New Year
£15 single, £35 double b&b
A pretty, white 17th-century inn overlooking Morecambe Estuary and the mountains beyond. Original beams, ship pictures and nautical maps adorn the inside, with good water views from four old windows. The pub is tied to Scottish and Newcastle and serves Theakston's ale, Younger's and Beck's. The food is reasonably priced and offers hot platters such as Cumberland sausage with traditional apple sauce. Several vegetarian items are on offer every day. Pool and darts are played in the pub. The bedrooms are attractive and light with pine furniture, and all overlook the estuary. A popular spot for bird watchers (heron can be spotted) and painters. Approach with care: at high tide water covers the road. The pub has disabled access but no special facilities.

Playground; walking; sailing in Arnside; sea fishing in Sandside; salmon fishing in Belar; bird watching in sanctuary; riding in Beatnam; summer guided walks from Arnside to Grange (takes four and a half hours); National Trust properties

MORECAMBE

🏨 12/33 ⌇ 🏠 ⌸ ▭

The Clarendon Hotel, The Promenade, West End,
Morecambe, Lancashire LA4 4EP   (Tel. 0524 410 180)
£29 single, £45 twin or double b&b
In a seaside town full of old-fashioned character, the Clarendon
has good sea views and plenty of space. Morecambe is
presently undergoing major improvements with the creation
of a large sandy beach, and a new tourism centre in the old
railway station. The hotel decoration is fairly average but the
'Davey Jones Locker' pub in the basement has a nautical
flavour, with ships' clocks, big barrels supporting the bar and
picture portholes. It is popular with locals and visitors alike.
The dining room seats 70 people, with seven tables overlooking the water. The three-course set dinner for £7.50 is
extremely good value for typical old-fashioned hotel food –
garlic mushrooms, roast lamb and a sweet trolley. The menu
changes nightly and offers four or five choices for each course.
Vegetarian meals can be prepared on request. The bedrooms
are comfortable, spacious and well equipped. No facilities for
the disabled, though there is a lift.
Walking; watersports; fishing; beach; golf; sea fishing

NEWBY BRIDGE

🏨 15/35 ⌇ 🏠 ⌿ ▭

Whitewater Hotel, The Lakeland Village, Newby Bridge,
Ulverston, Cumbria LA12 8PX   (Tel. 05395 31133)
On the A590 between the motorway and Barrow-in-Furness
£60 single, £85–£100 double b&b
Built around an old mill, from characteristic Lakeland stone
and slate, the hotel is right on the River Leven, and is an ideal
place to be pampered by day and fed to the gunwales at night.
Here you can indulge in a total health treatment: facilities
within the hotel include a swimming pool, a whirlpool, a gym,
sunbeds, squash courts, and two floodlit tennis courts. The
bedrooms are comfortable, and those facing the water have
one original stone wall. The dining room seats 70 people, and

four of the tables overlook the water. Bar lunches are available; a set dinner in the restaurant costs £16.50. Timeshare cottages and apartments can be rented for between £535 and £750 per week. There are no steps into the hotel, and there is a lift to the restaurant that is large enough to accommodate a wheelchair.
Walking; fishing; shingle beach; watersports nearby; riding; archery; clay pigeon shooting

NEWCASTLE

IOI 🍴₉ ⊗ ▭

Fisherman's Lodge, Jesmond Dene, Newcastle-upon-Tyne NE7 7BQ   (Tel. 091 281 3281)
Off the A1058, about three and a half miles east of central Newcastle, in Jesmond Dene Park
Open noon–2pm, 7pm–11pm Mon–Fri; 7pm–11pm Sat. Closed Sun and bank holidays
An extremely smart restaurant, sitting in a beautiful wooded dell which has the Ouse burn running through it. The building is a Victorian conversion, which is in earshot but unfortunately not in view of the babbling water. Nevertheless, this is a wonderfully picturesque setting and it is hard to believe you are so close to centre of Newcastle. The staff are friendly and there is plenty of parking. The restaurant offers innovative dishes built around fresh, local seafood. Other gastronomic possibilities include oriental-style duck breast, veal, partridge and Northumbrian lamb. The set lunch is £13.50, and à la carte main courses start at £16. There are 65 covers in the comfortable and nicely decorated dining area. Customers can enjoy a pre-meal walk in the spacious park to see the Ouse waterfall and old preserved mill. Booking is an absolute necessity. No facilities for the disabled.
Walking; Newcastle (three and a half miles away)

NEWTON-ON-OUSE

🛏 🍴 ◁ ▭

The Dawnay Arms, Newton-on-Ouse, York YO6 2BR
(Tel. 034 74 345)

Well signposted from the A19, seven miles north-west of York
Open 11.30am–2.30pm, 6.30pm–11pm Mon–Sat; noon–3pm,
7pm–10.30pm Sun. Closed Mon lunchtimes in winter
A pretty 18th-century whitewashed pub with black shutters on
the banks of the River Ouse. The pub stands near to Newton
parish church and the National Trust's Beningbrough Hall
is accessible from the village. Two traditional oak-beamed bars
are decorated with red carpets, copper tables and a log fire.
Tetley's Yorkshire Bitter, Theakston's hand-pulled beer and
Dawnay wine are the specialities of the house. The dining
room seats 50 people, overlooks the river and offers a candlelit
dinner of home-made duck pâté, Highland salmon, steaks and
vegetarian dishes. The traditional roast beef and Yorkshire
pudding served at Sunday lunchtime is very popular. A sunny
patio in the riverside garden is good for enjoying a drink and a
bite on warm days. The inn has fishing rights (mostly trout)
for its stretch of river and charges £1 per day. Private
moorings, a large car park and local bed and breakfast all add
up to make this an enjoyable place to visit. No facilities for the
disabled.
*Children's play house; North Yorkshire moor walks; fishing; boat
hire (Linton Lock half a mile away); Beningbrough Hall nearby*

NORTHALLERTON

Kirkby Fleetham Hall, Northallerton, Kirkby Fleetham
DL7 0SU   (Tel. 0609 748 226)
Two miles from the A1, signposted
£102–£175 per room b&b
This grand Georgian mansion, in its own 30-acre estate, nestles
in a deep valley between the North Yorkshire moors and the
Dales. There are no buildings in sight apart from a twelfth-
century church. A private lake offers fishing (the hotel can lend
equipment) and a place to watch wildfowl. A huge staircase
dominates the reception area, creating from the start a
gracious, country house atmosphere. The public rooms and
bedrooms, many of which still have their original decoration,

are very traditional and beautifully furnished. The dining room seats 40 people, and all tables overlook the lake. The sumptuous four-course dinner menu (£28) offers dishes such as 'A *delice* of sea bass baked with Welsh onions and fine celery on a rich port wine sauce'. The tranquil spot and discreet service make this a wonderfully peaceful retreat. No facilities for the disabled.

Walking; fishing; clay pigeon shooting; National Trust properties; York and Harrogate nearby

NORTH DALTON

inn 🏊 🏡 🚳 ▭

The Star Inn, North Dalton, Driffield, Humberside
YO25 9UX   (Tel. 037 781 688)
Village on the B1246, between Pocklington and Great Driffield
Open 11.30am–11pm Mon–Sat; noon–3pm, 7pm–10.30pm Sun
£37.50 single, £49 double/twin b&b

Right next to the village pond and opposite the Norman village church, this simple stone building has been an inn since Georgian times. The Star was originally a mail coach stop between York and Beverley minsters and lies on the famous Minster walk. All around are the undulating Yorkshire Wolds, an area as yet unspoilt by tourism. The snug ground-floor bar is the village pub, where welcoming staff serve Tetley's Bitter and John Smith's traditional ales. It is furnished with curiosities such as old sewing machines, a wooden till and Victorian family photographs. The restaurant has its own bar area where guests can enjoy an apéritif before dining. Interesting choices include rabbit pie followed by hot sticky toffee pudding. All drinking and eating areas overlook the pond. The pretty bedrooms are well equipped with added extras such as books, cassettes, and even bath toys. No facilities for the disabled.

Walking; gliding (Pocklington gliding club); clay pigeon shooting (48-hours notice); watersports; fishing and beach within 20 miles; tarot card readings

PIERCEBRIDGE

inn ☷ 8/40 ⚔ ⊘ ▭

The George Inn, Piercebridge, County Durham
(Tel. 0325 374 576)
On the B6275
£40 single, £50 double, £60 twin b&b
A lovely ancient coaching inn nestling on the banks of the River Tees and looking across to the graceful arches of Pierce Bridge. The area, once inhabited by the Romans, is steeped in history and archaeologists believe that the river here formed a basin where goods were transhipped from Dere Street to barges. The pub has four bars, one of which is reputed to have been a hiding place for Dick Turpin. Other features include a large, well-lit dining room with river views, a splendid 1920s function room with French windows to the river and a good-sized riverside garden for sitting out in fine weather. In the summer there is a ball in a marquee on the island. Bar meals are served all day, and the full dining menu is appropriately called 'The Feast' with a wide vegetarian choice, steaks and chicken dishes (a main course costing between £6 and £9), accompanied by a good wine list. The hotel rents two rods on the Tees for trout fishing. No disabled facilities but helpful staff.
Walking; fishing; Yorkshire Dales, Highforce and Aysgarth waterfalls nearby; Beamish Museum (working farm)

PRESTON

🏛 ☷ 58/72 ⚔ ⊲ ▭

The Tickled Trout, Preston New Road, Samlesbury, Preston PR5 0UJ   (Tel. 0772 877 671)
Near Exit 31 of the M6 (call for precise directions)
£65 single, £76 twin/double
A modern hotel, with standard decoration and piped music, which would make a good stopping off point on a north–south journey. You can just see the motorway, though more importantly there is a good view of the River Ribble. Bedrooms are large and well equipped, if a little characterless. Both of the bars overlook the river. Pets can be accommodated

by request. There are good leisure facilities – a jet pool and exercise machines – for anyone needing a stretch after too many hours behind the wheel, and also a sauna and solarium. The Kingfisher Restaurant, with the old beams of the original building, offers a variety of enticing dishes, and hosts a dinner dance on Friday and Saturday nights. No facilities for the disabled, though there are two ground-floor rooms.

Walking; golf; riding; lawn bowls; jet pool; sauna, solarium, gym and steam room

RICHMOND

Howe Villa, Whitcliffe Mill, Richmond DL10 4TJ
(Tel. 0748 85 00 55)
Off the A6108, half a mile out of Richmond
Open March to late November
£36–£42 pp dinner and b&b

Don't be put off by the less than tidy approach: the villa is an exquisite Georgian house tucked into a hollow and overlooking the River Swale. Lovingly restored by the owners, the public rooms and bedrooms are well proportioned and all are elegantly decorated. The first-floor sitting room and dining room command magnificent river views, though the bedrooms are on the ground floor, allowing only tall people to see the water. With just four bedrooms and 10 covers in the dining room, Howe Villa feels more like a private house than a hotel. Lunch costs £9.50, and a four-course dinner costs £23. The menu changes every night with a choice of starters and sweets, and a hearty main course in between. Guests are offered a drink and canapés before their meal, but are asked to bring their own wine, which will be served without a corkage charge. No facilities for the disabled.

Walking; fishing (day licence in town); golf course in Richmond; riding

ROWSLEY

🏨 ≈⁴/₂₀ 🚣 ⌂ 💳

The Peacock, Rowsley, Matlock, Derbyshire DE4 2EB
(Tel. 0629 733518)
On the A6 between Matlock and Bakewell
Bar open 11am–3pm, 6pm–11pm Mon–Sat; noon–3pm, 7pm–
10.30pm Sun; drinks service available in lounge from 11am–
11pm
£65 single, £75 twin/double (breakfast £5–£8)
Built in 1652 as a dower house for Haddon Hall, the Peacock
became an inn in 1828. The small cosy bar has oak beams, a
copper bar and stone walls; the atmosphere strikes a balance
between traditional character and modern smartness. The
bedrooms are pretty, decorated in a relaxed style with friezes
and matching bedcovers. More than four have river views
when the leaves drop in autumn. The restaurant has space for
45 diners, who can enjoy gazing at the garden and eating at
tables carved by the famous Mousey Thompson. Cold buffet
(£9.50) and other snacks are available at lunchtime; dinner
(£23) is a four-course affair offering an English menu with a
wide selection of wines. The garden, which grows herbs,
reaches down to the River Derwent, with views of two
bridges. No facilities for the disabled.
*Walking; fishing (hotel has 12 rods on a seven-mile stretch of the
River Wye, fishing for brown and rainbow trout from 1 April to 31
October*

SCARBOROUGH

🏨 ≈⁵³/₇₃ 🚣 ⌂ 💳

The Esplanade Hotel, Belmont Road, Scarborough
YO11 2AA   (Tel. 0723 360 382)
£33–£60 b&b
Conjure up in your mind the image of a typical English seaside
hotel, and there you have the Esplanade. An early Victorian
building dating from 1830, it stands on a cliff, overlooking
Scarborough harbour and the sea. The views from the
restaurant, the terrace and the majority of the bedrooms are

superb. The decor is very English, with lots of patterned wallpaper and reproduction furniture, though the restaurant, with 20 sea-view tables, is modern. The bedrooms are well furnished though the corridors have a slightly shabby feel. The hotel caters well for families with family suites and laundry facilities. Bar meals are available at lunchtimes in the Parlour bar, which overlooks the sea, and there is also a terrace with sea views. Scarborough beach is five minutes' walk away. Guests can fish from the town harbour. Pets can be accommodated by arrangement. The hotel can make arrangements for guests who want to visit the Stephen Joseph Theatre in the Round. No facilities for the disabled.

Walking; watersports; fishing; beach (five minutes' walk away)

SCARBOROUGH

The Holbeck Hall Hotel, Sea Cliff Road, Scarborough
YO11 2XX   (Tel. 0723 374374)
£47.50–£55 pp

Once a fine 1880s Victorian mansion, now a luxury hotel, Holbeck Hall is set high on the south cliff overlooking the sea in three acres of lawns, gardens and woodland. The most striking feature is a magnificent baronial hall complete with an enormous stone fireplace, original painted frieze, and minstrel's gallery. Many of the bedrooms overlook the sea as does the dining room, the Rose Lounge and adjacent conservatory. Bedrooms are fitted out to a high standard. The original sumptuous decor makes this a good place for those who seek a top-class hotel on the coast with a slightly unusual country house character. The restaurant serves good English food. No facilities for the disabled.

Walking; watersports; yachting; boating by arrangement; fishing (two rods on River Derwent, 25 minutes' drive away); beaches (20 minutes' walk, five minutes by car)

SEAHOUSES

The Beach House Hotel, Sea Front, Seahouses,
Northumberland NE68 7SR   (Tel. 0665 720 337)
Open April–October
£24–£29.50 pp b&b
In an enlarged and altered 1920s bungalow villa, this quiet and comfortable guest house has ravishing views of the Farne Islands. Downstairs there are two comfortable lounges and a dining room with huge picture windows making the most of the views. The bedrooms are individually decorated; only three of them face the sea. There is a large back garden, and from the green in front of the house you can see Bamburgh Castle to the north and Seahouses harbour to the south. There are regular boat trips from the harbour to the Farne Islands (and visits to Lindisfarne Priory) during the summer season. The owners say that they try to create a dignified yet laid back atmosphere, but cannot control the dining room stampede every evening. The food is imaginative and English, with home-baked bread, and fish dishes are a speciality. There is a large ground-floor room, with bathroom and ramps, that is suitable for disabled visitors.
Walking; beach; watersports (two miles away)

SEAHOUSES

The Olde Ship, Seahouses, Northumberland NE68 7RD
(Tel. 0665 720 200)
Village on the B1340
Open 11am–3pm, 6pm–11pm
£27.50 b&b, £72 pp for two nights dinner and b&b
A stone's throw from the harbour, this 18th-century hotel, originally built as a farmhouse, is not quite on the waterfront, but has a nautical character all its own. There is a fantastic collection of maritime memorabilia, collected over three generations, which fills every spare corner of the building; upstairs, the long gallery has a collection of model ships. Of the

public rooms, only the first-floor residents' lounge, with a fine bay window, has harbour views. Three of the bedrooms are in an annexe to the pub. The terraced garden, with a small putting green, and the summer house overlook the harbour. The restaurant (no sea view) serves good home cooking; dinner costs £11.50. Bar meals are also served. No facilities for the disabled.

Walking; fishing; beach; visits to Farne Islands bird sanctuary

SHARDLOW

Hoskins Wharf, London Road, Shardlow, Derbyshire
DE7 2GL   (Tel. 0332 792844)
On the A6, south-east of Derby
11am–11pm Mon–Sat in summer (11am–2.30pm, 6.30pm–11pm Mon–Sat in winter); noon–3pm, 7pm–10.30pm Sun
A well-converted mill, with thick walls and original timbers, in an attractive setting by the Trent and Mersey canal: water actually runs underneath the restaurant. Large windows give the clientele good views of the canal from the two bars. There are moorings on the canal for those passing by boat who want to stop for a drink. Meals are available in the grill room restaurant at lunchtimes and in the evenings (main courses cost between £6.25 and £10.75). Children are allowed into the restaurant, but not into the bars. A motel is being built alongside the pub, which will add 28 bedrooms. No facilities for the disabled.

Walking along towpaths; watersports at Shardlow Marina; fishing on canal; barges can be hired next to the pub

SHARDLOW

Malt Shovel, Shardlow, Derbyshire DE7 2HG
(Tel. 0332 792392)
Off the A6
Open 11.30am–3pm, 5.30pm–11pm Mon–Sat; noon–3pm, 7pm–10.30pm Sun

A comfortable, cosy and traditional English pub, just across the road from the Trent and Mersey canal. The building is interesting inside, with many odd angles and ceilings of variable height. Good bar food is available at lunchtimes: as well as the standard menu, there are daily specials such as game pies (£3.60) and Mediterranean chicken in lobster sauce (£4.50). The pub offers a good range of malt whiskies. The pub is said to be haunted by the ghost of Humphrey, a tramp who drowned in a vat of beer at the brewery next door. There is a patio area at the front of the pub, where you can sit and admire the canal. No facilities for the disabled.
Walking; coarse fishing; Donington Racing Museum

SKELWITH BRIDGE

IOI 🏠 ⌦ ⊟

Chesters Coffee Shop, Skelwith Bridge, nr Ambleside, Cumbria LA22 9NN   (Tel. 05394 32553)
Open 10am–5pm all week in summer; 10am–4.45pm all week in winter. Closed five days at the end of January
This friendly coffee shop is set in a gallery of shops by the River Brathay (which is just across the car park). There are wood-panelled walls, pine tables, a cosy wood-burning stove and burgundy festoon blinds, and a licensed restaurant is attached. It is well worth visiting for the mouth-watering cakes alone, if not for the pretty location. Hot lunches, teas and cappuccinos are also on offer. The lunchtime menu changes daily with temptations such as chicken and asparagus seasame pie, and walnut and stilton profiteroles followed by banana toffee flan and lemon double layer cake, all at reasonable prices. You can sit outside in summer, though the tables are not directly over the water. After eating visitors can easily spend all their money in the gift shop and the slate showroom. Tends to heave with people in the high season. No facilities for the disabled.
Walking; fishing

SOWERBY BRIDGE

🍺 🏠 ⌖ ▭

The Moorings Inn, (Bolton Brow), Sowerby Bridge, West
Yorkshire HX6 2AG   (Tel. 0422 833940)
Off the A58
Open 11am–3pm, 6pm–11pm Mon–Sat; noon–3pm, 7pm–
10.30pm Sun
An unusual place, in that the surroundings smack of industry
rather than leisure. The Victorian industrial buildings seem to
be black with soot even now. The Moorings is a converted
1790 canalside warehouse at the canal basin between the
westbound Rochdale canal and the eastbound Calder and
Hebble Navigation canal. Inside is a restaurant, which seats 60,
and a bar. The canal is visible from both; and food ranges from
simple snacks through to steaks, with the daily special costing
about £7. From the bar you can see a collection of painted
barges (you can also see a used-car dump, but only in the
distance). You cannot hire barges from the Moorings itself but
a boathouse nearby hires out barges by the week. There is
wheelchair access to the inn, though the lavatory is up two
steps.
Walking; fishing; barge hire nearby

SPARK BRIDGE

🏨 ^4/5^ 🏠 👌 ▭

Bridgefield House, Spark Bridge, nr Ulverston, Cumbria
LA12 8DA   (Tel. 022985 239)
£37 pp b&b; £56 pp dinner and b&b
An elegant, 19th-century residence in a pretty situation with
lawns stretching down to fields and the River Crake. The hotel
has three acres of wooded grounds and a vegetable garden
which supplies the restaurant. The decoration is comfortable
but not ostentatious, with log fires and armchairs to revive the
weary walker. The bedrooms are simply furnished and are
particularly peaceful as they do not house televisions. Mr and
Mrs Glister are very welcoming and friendly: she has been

named as one of the top five female chefs in England. Four tables in the dining room (which seats 30) have river views. Non-residents are welcome at dinner, which will cost them £22. The emphasis is on local dishes, and the daily menu runs to six mouth-watering courses, including sorbet and savouries, followed by coffee and Kendal mint cake. No facilities for the disabled.
Salmon and sea trout fishing available through hotel; windsurfing, sailing and canoeing (bring equipment); shore beach (two miles away); sandy beach (nine miles away)

SPROTBOROUGH

The Boat Inn, Sprotborough, Doncaster, West Yorkshire DM5 7NB   (Tel. 0302 857 188)
By the bridge over the River Don at the south end of Sprotborough village
Open 11am–3pm, 6pm–11pm Mon–Sat; noon–2.30pm, 7pm–10.30pm Sun
The Boat inn is situated in a secluded spot by the river, though it is quite difficult to see the river from the inn thanks to the high embankment. The attractive stone building was once a farmhouse, and has its own courtyard, with tables where guests can drink in summer. Inside there is a bar where food is served and a separate restaurant. The bar has open stone fireplaces, and stools and wheelback chairs clustered round tables: very much the traditional country pub save for the odd garish touch which spoils the total effect. In the restaurant, a four-course meal with coffee costs £18.50. Barges and a water bus plough down the Don in summer. Literary sleuths may like to know that Walter Scott is said to have written *Ivanhoe* here. There is wheelchair access to the pub, and a lavatory for the disabled.
Walking; boating; fishing; Conisbrough Castle

STAMFORD BRIDGE

The Corn Mill, Main Street, Stamford Bridge
YO4 1AE   (Tel. 0759 71274)
In the centre of Stamford Bridge, north-east of York on the
A166
A very handsome, 18th-century industrial building on the
River Derwent. Built on rock foundations, it was one of few
mills to have sufficient current to drive the wheel without
having to store up the water in a mill pond. Inside, one can see
the original wheel and gears, grindstone and millrace. There
are two bars and a restaurant, all overlooking the water. The
car park looks directly on to the weir, with hundreds of ducks
and pigeons. There is a good atmosphere, since so much of the
original building and its oak beams remain; touches such as the
coloured lights on the wheel, for example, seem a little naff by
contrast. The carvery and steak bar offer food from noon to
2pm, and 7pm–10pm; the small Kiln bar has a rounded stone
ceiling, completely covered with a mural of various faces and
scenes. Live Country and Western music on Sundays, and a
disco on Saturday nights are additional attractions. There is
wheelchair access to the bars only.
Fishing (licence available from the local Post Office); pleasure boats
for hire nearby

STAPLEFORD

Stapleford Park Hotel, Stapleford, Melton Mowbray,
Leicestershire LE14 2EF   (Tel. 057 284522)
Off the B676, three miles south-east of Melton Mowbray
£126–£300 per room b&b
A Grade I listed, 16th-century building in 500 acres of parkland
and woods, with fine views out over the lake. This country
house hotel is on a scale grand enough to put most of its rivals
to shame, with young, extremely friendly staff. The atmosphere is surprisingly warm for such an exclusive place. There

are 'signature' bedrooms, each decorated by a famous-name designer, from Turnbull and Asser to David Hicks. The bathrooms are palatial affairs in marble and mahogany with thick white towelling robes to wrap up in. The dining room seats 70 people, and the cuisine is described as 'Post Foodie', which perhaps translates best as 'a combination of styles from around the world'. Vegetables for the kitchen are grown in the walled garden. Breakfast is presented on Peter Rabbit china and is an unusually generous meal involving stilton and red Leicester soufflé and apple and raisin pancakes. Among other amusing luxuries are wellies and dogs on loan for walks in the woodland, and there is a helipad. No disabled facilities but helpful staff.

Clay pigeon shooting; stables; walking; watersports; coarse fishing (carp)

TYNEMOUTH

The Park Hotel, Grand Parade, Tynemouth, Tyne and Wear NE30 4JQ   (Tel. 091 257 1406)
On the A193 sea front between Tynemouth and Cullercoats
£49.50 pp b&b; £66 executive suite
Standing proud on the clifftop above a beautiful sandy bay, this hotel retains much of its original 1930s *joie de vivre*, and boasts the finest sea-front position in Tynemouth. There are no bay views from the restaurant, though this does have a fine tropical aquarium, but the bar, with its curved metal windows, has a fine view. The whole hotel has recently been upgraded, so that many rooms share this view from the first and second floors. It is a popular local spot, particularly for weekend weddings, so come for the Tyneside experience, rather than for peace and quiet. Pets can be accommodated at the manager's discretion. One bedroom has a ramp and widened doors, and may suit disabled visitors.

Walking; watersports; fishing; beach; sea fishing and yachting can be arranged

ULLSWATER

Sharrow Bay Country House Hotel, Ullswater, Penrith,
Cumbria CA10 2LZ (Tel. 07684 86301)
Off the A66 (call for specific directions)
Closed December–February
£70–£130 pp dinner and b&b
Reputed to be the first country house hotel in England,
Sharrow Bay is now celebrating its 43rd year in business. The
original managers still work alongside dedicated staff with a
policy to 'nurture, nourish, cosset and care for' their welcomed
customers. The hotel is a 17th-century converted farmhouse
with grounds leading to the lake shore. The views from the
main reception room look like a perfect picture, framed in the
window. There is plenty to look at within the rooms apart
from the views; chandeliers, old prints, dolls in dolls' chairs, a
pretty conservatory, and a fireplace bought from Warwick
Castle. Rooms in the Lodge and Bankhouse are more spacious
with sitting areas to relax in. In the baroque-style breakfast
room, converted from the old barn, guests sit at long tables on
high-backed tapestry chairs. The dining room seats 65 people,
with 15 tables overlooking the water. Non-residents are
welcome at dinner (£37), which is a lavish six courses, with a
good selection for a set menu. There are no special disabled
facilities but there is a downstairs bedroom.
Walking; watersports; fishing; lake beach

ULVERSTON

Bay Horse Inn and Bistro, Canal Foot, Ulverston, Cumbria
LA12 9EL (Tel. 0229 53972)
Follow signs to Canal Foot off the A590, the Barrow to
Greenodd road
Pub hours: 11am–3pm, 6pm–11pm Mon–Sat; noon–3pm,
7pm–10.30pm Sun. Restaurant closed Sun, and Mon lunch
The approach to this wonderful inn on Morecambe Bay is
unpromising – through a chemical industrial estate – but

persevere. You will find a cosy pub with coal fires, old horse brasses, and plates and dried flowers on the walls. Two hundred years old, the building was originally a row of fishermen's cottages with a small brewery and pub attached. The Bistro has a different atmosphere; most of it is in a light conservatory overlooking the estuary. Chef Robert Lyons used to work at the Miller Howe and people travel from far afield to sample his cuisine. His policy is to produce quality English food using as much local produce as possible. Children over 12 are allowed in the restaurant, which seats 28 people. The set lunch costs £12.50; dinner main courses cost £10 to £13. There are two dinner sittings: 6.30pm for 7pm, and 8.30pm for 9pm. The clientele is half business from the chemical works and half visitors who have come to check out the good reputation of the inn for themselves. Intrepid adventurers can test their nerves as there are guided tours over the quicksands when the tide is out. There is wheelchair access and a lavatory for disabled visitors.

Walking; sea trout and salmon fishing (bring equipment); visits to famous crystal factory in Ulverston which supplies all the British embassies around the world

WALTON

The Waterton Park Hotel, Walton Hall, Walton, Wakefield
WF2 6PW   (Tel. 0924 257 911)
Off the A61, the Wakefield to Barnsley road
£48–£56 single, £60–£72 double b&b

The hotel is a beautiful 1764 building, situated on a small island in the middle of a lake surrounded by fine countryside, though slightly spoiled by a range of modern squash courts built opposite the entrance, and a modern leisure centre attached to the back of the hotel. However, it is a very comfortable place to stay with all modern conveniences and wonderful views over the lake from all the public rooms. Inside the decor is fairly anonymous though some of the original plasterwork survives. The restaurant seats 60; most tables have lake views. Two menus are on offer, one at £13.25 for four courses including a choice of a roast, fish, steak and a vegetarian dish, or a larger selection of five courses for £21.50. The coffee shop serves sandwiches, spaghetti and snacks which can be consumed on the waterside patio next to the barbecue. No facilities for the disabled.

Indoor swimming pool, sauna, spa bath, solarium, gymnasium and steam room; old sand pit; squash; fly fishing on lake (equipment can be hired); walking; watersports with tuition on reservoir nearby (windsurfing, sailing and canoeing) – advance booking available

WATERMILLOCK-ON-ULLSWATER

Rampsbeck Country House Hotel, Watermillock-on-Ullswater, Cumbria CA11 0LP   (Tel. 07684 86442)
Fifteen minutes from Junction 40 of the M6 (call for precise directions)
Closed January–February
£30–£45 pp b&b, £58–£70 pp dinner and b&b
A very pretty, comfortable, early 18th-century country house hotel, standing in 18 acres of tranquil parkland and gardens on the shore of Lake Ullswater, with its own meadow running down to the lake. There is a beautiful, well-kept garden: in summer, the French windows of the drawing room open on to it for evening strolls. The main reception rooms are decorated in warm floral prints, while the bedrooms continue the flowery theme but in a lighter tone. Some of these rooms have magnificent views of garden, marina and lake together. The dining room seats 40; non-residents are welcome at dinner (set dinner £27), which is based on award-winning modern classical English and French cookery, with ideas such as a 'Symphony of Seafood' followed by hot mango soufflé. Packed lunches can be made up for guests (£6), and special diets can be catered for. Children can be accommodated by arrangement. The management need prior warning if you are to be accompanied by four-legged friends – and they will be charged £2 per night. No facilities for the disabled.
Walking; fishing; watersports (hotel has its own marina; bring own

equipment, no waterskiing); yacht tuition and charter £50 a day; beach; lake trips available

WHITBY

inn ≈ 3/3 ⌂ ◇ ▱

The Duke of York Inn, 124 Church Street, Whitby
YO22 4DE   (Tel. 0947 600 324)
Open 11am–11pm Mon–Sat May–October (11am–3pm,
7pm–11pm Mon–Sat November–April); noon–3pm, 7pm–
10.30pm Sun
£24 double (room only, no breakfast available)
The Esk Estuary is an area that is swimming in history and curious tales of bygone times. Captain James Cook sailed from the harbour on his voyage to the South Pacific; Bram Stoker wrote the original Dracula story here; and Church Street in the past has been the haunt of smugglers, whalers and press gangs. The Duke of York inn is at the foot of a Norman abbey, and overlooks the picturesque harbour, with some of the best views in Whitby. A traditional pub, and apparently a favourite haunt of local fishermen, it is well known for its excellent beers; John Smith's cask-conditioned Yorkshire Bitter and Magnet Ale among others. The bar food specializes in local fish, fresh from the market opposite, available for lunch and dinner. The rooms are unsophisticated but pretty, but be warned, guests have to venture outside to find their own breakfast in one of the nearby cafés. No specific disabled facilities, though the inn is all on one level.
Walking; watersports; jetskiing; waterskiing; boating; fishing at the end of the pier (parties of fishermen can be taken out to sea very early in the morning, £20 pp); beach just below hotel

WHITBY

|O| ⌂ ◈ ▱

The Magpie Café, 14 Pier Road, Whitby YO21 3JN
(Tel. 0947 602 058)
Distinctive black and white building by the harbour
Open 11.30am–6.30pm mid March–November

A delightful restaurant, not unlike a country teashop inside and out. The Magpie is a simple, modestly furnished establishment with excellent, good-value food and seating for 100. It was built in 1750 as a private home, converted into a restaurant in 1937, and has been run by three generations of the same family since 1950. The menu is dominated by all varieties of fish and chips (fresh off the boats), with plenty of options for weight-watchers. A three-course meal costs from £6.50. An ideal place for a family outing as there are children's menus, high chairs, and toy boxes. Sit upstairs by the window for the picturesque sea view with fishing boats chugging in and out of the harbour. No disabled facilities but helpful staff.

Boat hire from harbour; fishing parties in mid-summer; marina and yachting club; fishing; fossil and jet hunting; swimming; sunbathing; walking; waterskiing in harbour; sandy beach (two minutes' walk)

WHITEWELL

inn ≈ 6/10 ⚐ ⬥ ▭

The Inn at Whitewell, Forest of Bowland, nr Clitheroe,
Lancashire BB7 3AT   (Tel. 02008 222)
Village in the Forest of Bowland
Bar open 11am–3pm, 6pm–11pm Mon–Sat; noon–3pm, 7pm–10.30pm Sun
£38 single, £52 double b&b

An ancient inn, dating from 1380, with lawns stretching down to the River Hodder, deep in the country but close to main cities. The sport of orienteering was devised and originated in the surrounding forest. The atmosphere is unpretentious, the staff are friendly and the overall feeling is of a comfortable country home. The superb, newly refurbished rooms have beautiful views, and seriously good (Bang & Olufson) sound systems, and local artists' work is displayed on the walls. The large dining room has river views, specializes in local game and lamb (dinner £17.50), and offers an extensive wine list. Hearty bar meals are also served, rounded off with home-made puddings or 'a confusing selection of little known cheeses'. The Tap Room bar overlooks the water and houses pub games. The owner, Mr Bowman, has set up something of a cottage industry, producing wine, shoes, shirts, and shooting stockings which are all sold on the premises, alongside other quality goods. No facilities for the disabled.

Walking; fishing nearby (hotel has six miles of fishing rights: sea trout, £9 a day; salmon, £20 a day; equipment available); clay pigeon shooting, pheasant and grouse shooting arranged for parties (bring equipment)

WINDERMERE

Langdale Chase Hotel, Windermere, Cumbria
LA23 1LW   (Tel. 05394 32201/32604)
Off the A591, the Windermere to Ambleside road
£43–£57 pp b&b

A Victorian country house, built in 1896 by a Manchester cotton merchant, and turned into a hotel in 1933. It is a beautiful building, set in four acres of landscaped gardens on the edge of Lake Windermere, though unfortunately spoilt on the outside by modernizing of the windows. The interior feels very Victorian, with a grand imitation of a panelled medieval hall-gallery, and a real log fire in reception hall. Two of the rooms have four-poster beds, and in addition to the hotel rooms there is a garden bungalow available. The dining room seats 60 people, with 12 tables overlooking the lake (set lunch £9.95, Sunday lunch £10.50, set dinner £19.95). Bar lunches are available from £2. Guests have the use of a leisure club nearby, where there is a swimming pool, spa bath, gym, squash courts and table tennis. Twin room on ground level for disabled use.

Croquet; two grass tennis courts; two rowing boats for residents' use; two jetties and boathouse; walking; watersports; fishing

WINDERMERE

Miller Howe Hotel, Rayrigg Road, Windermere, Cumbria
LA23 1EY   (Tel. 09662 2536/5664)
Off the A592
Open March–December

£81–£136 pp dinner and b&b

A very comfortable and well-thought-out hotel, built in 1916, with a fine terrace, three lounges and a conservatory all overlooking the lake. The decor is interesting, with collections of plates on the walls, and flying golden cherubs above the stairs. The rooms have good stereos with classical music, rather than televisions, and puzzles and books: room prices vary with view, and bookings need to be made two months in advance. The dining room, with an attractive mural, seats 70 people. Sixteen tables have a lake view (most of these tables go to residents). John Tovey's English country cooking is widely renowned; dinner is at 8pm for 8.30pm (£27.50), and the menu changes daily. No direct access to lake from hotel grounds. Packed lunches can be made for guests, and special diets can be catered for. No facilities for the disabled.

Walking; watersports and fishing nearby; cookery courses

YORK

🍴 🏨 ⬦ 🟰

The Bonding Warehouse, Skeldergate, York YO1 1DH
(Tel. 0904 622527)
On the west side of Skeldergate bridge
Open 11am–11pm, Easter–Christmas; closed 3pm–6pm, Christmas–Easter

The Bonding Warehouse was originally just that – a place of storage for cargo brought up the Ouse and for produce of York to be transported out via the river. The original cargo chutes used to get the sacks from floor to floor are still in the building. Inside are a restaurant, tastefully styled allowing one to see the original features like columns and brickwork, and three bars, with great views of the river and Cliffords Tower opposite. In summer guests can eat and drink on the balcony overlooking the river. The Bonding Warehouse's speciality is live jazz – always at weekends and sometimes throughout the week too – in the Riverside Bar and restaurant, so you can eat your dinner on the balcony overlooking the river while the voice of a female jazz singer wafts out from the restaurant. The reasonably priced bistro food costs about £10 to £12 for three courses. No facilities for the disabled.

YORK
🏠 73/188 ⚓ ✗ ▭

The Viking Hotel, North Street, York YO1 1JF
(Tel. 0904 659822)
By Ouse bridge
£75 single, £95 double b&b
The Viking hotel is a perfectly good hotel of its kind: modern, big, efficient with all the facilities you could need. But as with other hotels of this kind it does lack personality. However, it is right on the River Ouse and many of the bedrooms, the Regatta restaurant (à la carte) and the Garden Court restaurant (set dinner £12.50) all look over the water; the lounge enjoys views of York. The hotel has its own moorings on the water below and can arrange for large parties of people to take boat rides down the Ouse from the hotel. A comfortable modern hotel to use as a base to discover York, but don't expect it to reflect York's history. There is a gym, sauna and solarium for guests' use, and themed evenings are a speciality. No facilities for the disabled.
Health and leisure club; walking; fishing; own moorings just below hotel, can arrange for large parties

Index

Index

European City Breaks

'Weekend' Escapes to Europe's 20 Major Cities

Katie Wood

As flight times decrease and air fares tumble, and with the approaching reality of the Channel Tunnel, the cities of Europe are becoming as accessible for short breaks – of three or four days, or maybe even a week – as those of Britain. Now, within a matter of hours you can escape the rigours of everyday life and find yourself strolling up the Champs-Elysées or dining in Budapest, rapt in the Rijksmuseum, shopping in Munich or having a drink in St Mark's Square.

Full of advice on how to get there, which tour operators to use, where to stay and eat and what there is to see and do, this is an invaluable handbook for every enthusiastic traveller. Whether you want to wander in your own way, cram in culture, arrange a romantic weekend or visit two cities in a week, *European City Breaks* – the result of several years of research – will help you decide where to go and when, and tells you all you need to know both before you go and when you're there.

Covers every city break operator for:

Austria – Innsbruck, Salzburg, Vienna; **Belgium** – Bruges, Brussels; **Czechoslovakia** – Prague; **France** – Nice, Paris; **Great Britain** – London; **Hungary** – Budapest; **Ireland** – Dublin; **Italy** – Florence, Milan, Rome, Venice; **Netherlands** – Amsterdam; **Portugal** – Lisbon; **Spain** – Madrid; **West Germany** – Munich, West Berlin

FONTANA PAPERBACKS

Ken Walsh

Hitch-Hiker's Guide to Europe

An invaluable guide for anyone wanting to travel cheaply in Europe, including the British Isles, Western Europe, Scandinavia, Iceland, the Eastern Bloc, North Africa, Turkey and the Middle East.

Packed with useful information on:

* What to take	* Routes
* How to travel	* Useful phrases
* Where to sleep	* Emergencies
* What to eat	* Local transport
* Best buys	* Working abroad
* Roughing it	* Currency hints

'Practically researched . . . colossal fun to read'
Observer

Fontana Paperbacks: Non-fiction

Fontana is a leading paperback publisher of non-fiction. Below are some recent titles.

☐ The Round the World Air Guide *Katie Wood& George McDonald* £9.95
☐ Europe by Train *Katie Wood& George McDonald* £4.95
☐ Hitch-Hiker's Guide to Europe *Ken Walsh* £3.95
☐ Eating Paris *Carl Gardner& Julie Sheppard* £2.95
☐ Staying Vegetarian *Lynne Alexander* £3.95
☐ Holiday Turkey *Katie Wood& George McDonald* £3.95
☐ Holiday Yugoslavia *Katie Wood& George McDonald* £3.95
☐ Holiday Portugal *Katie Wood& George McDonald* £3.95
☐ Holiday Greece *Katie Wood& George McDonald* £3.95
☐ Holiday Coastal Spain *Katie Wood& George McDonald* £3.95
☐ British Country Houses *Katie Wood* £5.95
☐ The Life and Death of St Kilda *Tom Steel* £5.95
☐ Back to Cape Horn *Rosie Swale* £3.95
☐ Fat Man on a Bicycle *Tom Vernon* £2.50

You can buy Fontana paperbacks at your local bookshop or newsagent. Or you can order them from Fontana Paperbacks, Cash Sales Department, Box 29, Douglas, Isle of Man. Please send a cheque, postal or money order (not currency) worth the purchase price plus 22p per book for postage (maximum postage required is £3).

NAME (Block letters) _____

ADDRESS _____

_____

_____